Environmental politics
the European Union

Manchester University Press

IIssues in Environmental Politics

series editors Mikael Skou Andersen and Duncan Liefferink

At the start of the twenty-first century, the environment has come to stay as a central concern of global politics. This series takes key problems for environmental policy and examines the politics behind their cause and possible resolution. Accessible and eloquent, the books make available for a non-specialist readership some of the best research and most provocative thinking on humanity's relationship with the planet.

already published in the series

Science and politics in international environmental regimes   *Steinar Andresen, Tora Skodvin, Arild Underdal and Jørgen Wettestad*

Animals, politics and morality (2nd edn)   *Robert Garner*

Implementing international environmental agreements in Russia   *Geir Hønneland and Anne-Kristin Jørgensen*

Implementing EU environmental policy   *Christoph Knill and Andrea Lenschow (eds)*

Sweden and ecological governance: straddling the fence   *Lennart J. Lundqvist*

Global warming policy in Japan and Britain: interactions between institutions and issue characteristics   *Shizuka Oshitani*

North Sea cooperation: linking international and domestic pollution control   *Jon Birger Skjærseth*

Climate change and the oil industry: common problem, varying strategies   *Jon Birger Skjærseth and Tora Skodvin*

Environmental policy-making in Britain, Germany and the European Union   *Rüdiger K. W. Wurzel*

Environmental politics in the European Union

Policy-making, implementation and patterns of multi-level governance

Christoph Knill and Duncan Liefferink

Manchester University Press

Manchester and New York

distributed exclusively in the USA by Palgrave

Published by Manchester University Press
Oxford Road, Manchester M13 9NR, UK
and Room 400, 175 Fifth Avenue, New York, NY 10010, USA
www.manchesteruniversitypress.co.uk

Distributed exclusively in the USA by
Palgrave, 175 Fifth Avenue, New York,
NY 10010, USA

Distributed exclusively in Canada by
UBC Press, University of British Columbia, 2029 West Mall,
Vancouver, BC, Canada V6T 1Z2

British Library Cataloguing-in-Publication Data
A catalogue record for this book is available from the British Library

Library of Congress Cataloging-in-Publication Data applied for

ISBN   0719075807 *hardback*
EAN   978 0 7190 7580 3

ISBN   0719075815 *paperback*
EAN   978 0 7190 7581 0

First published 2007

16 15 14 13 12 11 10 09 08 07   10 9 8 7 6 5 4 3 2 1

Typeset
by Action Publishing Technology Ltd, Gloucester
Printed in Great Britain
by CPI, Bath

Contents

List of boxes, tables and figures   *page* vii

Preface   ix

List of abbreviations   xi

1 Introduction and historical overview: the establishment
   of environmental policy as a European policy domain   1
2 Patterns of regulation   27
3 Central institutions and actors   57
4 Political processes and decision-making procedures   77
5 Typical interest constellations and patterns of interaction   102
6 Making EU environmental policy in practice: three
   case studies   121
7 Implementation effectiveness of EU environmental policy   145
8 Strategies to improve implementation effectiveness:
   'new' environmental policy instruments as a panacea?   162
9 The implementation of EU environmental policy in
   the UK, France, Germany and Spain   179
10 Taking stock: the environmental problem-solving
   capacity of the EU   196
11 Conclusions   214

   References   223
   Index   243

Boxes, tables and figures

Boxes

4.1 The consultation procedure   *page* 96
4.2 The cooperation procedure   97
4.3 The co-decision procedure   100

Tables

2.1 Principles of European environmental policy   28
2.2 Major overarching measures in EU environmental
     policy   47
2.3 Major measures in the area of water protection   48
2.4 Major measures in the area of air pollution control   50
2.5 Important measures concerning waste management   51
2.6 Important measures in the area of chemical control   51
4.1 Voting weights and power distribution in the
     Council of Ministers after the Nice Treaty   89
6.1 Emission limits for motor vehicles after the
     Luxembourg compromise of 1985   124
7.1 Investigative criteria for the introduction of
     infringement proceedings   149
8.1 Implementation effectiveness of 'old' and 'new'
     instruments   165
9.1 Administrative implications of the policies under study   182
9.2 National responses to EU policy requirements in four
     member states   183
9.3 European adaptation pressure and implementation
     effectiveness in four member states   186

10.1 Development trends in environmental quality in the
     member states for selected areas   210

Figures

2.1 Basic categories of instruments used in EU
    environmental policy   42
7.1 Different concepts of effective implementation   152
7.2 Complaints under investigation (end of 2002,
    by sector)   156
8.1 Institutional adaption pressure and implementation
    effectiveness   175
10.1 Number of environmental policy directives,
     regulations and decisions passed annually   198

Preface

The environmental policy of the European Union (EU) has made impressive progress during the last three decades. Since the early 1970s, there has been a growing expansion of regulatory activities and policy competences at the European level. Environmental policy, which started off as little more than a by-product of economic integration, has thus developed into a central area of EU policy-making.

Notwithstanding this success story, EU environmental policy is often subject to far-reaching criticism. In this context particular emphasis is placed on ineffective and long-winded decision-making processes as well as severe deficits emerging during the implementation of EU measures at the national level. Moreover, it is argued that EU environmental policy suffers from regulatory centralization, thus leaving national authorities insufficient discretion to adjust European requirements to specific domestic problem conditions.

In this book, we give a comprehensive overview of central features and developments of EU environmental policy and give explanations for the somewhat ambiguous assessments mentioned above. In particular, we focus on the following aspects: How can we explain the impressive development of environmental activities at the EU level? What are the central areas and instruments of EU environmental policy? What about the effectiveness and problem-solving capacity of the EU in the environmental field? Which factors influence the formulation and implementation of EU environmental policy?

In addressing these questions, we at the same time provide an overview of the theoretical state of the art of political science analyses of EU environmental policy-making and EU policy making more generally. The theoretical discussion is illustrated by a broad range of empirical findings with regard to the formulation and implementation of environmental policy.

The book is structured as follows. We begin with an overview of the historical development of EU environmental policy (Chapter 1) and the central policy areas, policy instruments and regulatory approaches (Chapter 2). In a second step, our focus is on the actors, institutions, processes and interest constellations which shape the process of environmental policy-making at the European level (Chapters 3–6). The third part, consisting of Chapters 7–9, takes a closer look at the implementation stage, illuminating central problems of enforcement and compliance underlying EU environmental policy both from a theoretical and an empirical perspective. In the concluding Chapters, 10 and 11, we provide an overall assessment of the problem-solving capacity of EU environmental policy. In doing so, we place particular emphasis on potential effects of recent and future enlargements of the Union.

This book is a rigorously revised and updated version of an introduction to EU environmental policy published by Christoph Knill in 2003 in German (Knill, C. 2003, *Europäische Umweltpolitik. Steuerungsprobleme und Regulierungsmuster im Mehrebenensystem*. Opladen: Leske und Budrich). Even though, after all, the book was almost entirely rewritten, we would like to thank Leske und Budrich for allowing us to use the German book as a starting point for this project. We very much appreciated the pleasant collaboration with Lucy Nicholson and Tony Mason at Manchester University Press, as well as the very helpful comments on our first draft by Mikael Skou Andersen and an anonymous reviewer. In addition to that, we gratefully acknowledge the financial support provided by the research programme 'Governance and Places' and the Department of Political Sciences of the Environment at Radboud University Nijmegen. Finally, we are grateful to Michael Dobbins for translating parts of the original German book and to Helen Foerster for preparing the final manuscript. It goes without saying that we alone are responsible for any remaining errors.

Christoph Knill   Konstanz/Nijmegen
Duncan Liefferink   September 2006

Abbreviations

CFSP	Common Foreign and Security Policy
COP	Conference of the Parties
COREPER	Committee of Permanent Representatives
DG	Directorate-General
EAA	European Atomic Agency
EC	European Community
ECE	United Nations Economic Commission for Europe
ECJ	European Court of Justice
ECSC	European Coal and Steel Community
EEA	European Environment Agency
EEB	European Environmental Bureau
EEC	European Economic Community
EIA	Environmental Impact Assessment
EIONET	European Information and Observation Network
EMAS	Environmental Management and Audit Scheme
EMU	European Economic and Monetary Union
EP	European Parliament
EQO	Environmental Quality Objective
EU	European Union
IPPC	Integrated Pollution Prevention and Control
JHA	Justice and Home Affairs
NGO	Non-governmental Organization
OECD	Organisation for Economic Co-operation and Development
OMC	Open Method of Coordination

PCB	Polychlorinated Biphenylene
PCT	Polychlorinated Terphenylene
QMV	Qualified Majority Voting
SEA	Single European Act
SRU	Rat von Sachverständigen für Umweltfragen
TEC	Treaty establishing the European Community
TEU	Treaty on European Union
UK	United Kingdom
UN	United Nations
UNCED	United Nations Conference on Environment and Development
UNEP	United Nations Environmental Program
UNFCCC	United Nations Framework Convention on Climate Change
UNICE	Union des Industries de la Communauté Européenne

1

Introduction and historical overview: the establishment of environmental policy as a European policy domain

The environmental policy of the EU[1] has developed in remarkable fashion in the past three decades. Since the beginning of the 1970s we have witnessed a steady expansion of environmental policy activities at the European level. An increasingly dense network of European legislation has emerged, which has now been extended to all areas of environmental protection. This holds not only for air pollution control, water protection and waste policy, but also for nature conservation and the control of chemicals, biotechnology and other industrial risks. Environmental policy has thus become a core area of European politics. A development which was still regarded as a 'fad' or as 'politically irrelevant' at the beginning of the 1970s, 'is now seen as an important policy area within the EU's policy portfolio' (Jordan 1999, 5).

The increased significance of this European policy area is demonstrated in particular by the extensive influence which Brussels exerts on the environmental policies of the member states (Sbragia 2000, 294). Due to the overall very high density of regulations and the broad spectrum of European environmental policies, the member states are frequently forced to adjust the content of their national regulations, policy instruments, and administrative structures to the European guidelines (Héritier, Knill and Mingers 1996; Knill 2001).

Such dynamic developments in EU environmental policy could hardly be expected in light of the legal and institutional conditions which existed at the beginning. After all, the EU was founded in the Treaty of Rome in 1957 as the European Economic Community (EEC). Apart from the fact that environmental problems were not yet a politically significant topic at this point in time, the founding fathers of the EU were primarily concerned with economic integration. Thus the groundwork of the Treaty did not grant the European institutions any authority to act or any responsibilities with respect to environmental policy.

Due to these unfavourable starting conditions, the continuously increasing environmental activities of the EU, which we have witnessed since the beginning of the 1970s, are certainly surprising. How can it be that 'completely unanticipated in 1957, environmental policy had moved from silence to salience within thirty years' (Weale 1999, 40)? This question will be answered in the course of the following sections.

In doing so, we will illustrate how policy-makers acting without any legislative authority initially made a clever move to increase the EU's capacity to act in environmental matters: environmental policy was 'defined' as trade policy, meaning that it became legitimate in legal terms not so much on the basis of realizing environmental policy goals, but rather as a means of dismantling economic trade barriers between the member states.

In the course of time, however, environmental policy increasingly emancipated itself from its status as a 'by-product' of economic integration. Environmental protection developed into its own policy area in the context of European integration, independent of economic policy goals. This development, which can be regarded in particular as a consequence of cross-border environmental pollution, resulted in environmental policy being legally confirmed as an independent area of action of the EU in the Single European Act (SEA) of 1987.

The growing importance of EU environmental policy has ultimately also been underpinned by the further expansion of the EU's authority and capacity for action in subsequent institutional reforms. The Treaties of Amsterdam and Maastricht as well as the establishment of a European Environmental Agency in Copenhagen in 1994 are particularly worthy of mention here.

The beginnings: environmental policy as trade policy

The Paris Summit meeting of heads of state and government of the European Community (EC) in October 1972 can be viewed as the beginning of an independent EU environmental policy. Just a few weeks before the enlargement of the Community to Denmark, the United Kingdom (UK) and Ireland (on 1 January 1973), a declaration on environmental and consumer policy was adopted at this conference. The declaration granted the European Commission the task of drawing up an action programme for environmental protection. To this end, a 'task force group' was created in the Commission, from which today's Directorate-General (DG) for the Environment has emerged.

This very first environmental action programme was adopted by national governmental representatives in July 1973 during the first meeting of the Council of Environmental Ministers and formally enacted a few months later. Thus, for the first time, the governments of the member states had granted the Union an environmental policy mandate (Hildebrand 1993; Liefferink, Lowe and Mol 1993, 2ff.).

Reasons for environmental policy action at the European level
What were the causes and motives for the member states and Commission to promote the development of a common environmental policy? Which factors explain the environmental activities at the European level at the beginning of the 1970s? We can trace this back to economic and ecological as well as socio-political reasons.

The most important cause for the introduction of a common environmental policy was based on the fear that trade barriers and competitive distortions in the Common Market could emerge due to the different environmental standards (Johnson and Corcelle 1989). Diverse national standards for certain products, such as limitations on automobile emissions or the lead content of petrol, posed formidable obstacles to the free trade of these products within the Community.

In establishing the EEC, the member states had in fact agreed on a general ban on so-called non-tariff trade barriers (Articles 29 [ex-Article 34] and 30 [ex-Article 36] TEU[2]). In Article 30, however, exceptions to this general ban were specified. Thus, among other things, such trade restrictions which are justified for the 'protection of the health and life of humans, animals, or plants' are exempted. Although Article 30 stipulates that such trade restrictions may not constitute random discrimination, this allowed the member states to a large extent to design their own environmental policy after all, even if this led to trade obstacles (Holzinger 1994, 68; Rehbinder and Stewart 1985, 29ff.).[3]

Against this background, EU environmental policy was primarily a 'flanking policy' to create a Common Market. This is also evidenced by the fact that even before the beginning of the actual EU environmental policy, individual environmentally relevant measures were passed in the area of chemicals control and the regulation of automobile emissions. However, these measures were not part of a coordinated and goal-oriented European environmental policy (Jordan 1999, 3). They were motivated instead by competition policy, or to be more precise, the realization of the Common Market by harmonizing national legal and administrative regulations.

Besides competition policy motives, an additional factor which has led to the establishment of EU environmental policy is the fact that since the middle of the 1960s numerous environmental catastrophes have not only led to the increased international politicization of environmental problems, but also underlined the cross-border nature of certain forms of environmental pollution (Liefferink, Lowe and Mol 1993, 1). The growing international perception of environmental problems was brought to light at the United Nations Conference on the Human Environment, which took place in Stockholm in 1972. Within the framework of this conference the member states of the EU increasingly began to deal with the environmental policy consequences of the European integration process (Jordan 1999, 3).

The main focus was placed here on the problem of cross-border air pollution. It had become evident that the efforts of individual states on a national basis alone are not sufficient to effectively solve certain environmental problems. One of the most widespread air pollutants is sulphur in the form of sulphur dioxide (SO_2), which primarily is produced when sulphurous fossil fuels such as petroleum are burnt. Once it is emitted into the air, SO_2 is 'gone with the wind' in the truest sense of the phrase. When mixed with the dampness contained in clouds, acid rain develops, which contributes to the acidification of the earth and water often far away from the original site where the pollutants were emitted.

Cross-border pollution became an international issue for the first time when the acidification of Scandinavian lakes came to light. It had become evident that the cause for the acidification and the resulting decline in the fish stock could not be attributed to Swedish emissions. The cause of the acid rain was instead the air pollution in other countries – in particular the UK as well as the industrial areas of Central and Eastern Europe – (Boehmer-Christiansen and Skea 1991).

Thus, from the beginning of the 1970s the problem of acid rain increasingly led to the realization that environmental pollution did not stop at national borders, but had to be addressed by cross-border measures. The relevance of this notion for the development of EU environmental policy is also expressed in the related documents from the EU Commission (European Commission 1984, 11).

Along with the economic and ecological motives just described, the literature also frequently makes reference to an additional factor which has facilitated the creation and development of the EU environmental policy: the goal of improving the living conditions in the EU. This objective results from the preamble and Article 2 (ex-Article 2) TEU. The goals of a 'continual improvement of living and employment conditions' and 'rapid increase in the standard of living' mentioned here were interpreted by the Community institutions in terms of not only a quantitative, but also qualitative rise in the standard of living. This interpretation implies that the improvement of the state of the environment is also among the goals of the Community (Rehbinder and Stewart 1985, 20ff.; Holzinger 1994, 67; Krämer 2000).

The explicit orientation to these objectives is not only evident in the introduction to the First Environmental Action Programme from 1973.[4] In justifying its environmental policy activities, the Commission also retrospectively points out that this aspect – along with economic and environment policy motives – was of great significance: 'In 1972 it had become clear that we had to act because ... the development of completely different living conditions in the member states would not be politically justifiable' (European Commission 1984, 11).

Environmental policy without explicit legal basis

In political and legal terms, the environmental policy of the EU particularly distinguishes itself from other policy areas such as trade, agricultural, or transportation policy in that it was not mentioned in the Treaty of Rome establishing the Community. In other words, there was no explicit treaty basis which could have underpinned European environmental policy.

Due to these circumstances, the request made by the heads of state and government at the Paris Summit conference in 1972 to push forward with the development of a European environmental policy entailed an interesting question, for legal experts in particular. As there was no treaty basis, it was totally uncertain at that point in time what would serve as the legal foundation for the fulfilment of the political objectives.

The first discovery in conjunction with this was that if the treaty text were to be interpreted 'dynamically', environmental policy would be regarded as an essential goal of the Community, even though it was not explicitly mentioned. Otherwise, it would hardly be possible to fulfil the 'resolution' reinforced in the Treaty's preamble that living and working conditions must be improved under the changing circumstances of increasing environmental risks and increasing environmental awareness.

In the treaty text itself, the catalogue of measures formulated in Article 2 TEU in particular offered indications of a dynamic interpretation. This is voiced very clearly in the following statement by representatives of the national governments, which was formulated on the occasion of the adoption of the First Environmental Action Programme by the Council of Environmental Ministers:

> Whereas in particular, in accordance with Article 2 of the Treaty; the task of the EEC is to promote throughout the Community a harmonious development of economic activities and a continuous and balanced expansion, which cannot now be imagined in the absence of an effective campaign to combat pollution and nuisances or of an improvement in the quality of life and the protection of the environment; whereas improvement in the quality of life and the protection of the natural environment are among the fundamental tasks of the Community; whereas it is therefore necessary to implement a Community environment policy.[5]

This kind of dynamic interpretation was not only generally accepted by legal experts (Rehbinder and Stewart 1985, 20ff.), but also by the European Court of Justice (ECJ), which recognized this development as a legitimate further interpretation of the law and designated environmental protection as an essential goal of the Community in various decisions.[6]

Through this, the pursuit of environmental policy goals was legally supported by the Community for the first time. However, this did not solve the problem that a concrete treaty article still had to be found on which environmental measures could be based. It eventually turned out that the stipulations in Articles 94 (ex-Article 100) and 308 (ex-Article 235) of the TEU, which were usually drawn on together as a basis of authority, resulted in new opportunities for environmental policy action.

Along these lines, Article 94 TEU contains a general authorization for the Community to harmonize legal and administrative regulations in the member states which have direct ramifications for the establishment or the functioning of the Common Market. Accordingly, the adoption of environmental policy regulations could be substantiated by the fact that different environmental requirements in the member states constitute trade barriers in economic terms (Johnson and Corcelle 1989, 4).

Above all, product-related environmental regulations (product standards) – i.e. regulations of environmentally relevant features of goods – were affected by this provision. For example, the definition of limits for car exhaust emissions or the specification of standards with regard to the lead content of petrol falls under this. Here it was evident that deviant national product norms become technical trade barriers which disturb the functioning of the Common Market. However, supported by the case law of the ECJ, Article 94 was additionally used as a legal basis for the harmonization of production-related environmental regulations (production or process standards). These entail technical specifications, which must be taken into account when designing production sites and the production process, such as the definition of dioxin limits for waste incineration facilities (Rehbinder and Stewart 1985, 25).

However, several restrictions were associated with the use of Article 94 as a basis for environmental policy action. First, these resulted from its economic policy objectives, according to which only those measures are subject to the Community's harmonization authority which serve the purpose of completing the Common Market. Hence, Article 94 did not come into question as a legal basis for environmental activities without a concrete reference to economic matters. A second restriction resulted from the fact that this article requires the existence of legal or administrative provisions in at least one member state. European harmonization is not necessary or possible until at least one member state has preceded with this (Holzinger 1994, 68).

Third, from the standpoint of environmental protection, it was ultimately problematic that the authority for harmonization in Article 94 did not refer to the level of the environmental standards. Nothing about the targeted level of protection could be inferred from the article. The approximation of national environmental provisions for reasons of competition does not necessarily always have to lead to desirable results with respect to environmental policy. Thus, European harmonization at a weak level can serve to block more stringent national measures. A related problem is the fact that harmonized environmental standards frequently do not do justice to the ecological conditions which might vary from country to country.

In the areas in which Article 94 was not applicable, Article 308 TEU could be used as a subsidiary legal basis for EU environmental policy. Article 308 enabled the Community to pass 'suitable measures' in such cases in which action on behalf of the EU appears necessary to achieve its objectives, even if the Treaty does not explicitly include the authority necessary for doing so. As the objectives mentioned in Article 308 have to be achieved 'within the framework of the Common Market', though, it was generally assumed that the legal acts based on Article 308 must in some way be related to the economic objectives of the Community (Rehbinder and Stewart 1985, 26). Thus also Article 308 only covers economically related environmental problems at best.

We have seen that the two decisive foundations for European environmental policy activity were to a great extent pegged to the realization of economic objectives. The prevalence of economic objectives results from the original design and function of the EU as a purely economic community. Along these lines, the creation of a European environmental policy, which was taking shape fifteen years after the signing of the Treaty of Rome, was not founded exclusively, but for the most part, on economic objectives.

To be sure, besides the economic objectives, other motives also played a role: the awareness of the increasing significance of environmental problems, the view that a healthy environment is the basis for the prosperity which the Community strives for, and the conviction that the EU might be the suitable institution to solve various problems of cross-boundary and global environmental pollution. However, between these ecological objectives and the foremost goal of creating a Common Market, there was a disparity in favour of market integration, which resulted in a kind of 'economic bias' in European environmental policy (Holzinger 1994, 70). It was not until the middle of the 1980s and the signing of the SEA in 1987 that economic and ecological objectives were put on equal legal footing within the Community.

Growing policy output despite unfavourable legal conditions
In light of this constellation, there was no reason to be particularly optimistic with regard to the expected output of environmental measures by the EU. Acting on the legal foundations for trade policy, how was the Community supposed to be able to achieve the bold environmental objectives, as formulated in the First Environmental Action Programme of 1973?

An additional complicating factor was the fact that both Articles 94 and 308 TEU required a unanimous vote by the member states in the Council of Ministers. As a consequence, member states who believed themselves to be at a disadvantage due to the proposed measures (for example, because they feared economic harm for their industries), were generally able to block such decisions in the Council of Ministers.

Considering these relatively unfavourable starting conditions, the output of this first phase of European environmental policy can by all means be regarded as a success. Within about a decade, a very substantial set of European environmental laws emerged, with many important areas of environmental policy being regulated at the European level (see Haigh 2000). By the middle of the 1980s, not only had three additional environmental action programmes characterized by a constant broadening of environmental objectives and activities been passed, but also around 200 binding legal acts, primarily in the form of directives and regulations (Liefferink, Lowe and Mol 1993, 2ff.; Weale 1996, 597; Zito 1999). There existed manifestly at least a basic consensus between the member states on the necessity of a common environmental policy.

A comprehensive programme for European environmental policy had emerged from an initial series of more or less 'coincidental' and non-coordinated activities. In legal terms, this programme still relied on its trade policy foundations, but with regard to its political aims it had increasingly freed itself from purely economic motives. Even if environmental policy formally could only be substantiated as trade policy, on the informal level environmental policy goals had increasingly come to the fore as the motivation for joint environmental measures. European environmental policy had gradually developed into an independent policy domain of the Community, even without having a relevant legal basis (see Knill 1995, 132–3; Sbragia 2000, 294–5).

For instance, in the 1970s relatively strict limits with regard to water pollution control were passed, which went far beyond what would have been necessary for mere market harmonization. These entailed minimum requirements for the quality of surface water, bathing water, fishing water, shellfish water and drinking water. Some very far-reaching measures were also passed by the EU in the areas of waste law and chemical control. The same holds for air pollution control, for which important quality thresholds on individual pollutants were passed. From the beginning of the 1980s, these were supplemented by various and sometimes very extensive directives to combat air pollution by industrial plants (Jordan 1999, 10).[7]

Many of these measures were associated with great costs for the member states and their industries. For instance, complying with the strict quality thresholds for drinking water required the installation of expensive filter and purification technology by the national water supply companies. These policies also led to additional costs for the administrative and institutional adaptation of the member states in order to ensure the compatibility of national regulations with the European specifications (Héritier, Knill and Mingers 1996; Knill and Lenschow 1998; Knill 2001).

There is an array of reasons for the formidable development of the European environmental policy despite the difficult legal and institutional preconditions. Some observers point out that the member states were confronted with growing domestic pressure due to environmental issues, which strengthened their willingness to cooperate on the European level. In particular at the beginning of the 1980s, environmental problems were increasingly politicised in several member states. One might note here forest dieback (*Waldsterben*) due to acid rain, which triggered extensive environmental policy activities in Germany, above all.

The transnational character of the problem of acidification, but also the feared damage to the competitiveness of industries, which were now confronted with strict national environmental regulations, facilitated a very active role for Germany on the European level. Together with other 'green' member states such as the Netherlands and Denmark, the Germans attempted to enhance the level of protection and the regulatory requirements for European environmental policies. Despite the reservations of other member states, they triggered certain dynamics at the European level, leading to the adoption of European standards which in part went significantly beyond the existing provisions in the individual member states (Héritier, Knill and Mingers 1996; Sbragia 2000).

Furthermore, there are also indications that during the negotiations at the European level the representatives of the member states were frequently not able to properly assess the economic and administrative implications of the measures decided on, in particular during the initial phase of the European environmental policy. Or more bluntly: some of the member states were not totally aware of what they had got into during the European negotiations. Thus the member states accepted extremely strict quality standards for drinking water proposed by the Commission, whose implementation at the national level turned out to be highly problematic and only feasible with great costs. Individual member states also had false notions on the binding legal character of European directives. For example, the UK had accepted European directives assuming that the specified limits were to be interpreted merely as unbinding recommendations instead of legally binding requirements (Sbragia 2000, 296).

In individual cases these factors certainly may have played a role. However, as we will see later in Chapters 3–6, they alone do not suffice to adequately capture and explain the dynamics of European environmental policy-making. As we will demonstrate, there are several structural aspects as well, which influence the interest constellations and patterns of interaction of the central actors in European environmental policy.

Yet before we ultimately explain the puzzle of the relatively comprehensive environmental policy activities despite the unfavourable preconditions, we will first round off the historical overview of the development of the European environmental policy. As already indicated, the adoption of the SEA in 1987 brought about a few lasting changes.

The Single European Act: environmental policy as an official task of the Community

With the 1987 expansion of the Treaty through the SEA, environmental policy was explicitly declared a task of the Community. The uncertainty with regard to the legal basis of EU environmental policy was thus eliminated. The necessary legitimation for environmental policy activities, which had previously been based on economic integration, was replaced by legitimation on the basis of environmental policy goals. The background and concrete ramifications of this development will be examined more closely in the following sections.

The political background

The decisive motivation for the adoption of the SEA was rooted less in environmental than economic policy motives. The foremost goal of the SEA was to accelerate economic integration within the Community in order to complete the European Common Market. The explicit establishment of environmental policy as an official domain of the Union took place to a certain extent as a 'by-product' of economically motivated reforms.

In the middle of the 1980s the Community was still far from the goal of a Common Market as formulated in the Treaty of Rome, despite certain advancements. It appeared that the harmonization of national legal and administrative provisions necessary for the realization of the economic goals was often very sluggish. Above all, it was feared that the process of economic integration might also stagnate after the accession of Spain and Portugal in 1986. As it was difficult enough to bring about unanimous resolutions in the Council of Ministers with ten states (Greece had joined the EU in 1981), the situation was anticipated to further deteriorate with the accession of additional member states.

These concerns were additionally compounded by economic developments. Stagnating growth, high unemployment rates, as well as fears that the EU could lose ground economically against the USA and Japan, increased the willingness of the member states to endorse the institutional reforms aimed at completing the Common Market more quickly (Young and Wallace 2000).

With this constellation in mind, it seemed surprising at first glance that the SEA also strengthened the EU's basis for action in environmental affairs. Nevertheless, at the conference of heads of state and government which led to the SEA there was soon a consensus that environmental policy should be made an explicitly legitimated area of Community action (Sbragia 2000). This development can be explained on the basis of three factors.

Firstly, the previous developments had made it clear that a Common Market cannot be achieved by the member states merely transferring economic authority to the EU. The development had illustrated that market and trade obstacles result not exclusively from different customs and tax regulations, but also, among other things, from different environmental policies in a more general sense.

Secondly, the explicit mentioning of EU environmental policy in the Treaty ultimately only confirmed in legal terms what had already been accomplished *de facto* in the preceding years. The basic legitimacy of the joint environmental policy had already been acknowledged. In light of the considerable number of existing legal acts and action programmes it seemed only reasonable to use the opportunity of the SEA for anchoring this policy area in the Treaty (Holzinger and Knill 2002).[8]

Finally, it should not be overlooked that regardless of the necessity of environmental regulation as an aspect of the Common Market, the Commission and the European Parliament (EP), in particular, played a very active role in promoting the establishment of environmental policy authority in the Treaty. We will elaborate further on this aspect in Chapter 3. Here it suffices to mention that vital institutional interests on behalf of the Commission and the Parliament geared at gaining new capacity for action vis-à-vis the member states were crucial. In other words: both the Commission and the Parliament hoped for new means of political influence by enhancing their environmental policy authority.

This overall constellation of diverse interests and motives facilitated the emergence of relatively far-reaching legal and institutional reforms. Although these developments were primarily geared to complete the European Common Market, they went hand in hand with significant changes in the common environmental policy.

An explicit basis for EU environmental policy

With the adoption of the SEA, the goals and principles of EU environmental policy were defined for the first time in the Treaty. Moreover, this resulted in important changes in the decision rules for environmental policy. The concrete changes here were twofold: firstly, a new title – 'environment' – was added to the Treaty, comprised of Articles 174–6 [ex-Article 130r-t) TEU. Secondly, the introduction of new rules to accelerate economic integration had ramifications for the design of the European environmental policy. These legal changes were based, in particular, on Articles 18 (ex-Article 8a) and 95 (ex-Article 100a).

Basic principles of the common environmental policy

Articles 174–6 are to be regarded as the actual environmental articles of the European Treaty. They include not only provisions on the general significance and the goals of EU environmental policy, but also define the basic principles and decision-making procedures by which these goals are to be achieved. Furthermore, general conditions with regard to the allocation of European and national environmental policy responsibilities and possibilities for action are specified.

Article 174 (1) offers a relatively detailed definition of the objectives of EU environmental policy, including the following aspects:

- Preserving, protecting and improving the quality of the environment;
- Protecting human health;
- Prudent and rational utilization of natural resources.

Article 174 (2) codifies several main guidelines which serve as the basis for achieving the environmental policy aims. Interestingly, these principles for the most part had already been formulated in the First Environmental Action Programme from 1973. Their implementation up to then had only been successful to a certain extent. They entail the following principles, which will be further worked out in Chapter 2:

- The precautionary principle:
  Environmental policy action should not be taken only when concrete damage has been demonstrated, but instead should be directed at preventing dangers and risks.
- The principle of action at the source:
  Environmental damage should be combated at the source where it originates.
- The polluter-pays principle:
  He or she who pollutes the environment or creates a risk to it shall bear the costs for the prevention, removal of and compensation for environmental damage.
- The principle of integration:
  The demands of environmental protection should be taken into account during the formulation and implementation of measures in other policy areas of the Community (such as transport, regional or agricultural policy).

Article 174 (3) specifies criteria and restrictions which are to be considered during the development of environmental action programmes and individual measures. Hence the common environmental policy is supposed to consider the current state of science and technology as well as the economic and social development of the Community and the regions. At the same time, the foundations are laid for the introduction of regionally differentiated environmental standards by establishing that the respective environmental conditions in the individual regions of the Community must be taken into account. Previously, the Community was under certain pressure to set uniform standards, because environmental protection measures usually had to be based on the harmonization stipulation of Article 94.

Moreover, the 'subsidiarity principle for environmental policy', which had already essentially been formulated in the First Environmental Action Programme,[9] was added to the Treaty. According to this principle, the Community is only allowed to become active in the area of the environment, when the 'objectives can be better reached at the Community level than at the level of the individual member states' (Article 174 (4) TEU).

Article 176 authorizes the member states to maintain or introduce stricter environmental rules than those of the Community. However, the member states are only granted this possibility to the extent that national specifications exceeding those of the European provisions are in accordance with the goals of the TEU. The result of this is that unilateral national policies are not allowed, in particular, when they stand in the way of the goal of completing the European Common Market. This kind of 'Common Market relevance' comes into play, in particular, when tradable products are affected by demands for environmental protection.

Legal arrangements and decision rules
The SEA serves not only to explicitly anchor the basic features of EU environmental policy. It also offers a concrete basis for action at the Community level. In this regard, two articles should be particularly emphasized: the general legal basis of Article 175 and the special authorization for action for trade-related environmental measures of Article 95 of the TEU. The two articles differ above all in terms of their stipulations with regard to the decision-making procedure in the Council of Ministers.

The general authorization for the Community to decide on the necessary measures to fulfil the environmental policy objectives specified in the Treaty can be found in Article 175. As for the decision-making rule, the article stipulated that as a rule the resolution in the Council of Ministers must be reached unanimously. Thus, as far as this section of the Treaty is involved, the SEA did not bring about any change with respect to the decision-making procedure for environmental policy matters. As had been the case with the environmental measures on the basis of Articles 94 and 308 of the TEU, each member retained a power of veto and could block political decisions, if necessary.

However, Article 175 is only significant in cases where there is no other treaty basis for action. Such basis exists, in particular, for environmental regulations which have an impact on the realization of the Common Market, i.e. all rules which previously had to be based on the harmonization provision of Article 94 of the TEU. The SEA introduced a new legal basis for such measures.

Article 95 facilitates the harmonization of national legal and administrative regulations in the course of the completion of the European Common Market, which are defined more precisely in Article 18 TEU (i.e. creation of an area without internal borders, free movement of goods, services, people and capital). Like

Article 94, Article 95 is therefore motivated purely by trade policy (Holzinger 1994, 73). Accordingly, Article 95 is always taken into consideration as a special legal basis for environmental protection measures by the Community, if they are relevant to the completion of the Common Market.

The question of whether European environmental regulations are of relevance for the Common Market, and thus must be decided on according to Article 95, had significant implications for the decision-making process in the Council of Ministers. While under Article 175 the principle of unanimity applied, Article 95 provided for a new decision-making procedure, the so-called cooperation procedure, for all decisions on regulations concerning the completion of the Common Market. To accelerate the process of European market integration, decisions were to be taken by qualified majority voting (QMV), implying that individual member states could no longer rely on a veto position in order to block environmental policy proposals.

At the same time, the cooperation procedure enhanced the EP's right to participate in the legislative process. This was a significant change because the Parliament had always been a progressive driving force for environmental protection, since it hoped to receive a positive response from the public and from voters. Under the new procedure it became directly involved in legislative decisions of the Council and received a right to suspensory veto.[10]

The political effects: new opportunities for action

What were the concrete effects of the SEA for the structure and development of the European environmental policy? On the one hand, the changes initiated by the SEA

> helped to entrench and formalise the EU's involvement by placing environmental protection on a firm legal footing and enunciating a set of guiding principles. In some respect, they merely formalised ideas and rules that were already an integral feature of day-to-day policy-making in the EU. (Jordan 1999, 11)

On the other hand, the SEA opened new possibilities for environmental policy action at the European level. Particularly noteworthy in this regard are the new articles on the environment which generally authorize the EU to act on environmental policy matters independently of trade policy motives. This way, the

Commission was no longer required to link its proposals for environmental measures to their significance for the completion of the Common Market. This enabled the Commission to protrude into new areas of environmental policy and develop measures which hardly would have been justifiable on the basis of earlier legal foundations (Articles 94 and 308). An important example of this is the directive passed in 1990 on the free access to environmental information. This measure, which entails extensive access rights for the public to environmentally relevant data from national authorities, could hardly have been legitimized by trade policy goals (Haigh and Baldock 1989, 21).

A second aspect which is significant with regard to the expansion of environmental policy authority concerns the introduction of majority decision-making on environmental measures relevant to the Common Market. It was generally expected that decisions by qualified majority would enable more innovative environmental policy-making which goes beyond the 'lowest common denominator'. It is frequently pointed out in this regard that in majority decision the states with the least interest in environmental protection can be outvoted and, consequently, the environmentally 'slowest' state no longer determines the pace and the stringency of European environmental policies (Jordan 1999, 11; Sbragia 2000). From the standpoint of the individual member states, searching for coalition partners to enforce national interests now turned out to be more promising than blocking negotiations (Knill and Héritier 1996, 228).

However, in the academic debate, there is little agreement on whether and the extent to which the change in the decision-making procedure at the European level has indeed contributed to the increased environmental policy dynamics. While on the one hand observers accepted the intuitively plausible hypothesis that a higher level of environmental standards could be expected with qualified majority decisions, Holzinger (1994, 1997) points out that such a scenario is not to be taken for granted. Rather this depends on the majority conditions and coalition possibilities in the Council of Ministers. With this in mind, it is absolutely plausible that more environmentally ambitious states in the Council of Ministers cannot produce a sufficient majority to enforce stricter environmental norms. There is even the potential danger of these countries being outvoted by the countries which are interested in less strict standards. Under the cooperation procedure, ambitious states no longer have a veto right either. Thus, they are no longer in a position to block the introduction of weak standards on the basis of Article 95.

From this theoretical standpoint, there are many reasons to assess the impact of majority decisions on European environmental policy in a more differentiated fashion. The effects vary with the concrete constellation of national interests in the Council of Ministers. In this regard, moreover, significant shifts in the balance of power have taken place after EU enlargements. For example, in 1995 the accession of environmentally ambitious states such as Sweden, Finland and Austria made the environmental policy 'forerunners' more influential (Holzinger 1997). The accession of ten predominantly Central and Eastern European countries in 2004, by contrast, might imply a reversal of this trend, given the fact that the new members might place a stronger interest on economic rather than ecological development.

However, it is difficult to test these theoretical considerations on the basis of empirical developments in EU environmental policy. There are no systematic findings, only investigations into individual areas. Nevertheless, these do include studies offering evidence of high standards in EU environmental policy even exceeding those of the most progressive member states. However, these investigations also show that the often extremely complicated environmental policy measures by the EU cannot simply be reduced to the concepts of 'high' and 'low' standards or 'lowest common denominator'. Thus, it is hardly possible to draw firm conclusions on the impact of different decision-making rules in the Council of Ministers on European environmental policy.

An additional complicating factor in this regard is that we have been witness to a fundamental transformation in the patterns of environmental policy regulation since the beginning of the 1990s. This change was set off in particular by the Fifth Environmental Action Programme, published in 1993. It manifests itself in the declining trend for the EU to specify strict and extensive limits. Instead emphasis is increasingly being placed on 'new instruments', which prioritize economic incentives and the self-regulation of industry as well as greater participation rights for the public.[11] These divergent regulatory concepts cannot easily be compared and contrasted with regard to their concrete ramifications for the level of European environmental protection.

Regardless of that, we must keep in mind that the SEA laid out crucial foundations for the establishment and expansion of the EU's capacity for action in environmental policy. This triggered a development which was subsequently enhanced by further legal and institutional reforms.

Institutional and political changes since the 1990s: gradual shifts

Compared to the reforms initiated by the SEA, which created a comprehensive legal basis for a joint environmental policy, more recent legal and institutional reform developments have resulted in relatively small changes for EU environmental policy. However, while the legal and institutional development thus offers evidence of a gradual, but constant increase in the significance of EU environmental policy, a certain weakening and stagnation of the environmental policy dynamics has become apparent in terms of the political activities. We are confronted with the paradoxical situation that the increasing legal and institutional 'anchoring' of EU environmental policy coincides with the stagnation of its political dynamics. This scenario is in stark contrast with the initial phase of EU environmental policy in which a respectable environmental policy programme was drawn up despite the weak legal and institutional basis.

Legal and institutional changes

As for the increased institutional and legal underpinnings of European environmental policy, one should particularly underscore the developments resulting from the Treaties of Maastricht and Amsterdam. The creation of the European Environmental Agency marks the further institutionalization and fortification of the EU environmental policy.

The Maastricht Treaty on the European Union (TEU), which has been in effect since 1993, was a continuation of the developments set off by the SEA. The centrepiece of the Treaty is the creation of the EU, which since then has provided the overall institutional framework for the entire European integration process. It is based on three pillars: as a companion to the Common Foreign and Security Policy (CFSP) and cooperation in the areas of Justice and Home Affairs (JHA), the so-called first pillar is most relevant here. It consists of the European Atomic Agency (EAA), the European Coal and Steel Community (ECSC) and the EEC. In the TEU, the EEC was renamed the European Community, the core of the newly founded EU.[12] Besides the introduction of European Economic and Monetary Union (EMU) and the concretization of European civil rights (Union Citizenship), the Treaty provides for new and expanded authority in individual policy areas. These entail not only consumer protection, health, research, technology, education and culture, but also environmental protection.

While the Treaty of Maastricht defined the basic parameters for the further integration process, the Treaty of Amsterdam ratified in 1999 brought relatively few innovations. Most importantly, the heads of state and government at the intergovernmental conference in Amsterdam could not agree on the necessary institutional reforms to facilitate the accession of new member states from Central and Eastern Europe.[13] Nevertheless, as a whole, the Treaties of Maastricht and Amsterdam provide for a series of new legal and institutional specifications for the common environmental policy, which essentially concern the decision-making procedure, goals and principles.

The increased significance of environmental policy becomes apparent in the changes in the decision-making procedure which the Maastricht Treaty provided for. Environmental policy measures on the basis of Article 175 were now to be decided by QMV, as was already the case for measures relevant to the Common Market on the basis of Article 95.[14] These changes in the decision-making procedure were followed by a further strengthening of the EP in the Amsterdam Treaty. The cooperation procedure introduced with the SEA was now replaced by the co-decision procedure, in which the Parliament and the Council of Ministers have equal power and the Parliament has a true veto right (Judge, Earnshaw and Cowan 1994).[15]

Moreover, the Treaty of Maastricht expanded the tasks of the Community, emphasizing that the task of the Community is to promote environmentally sustainable growth. This wording was once again modified in the Amsterdam Treaty to 'achieve a balanced and sustainable development' (Schröder 1998). The concept of 'sustainable development' thus applies as a guideline for policy-making in all policy areas of the EU (Jordan 1999).

The Treaty of Amsterdam additionally served to reinforce the further integration of environmental policy goals into other policy areas as a principle of the common environmental policy. This was primarily achieved by no longer hiding the transversal character of environmental protection in the environmental articles, and linking it directly to the description of the spectrum of tasks of the Community at the beginning of the Treaty (Article 3) (Lenschow 1999). This results in a general strengthening of environmental policy concerns vis-à-vis other policy areas of the Community. This holds in particular for the position of the DG Environment as compared to other DGs within the Commission (Haigh and Lanigan 1995).

The creation of the European Environment Agency (EEA), which began its work in 1994 in Copenhagen, implies an additional reinforcement and institutionalization of EU environmental policy. An essential task of the agency is the formation and coordination of an overarching European Environmental Information and Observation Network. On the basis of the information gathered through the existing environmental information systems of the member states, an improved intercommunity exchange of environmental data is supposed to be achieved by examining, collecting and evaluating them in a centralized manner. At the same time, this should ensure a better foundation for the formulation and implementation of European environmental policies (Dilling 2000).

Following the Treaties of Maastricht and Amsterdam, a further Treaty revision was adopted in Nice in 2000. The consequences of this revision for the environmental field were very limited, however. Since Nice, moreover, an attempt has been made to replace the existing Treaties by a new, comprehensive Constitutional Treaty. Due to failing referenda in France and the Netherlands in 2005, however, the Constitutional Treaty has so far not entered into force. If it had, the most significant change for the environmental policy field would have been the revision of the system of QMV. Considering the political complications surrounding the Constitutional Treaty, it is highly questionable if it will ever become effective in its present form (see Chapter 11).

The political development: reduced dynamics

If we look at the dynamics of EU environmental policy since the beginning of the 1990s, we find two opposite trends. While we can ascertain on the one hand a continual legal and institutional expansion and reinforcement of the basis for environmental policy action, we observe to a certain extent a 'cooling off of the environmental policy boom' at the European level. This holds, in particular, when compared to the rate of environmental policy activities during the 1980s. The increasing legal and institutional 'anchoring' of the European environmental policy thus paradoxically goes hand in hand with stagnating political dynamics (Zito 1999, 31).

This conclusion is based on two observations. Firstly, there appears to have been a certain decline in political significance both at the national and the European level despite all the legal and institutional enhancements. Problems associated with environmental protection no longer have the same priority on the political agenda of the EU and most member states as in the 1980s.

There are diverse reasons for this development. Besides the general slow-down in economic growth at the beginning of the 1990s and the persistent problem of high unemployment, we should also mention increased competition in the wake of international market liberalization. All these factors reduced the willingness of the member states to pass stricter environmental regulations which might have negative effects on the position of their industries in the midst of international competition. '[T]he political commitment to impose stringent and intrusive regulations through command and control processes has diminished very significantly' (Sbragia 2000, 294–5).

Secondly, as a consequence of this general political development, we can observe a certain reorientation of environmental regulation at the European level. In contrast to developments in the 1980s, the definition of uniform legally binding limits is no longer the main focus of EU environmental policy. Instead, the Commission increasingly focuses on more flexible and less harmonization-oriented regulatory concepts, which allow the member states greater room to manoeuvre with regard to the implementation of policies. These new instruments are marked in particular by the fact that they are legally less demanding for the member states than previous measures. They concentrate to a lesser extent on specifying detailed standards, which all member states must equally comply with, than on stimulating and enhancing national environmental policy reforms (see Knill and Lenschow 2000).[16]

As a whole, the consequence of these developments is that European environmental policy has partially lost its function as a driving force behind the constant increase in the level of environmental protection in the Community. This is the case despite the continually high number of environmental policy measures passed at the European level, of which a significant part is in fact still aimed at the harmonization of national environmental standards (Jordan 1999, 15). However, our assessment should not neglect the fact that the slow-down in environmental policy dynamics since the 1990s is not a genuine EU phenomenon. It can be observed at the member state level as well, as already indicated.

Summary: three phases of EU environmental policy

If we sum up the developments in EU environmental policy, we can distinguish three phases. In the first phase (1972–87) the European environmental measures were legally justified primarily by trade policy motives. The main focus was initially the goal of harmonizing different national environmental regulations, which might stand in the way of the completion of the Common Market. As a consequence of increasing cross-border environmental problems and the pioneering role of individual member states (Andersen and Liefferink 1997), a respectable programme of often very ambitious measures and activities emerged despite the weak legal and institutional basis. This was accompanied by the gradual emancipation of environmental policy as an independent Community policy domain detached from the area of economic integration, even though the corresponding legal foundations did not exist yet.

The second phase (1987–92) is primarily characterized by the legal and institutional consolidation and further development of the common environmental policy. The SEA formally codified what informally was already reality: environmental policy was anchored in the TEU as an official field of activity of the

Community, while a new treaty title served to lay down the aims, principles and decision-making procedures for environmental policy. This resulted in a considerable expansion of the EU's environmental policy authority. On the one hand, environmental measures no longer necessarily had to be substantiated by trade policy goals. On the other hand, a new decision-making procedure was introduced for environmental measures relevant to the Common Market, which allowed for qualified majority decisions in the Council of Ministers instead of unanimous decisions. Thus, it was generally expected (although only partly confirmed in practice) that stricter environmental standards would be passed that went beyond the lowest common denominator of the member states.

The third phase in which EU environmental policy has been since 1992 is characterized by two opposite trends: from an institutional and legal standpoint, the developments triggered by the SEA were gradually revised and updated, in particular in the Treaties of Maastricht and Amsterdam and through the creation of the EEA. Contrary to this trend, however, we have witnessed how environmental policy dynamics weakened to a certain extent. EU environmental policy lost momentum on the European agenda as opposed to other policy areas. This was associated with at least a partial decline of the EU's environmental policy as a motor for stricter and more far-reaching environmental regulations in the Community. It remains to be seen how this development will proceed in the future.

Notes

1 The EU was created with the Treaty of Maastricht, which has been in force since 1993. In order to use the simplest possible terminology, the term EU will be used universally throughout, even if references are made to earlier points in time.

2 Throughout this book we will use the current numbering of Treaty articles as introduced by the Amsterdam Treaty, in force since 1999. To facilitate reference to the older literature, however, we will also occasionally refer the former numbering (ex-Article ...).

3 However, in its jurisprudence the European Court of Justice has generally interpreted the exemption stipulation of Article 30 in favour of free trade and developed stricter criteria for the permissibility of national measures. Along these lines, national measures may

not have any significant consequences for interstate trade, and the pursued objective may not be reachable with other means which have lesser trade impact and the measures must pursue purely environmental policy purposes (Rehbinder and Stewart 1985, 29ff.).

4   Official Journal C 112, 12 December 1973, p. 5.

5   Official Journal C 112, 20 December 1973, pp. 1–2.

6   A decision of the ECJ on oil residues in 1985 should be particularly underlined here, cf. ECJ 7 February 1985, Case 240/83, *Procureur de la République / Association de défense des brûleurs d'huiles usagées (ADBHU)*, 1985 ECR 531, 549.

7   A more detailed description of the content and design of the various directives will be given in Chapter 2.

8   Incidentally, other policy areas, such as research and technology as well as regional policy, demonstrated similar developments.

9   Official Journal C 112, 20 December 1973, p. 7.

10 For more on the decision-making procedures, see Chapter 4.

11 See further Chapter 2 on this.

12 This new designation was particularly aimed at the increasing significance of other policy areas than economic integration (European Communities 1992, 8).

13 These unanswered questions returned as a main issue at the intergovernmental conference in Nice in December 2000.

14 However, the member states still upheld unanimous decision-making for vital areas. These include primarily tax regulations, spatial policy measures, land utilization (with the exception of waste disposal) as well as the utilization of water resources and measures which significantly affect a member state's choice between different sources of energy and the general structure of their energy policy.

15 See Chapter 4 for more on this.

16 However, the development of new regulatory concepts cannot be viewed exclusively against the background of the stagnating environmental policy dynamics at the European level. They are also a reaction to the often ineffective implementation of harmonization measures at the national level (see Knill and Lenschow 2000 as well as Chapters 7–9).

2

Patterns of regulation

Following the historical overview of the first chapter, this chapter employs a more analytical perspective on the main characteristics of the EU environmental policy field. The discussion is organized by a decreasing level of abstraction, i.e. starting with general principles, via regulatory approaches and instruments, going down to an overview of concrete policies and measures. First, the main principles of making environmental policy in the multi-level system of the EU are presented, such as the precautionary principle, the principle of subsidiarity, and the integration of environmental considerations into other policy fields. Second, the main regulatory approaches or 'paradigms' underlying the EU's environmental policies are explained. This is done with the help of two basic dichotomies: technology versus cost orientation, and intervention versus context-oriented governance. Third, a simple taxonomy of environmental policy instruments applied by the EU is developed. This is followed by an overview of the range of environmental problems covered and the principal measures taken by the EU and a brief conclusion.

General principles

The environmental policy of the EU is oriented towards an array of different principles and guidelines. These form, in turn, the basis for policy programmes such as the environmental action programmes as well as for individual policy measures. Following Weale et al. (2000, 62) these principles can be analytically divided into four different categories (see Table 2.1).[1] These categories will be discussed in detail on the following pages.

Table 2.1   *Principles of European environmental policy*

Environmental management	• Prevention • Action at source • Integrated pollution control
Specification of environmental standards	• Resource conservation • High level of protection • Precaution
Allocation of authority	• Appropriate level of action • Subsidiarity
Integration of environmental protection into other policy areas	• Polluter pays • Integration

Source: Weale et al. 2000, 62–3.

Environmental management
An important principle in European environmental management is that of prevention. This means that political measures are basically aimed at preventing damage to the environment before it arises. Thus, preventive policies are given priority over more reactive policies, i.e. measures aimed at eliminating already existing damage to the environment. In this respect the principle of prevention poses considerably greater demands than the 'polluter pays' principle, on which we will further elaborate below. In principle, the latter ultimately allows for the environment to be affected and potentially harmed, as long as the polluter compensates for the damage caused.

Applying the notion of prevention is generally substantiated by the idea that it is more efficient to design products and production processes so as to minimize harm to the environment from the beginning than to install so-called 'end-of-pipe' technologies. The latter do not eliminate pollution until the very end of the production chain (Weale et al. 2000, 64). Examples of measures aligned with this principle can be found in the area of chemical control, for example, where the manufacturers of chemical products are required to identify potential dangers which might arise during the circulation and transportation of these products and take the appropriate preventive measures.[2] The notion of prevention also plays an important role in European waste policy. Here waste prevention before it accumulates was already anchored as the foremost principle in the 1970s (Krämer 1992, 32).

Closely related to the idea of prevention is the principle of action at the source, according to which damage to the environment is to be combated directly when and where it originates. This principle comes to play for instance in measures that stipulate uniform limits for the discharge of pollutants, such as the series of directives on car emissions. The primary goal here is to reduce harm to the environment at the source to the greatest extent possible, regardless of the state of the environment in the area surrounding it. The principle of action at the source thus favours an emission-based rather than a quality-based understanding of environmental protection.[3]

The concept of integrated pollution control implies that environmental regulation and control is founded upon an 'integral approach'. Instead of dealing with individual environmental compartments, media or sectors (such as soil, water and air), overarching policies should be pursued which take the possible interactions between different measures into account. Along these lines, it should be ensured that the installation of filter technologies to prevent air pollution does not lead to increased water pollution when the toxic substances extracted from the air are 'disposed of' in the sewage of an industrial firm. The comprehensive approach to environmental problems across different sectors of the environment is intertwined with the goal of legal and administrative integration. Thus, also regulatory requirements and licensing procedures for different compartments of the environment are supposed to be approximated and consolidated.

Due to the high degree of scientific complexity associated with the assessment of reciprocal effects on different sectors of the environment as well as the highly diverse regulatory approaches, the efforts at implementing an integrated programme of environmental protection have progressed relatively slowly up to now. Two major measures stand out: the Directive on Environmental

Impact Assessment (EIA), which calls for an overarching *ex ante* evaluation of environmental effects as a prerequisite for the approval of certain projects, and the Directive on Integrated Pollution Prevention and Control (IPPC), which requires the member states to ensure a full coordination of sector-specific regulatory requirements and licensing procedures (Héritier, Knill and Mingers 1996, 241ff.).

Specification of environmental standards
This category includes environmental principles which define the general significance of environmental policy goals as compared to others, such as economic or socio-political goals. One important canon which comes to play here is the principle of conserving natural resources. This was already mentioned in the First Environmental Action Programme and then fixed in the SEA as an official Treaty objective (Article 174(1)). The principle underlines the significance of environmental policy objectives in their own right, i.e. independent of other objectives. The exploitation of natural resources must not be merely aimed at short-term economic benefits, but also has to take the long-term impact on the ecological equilibrium into account.

The significance of environmental protection as a goal in its own right, apart from other policy areas, is additionally manifested in the demand by the SEA for a high level of protection in the context of environmental policy harmonization. This is to be considered particularly when developing the Common Market (Article 95(4)). While market integration as such is primarily geared at the approximation of national legal and administrative provisions (regardless of the concrete level of regulation at which this harmonization takes place), this principle poses demands on the stringency of European environmental policies. It thus again emphasizes the significance of environmental protection as a regulatory objective independent of economic integration (Weale et al. 2000, 66).

Nevertheless, the question of how exactly the level of environmental regulation should be set in individual cases remains unanswered. How strict should European environmental standards be? Or in other words: When does a 'high level' of protection exist? This question is of even greater significance if we recall that many environmental standards are characterized by decreasing marginal utility: the additional benefits for the environment resulting from stricter regulations tend to decrease as of a certain regulatory level.

From a political standpoint, this question is particularly explosive when there are no firm scientific findings on whether stricter environmental standards are at all suitable to solve a certain problem, as was the case in the 1980s with regard to the problem of acidification, or acid rain. A similar problem exists in relation to climate change, the extent and causes of which are still disputed.

In the course of the discussion around acidification and due to the active role of Germany, in particular, the precautionary principle was established as a basis for European environmental policy. It was formally institutionalized by the Treaty of Maastricht. The precautionary principle serves to justify environmental policy action in situations of high scientific uncertainty (O'Riordan and Cameron 1994). It tips 'the burden of proof in favour of stringent environmental regulation where no clear-cut decision could be made' (Weale et al. 2000, 67). Hence this principle distinguishes itself from the prevention principle, which does not directly require any action in the case of scientific uncertainty (Rehbinder 1991).

Allocation of authority

In a multi-level system such as that of the EU the basic question arises of on which institutional level (European, national, subnational) the respective authority and decision-making capacity should be located. The allocation of environmental policy authority is aligned with functional efficiency criteria. Environmental policy standards, as a rule, should be defined at the level which is most capable of dealing with the problem at hand (see Holzinger 2000).

This policy orientation was expressed initially by the principle of the appropriate level of action, which was already laid down in the First Environmental Action Programme of 1973. It stipulates that for each category of environmental problems, in view of their scope and nature, the level of action should be chosen which is most suitable for formulating and implementing the necessary measures. Thus, it is recognized that environmental conditions and constellations that vary nationally, regionally or locally demand different political activities and measures. However, the notion of environmental policy differing from region to region was not explicitly anchored in the Treaty until the SEA was passed (see Chapter 1).

These demands were further substantiated by the subsidiarity principle, formally established for the environmental policy field by the SEA (Article 174[4]) and elevated to a general principle of joint action in the Treaty of Maastricht (Article 3b). According to this, a prerequisite for the Union to become active in a certain area is that the targeted objectives can be better met at EU than at member state level. Or phrased differently, authority should only be allocated to the European level when the problems to be solved are of a global, Europe-wide or cross-border character.

However, the application of both principles is characterized by multiple problems. Firstly, the emphasis on the appropriate level of action and the inherent preference for the national level which the subsidiarity principle entails should not detract attention from the fact that in the age of internationalized markets and global environmental problems the majority of all necessary political and legal measures meet the mentioned conditions and hence should be transferred to the European level. Despite the focus on subsidiarity, there is thus a general tendency to centralize authority at the European level (Scharpf 1994, 137; Holzinger and Knill 2002).

Secondly, these principles, which are definitely meaningful in designing the most efficient environmental policy possible, entail the risk of protracted political conflict in individual cases. Member states who fear the restriction of their own political authority or reject a certain EU regulation for economic reasons can attempt to prevent the EU from becoming active in this area by appealing to the subsidiarity principle (Holzinger 1994, 72). In fact, individual member states (the UK in particular) did attempt to promote the re-nationalization of European environmental policies by referring to the subsidiarity principle (Jordan 1999a). For example, the British have pointed out that the regulation of the quality of bathing water is an issue which can be better regulated at the national than at the European level (Wurzel 2002, 238–9). Despite these efforts, though, environmental policy authority between the EU and the member states has not been fundamentally redistributed. Instead, the emphasis on the subsidiarity principle, among other factors, has facilitated a change in environmental governance patterns at the European level. This pertains in particular to the greater emphasis placed on non-hierarchical policy instruments, which aim to incorporate diverse public and private actors at all institutional levels of action (Lenschow 1999; Knill and Lenschow 2000; Weale et al. 2000, 69; see also below, Regulatory approaches, and Policy instruments).

Integration of environmental protection into other policy areas
Environmental pollution typically is a side effect of an array of other activities, such as industrial production, agriculture or transport and traffic. This observation generally leads us to believe that an effective environmental policy must be aimed at integrating environmental policy concerns and objectives into these other policy areas. At the European level, two principles can be distinguished which serve to meet this goal: the polluter pays principle and the integration principle.

The polluter pays principle aims at preventing the environment from being treated as a free commodity. By imposing the costs for the prevention of, elimination of or compensation for environmental damage on those who cause it, the EU creates incentives for environmentally friendly behaviour. Measures aimed at shifting environmental costs to those responsible entail first and foremost economic instruments, such as taxes on emissions, additional charges, or compensation payments. It is widely claimed in the economics literature, although not fully uncontested, that economic instruments can reach the targeted regulatory goals more efficiently than classical forms of 'command-and-control' regulation. Apart from economic instruments, however, also bans, special requirements or liability or injunctive claims by civil law can be used to internalize environmental costs (Tsekouras 2000; Holzinger, Knill and Schäfer 2006).

The polluter pays principle was legally anchored in the SEA, but its significance was already emphasized in the EU's First Environmental Action Programme. Both the Fourth (1987–92) and the Fifth Action Programme (1993–2000), moreover, pushed for the increased application of economic instruments. However, these declarations of political intent have yet to be translated into corresponding policies (Weale 1999, 40–4). For instance, efforts to introduce a European energy tax have so far failed due to the resistance of the member states (Héritier, Knill and Mingers 1996, 314–15; Jachtenfuchs 1996; Grant, Matthews and Newell 2000; Klok 2002).

While the polluter pays principle is primarily geared at enforcing environmental objectives by offering appropriate incentives for individual behaviour, the integration principle is based on a much more comprehensive concept. It rests upon the conviction that effective environmental policy cannot be carried out if it is detached from other policy areas, given that decisions in other policy sectors, such as regional, transport, or agricultural policy, frequently have considerable ramifications for the environment. Thus, this principle emphasizes

> that environmental protection cannot be the responsibility solely of a separate branch of environmental policy and administration, but that it has to be integrated into a wide range of public policies, if harmful effects from those policies are to be anticipated and counteracted. (Weale et al. 2000, 69)

Even if it also has its foundations in the First Environmental Action Programme, the integration principle only gained greater political significance at the European level in recent years. This is demonstrated not only by the fact that the principle is mentioned in the SEA and its scope was extended in the Amsterdam Treaty, but also by the way it was concretized in the Fifth Action Programme (Lenschow 1999, 92). On the one hand, this document underlined the necessity of improved horizontal coordination between the DGs of the Commission responsible for different policy areas. On the other hand, it stressed the goal of enhancing vertical coordination, incorporating state as well as private actors at different institutional levels (European, national, regional, local) within the framework of so-called dialogue groups (Favoino, Knill and Lenschow 2000, 39–40).

However, until now the practical realization of these goals has proven to be fairly difficult. This holds both for the better incorporation of environmental policy goals into the policies of other DGs and for the integration of environmental policy goals into policy formulation at the national and sub-national level (see European Commission 1996; Lenschow 1999, 2001; EEA 2005). These difficulties can be explained, among other things, by the weak position of DG Environment as compared to other DGs within the Commission and the relatively low priority attached to environmental policy goals and their implementation as opposed to other objectives of the Union. Furthermore, observers have pointed out that the organizational requirements for the effective integration of environmental policy goals into other fields is only seldom compatible with institutional routines and procedures that have evolved over the years in other policy areas (Lenschow 1997, 1999; Favoino, Knill and Lenschow 2000).

All in all, the remarks up to now indicate that the European environmental policy can by no means be conceived as a conglomeration of relatively unconnected and uncoordinated measures. Instead, it is based on a range of quite fundamental principles. These entail not only general environmental management, the definition of standards and the allocation of authority, but also the integration of environmental protection into other policy areas. However, these principles are not static or fixed. Their political significance and impact fluctuate in the course of time as well as across the various measures taken. This aspect becomes particularly apparent when we take a closer look at the regulatory approaches that underlie concrete policies and at the instruments chosen to implement those policies.

Regulatory approaches

In European environmental policy we can identify not only principles that shape the substance of policy-makers' actions, but also paradigms pertaining to the modes of regulation which are deemed appropriate. Such regulatory approaches can be distinguished, in particular, along two dichotomies: (1) technology versus cost orientation and (2) interventionist versus context-oriented governance.

Technology versus cost orientation
The question of whether environmental policy in the EU should be more oriented towards the technological means of preventing environmental pollution, i.e. the current state of technology, or based on the careful consideration of the economic and ecological costs and benefits associated with the implementation of environmental policy measures, has been an object of protracted political

controversy between individual member states (Sbragia 2000, 308–11). In this context, 'regulatory competition' between Germany and the UK was (and to some extent still is) a main factor (Héritier, Knill and Mingers 1996).[4] Both states have highly divergent views with respect to the character of environmental governance and have continually attempted to put those views into practice at the European level.[5]

The German understanding of environmental governance is closely aligned with the current state of technology. Regardless of local conditions which might vary (e.g. the state of the environment or the economic situation of an industrial firm) the 'best available technology' (BAT) should be used uniformly in order to reduce the emission of pollutants. The principles of precaution and action at the source lie at the heart of this emission-oriented conception of environmental policy (Boehmer-Christiansen and Skea 1991; Weidner 1996; Jänicke and Weidner 1997).

The German point of view stands in stark contrast with that of the British. The latter emphasizes the quality of the environment and not – as is the case in the Federal Republic of Germany – the quantity of pollutants as such. The main focus is placed not on whether certain hazardous substances exist, but rather on the extent to which these substances produce adverse effects for the environment. Inherent to this quality-oriented approach is the premise that the environment can absorb a certain degree of damage imposed by emissions without any harmful side effects arising. Thus, arguments based on cost–benefit analysis come to the fore: the objective is not the prevention of emissions at (almost) any price, but rather the definition of an optimal, i.e. most cost–effective, way of managing the environment. This optimum may fluctuate depending on local circumstances, the cost of the preventive technology, and the economic situation of the company (Weidner 1987; Jordan 1993; Knill 1995, 76f.).

The result of this competition between different regulatory approaches is that elements of both can be identified at the European level. Classic examples of the German brand of European environmental policy are, for example, the Directive on the Incineration of Hazardous Waste, which is closely oriented towards the current state of technology and the reduction of emissions, and the Directive on Air Pollution from Large Combustion Plants (i.e. power plants and other large industrial installations such as refineries and steel works). The British style, on the other hand, is best represented by the various directives on air quality and by the IPPC Directive, in which the use of the best available technology is subject to a cost analysis, following the concept of 'best available technology not entailing excessive cost' (BATNEEC) (Héritier, Knill and Mingers 1996; Sbragia 2000). In the 1976 Directive on Water Pollution by Dangerous Substances the two approaches were both included as alternative options, giving rise to a fair amount of confusion in the implementation phase (Wurzel 2002, 17–30).

The fact that 'German' and 'British' elements are about equally reflected in EU environmental policy by no means implies that technology and cost orientation were always of the same political relevance. Instead, a closer analysis reveals a shift in focus over time. While German regulatory models dominated the 1980s, policies emphasizing the quality of the environment and the local context and conditions gained influence from the 1990s. More recent EU policies thus coincide to a greater extent to the British notions (Knill and Héritier 1996; Sbragia 2000).

This shift can be traced back to several factors. Obviously, it is relevant to ask to what extent a member state has developed innovative governance concepts at the national level at all, which may then serve as a model for corresponding European activities. For Germany, this was the case during the 1980s, when relatively extensive measures to combat forest dieback were passed at the national level. In the UK, on the other hand, there were far-reaching environmental policy innovations in the 1990s due to domestic developments and European demands for compliance. This enabled the British to take over the role of a forerunner in EU environmental policy (Héritier, Knill and Mingers 1996, 207ff.).

However, national innovations alone do not suffice to exert a positive influence on EU environmental policy. Instead, the national viewpoints must be compatible with the general ideas and objectives prevalent in the Commission, which is in charge of drawing up concrete policy proposals. In the 1980s, the Commission offered a fertile soil for the German conceptions based on uniform emission reductions. From the 1990s, however, a number of factors discussed in more detail in the next section led to a search for more flexible and context-oriented alternatives.

This made the Commission more responsive to the British approach.

Intervention versus context-oriented governance

In the first two decades after its emergence as an independent policy area in the early 1970s, EU environmental policy was predominantly built upon hierarchical intervention. Most policies were characterized by detailed, mostly substantive regulatory requirements, which allowed the member states relatively little leeway for their implementation.

Typical examples of this 'command-and-control' approach are the European directives which were passed in the area of air pollution control and water protection. They set strict limits that were aligned with the best available technologies. As we will discuss in more detail below, directives are formally supposed to be restricted to the definition of goals and to leave the specification of the means by which these goals should be reached to the member states. However, with some exceptions, the first genera-tion of EU environmental directives in fact tended to lay down both goals (i.e. standards) and means (i.e. best available technol-ogy). This reduced the individual countries' room to manoeuvre in the implementation process to a considerable extent (Knill and Lenschow 2000a).

However, the emission-oriented approach, based on the current state of technology, conceded its dominant role at the beginning of the 1990s. Instead, so-called context-oriented forms of environmental governance gained prominence. They first did so in the Fifth Environmental Action Programme, adopted in 1993 (Kronsell, 1997; Lenschow 1999a). Since then, the 'new' approach has received particular attention in the literature (Golub 1998; Knill and Lenschow 1999, 2000; Mol, Lauber and Liefferink 2000; Sbragia 2000, 311; Héritier 2002; Jordan, Wurzel and Zito 2003). This is certainly not to say that the 'old' approach has entirely disappeared from the scene. Traditional emission limits, based on the best available technology, are still widely used in Brussels alongside the 'new' generation of policies (Héritier 2002).

The 'new' governance concept is explicitly oriented towards the diversity of national conditions. Instead of imposing detailed guidelines 'from above', the 'new' approach allows states more flexibility in adapting national arrangements to European requirements. Furthermore, it aims to create positive incentives for the voluntary participation and cooperation of societal actors.

The 'new' approach is reflected firstly by a renewed focus on the definition of policy goals (e.g. with respect to air quality), leaving the decision on the means by which these goals should be reached (e.g. limitation of industrial emissions or automobile exhaust fumes) to the member states. Secondly, there are more and more measures which strive for better information and participation of the broadest possible array of state and private actors, such as the Directive on Access to Environmental Information, the Environmental Management and Audit Scheme (EMAS)-Regulation or the scheme for greenhouse gas emissions trading. Thirdly, forms of hierarchical regulation are increasingly enhanced by cooperative arrangements and legally non-binding agreements between public and private actors.

> [The new approach] works bottom-up towards the creation of environmental responsibility and awareness on the part of the polluting actors ... as well as towards the integration of the typically rather diffuse environmental interests in the policy formulation, implementation, and evaluation processes ... Its link to the policy addressees (businesses, consumers, general public) is often indirect, providing incentives or establishing new communication and participation channels; the obligations for the immediate implementation actors (local public authorities) are supposed to be flexible, permitting the instrument's integration in the local political, socio-economic and institutional context. (Knill and Lenschow 2000b, 4)

While the impact and effectiveness of the 'new' approach will be evaluated in considerable detail in Chapters 8 and 9 of this book, we will for now restrict ourselves to the causes of this important change in the regulatory orientation of EU environmental policy. Four aspects are of particular significance.

Firstly, given the different national conditions and interest constellations, the detailed definition of issue-specific 'command-and-control' requirements often entailed tedious and problematic decision-making processes at the European level. The negotiations on the Directive on Large Combustion Plants, for instance, lasted more than five years. Thus, interventionist governance proved to be detrimental to the EU's capacity to act.

This applied not only to the adoption of new measures, but also to the adaptation of existing regulations to new technological developments or environmental policy issues. For example, if one wanted to tighten emission limits in light of the development of improved filter technologies, a separate directive or regulation would have to be passed to change the existing legislation. Thus, even minimal modifications meant that the entire decision-making process had to be repeated from beginning to end (Knill 1995, 241).

A restriction to general objectives, e.g. in the form of framework directives or quality standards,[6] was supposed to reduce the complexity of the decision-making process. Furthermore, the EU hoped that the more widespread use of voluntary agreements with industries, aiming for instance at reducing automobile emissions (Wurzel 2002), would help to circumvent the tedious and complicated European legislative process (Mol, Lauber and Liefferink 2000; Héritier 2002).

A second problem that was supposed to be overcome by switching from interventionist to context-oriented governance is the 'implementation deficit' in EU environmental policy. Even if this problem had been well known for a long time, it did not gain significance on the political agenda until the beginning of the 1990s. One of the main reasons for this was that some member states started to question the overall legitimacy of the European environmental policy and urged for the 're-nationalization' of regulatory authority. In doing so, they explicitly referred to the negative results in implementing common policies (Golub 1997; Jordan 1999; see also Chapter 7).

In spite of the often very detailed and ambitious policy demands posed by European directives, problems of ineffective formal and practical implementation at the national level continually escalated (European Commission 1996). Apart from the fact that the monitoring and control of implementation across the EU was a difficult matter, it turned out that the detailed requirements contained in European legislation were not always the most effective means of reaching the targeted policy effects due to varying geographical, political, social and economic conditions at the national, regional or local level (Knill and Lenschow 2000a).

With the 'new' governance approach, explicitly aimed at taking different national contexts and conditions into account, the EU attempted to reduce these problems. Furthermore, it was assumed that a closer cooperation with those affected by the policies would lead to their greater acceptance and, as a consequence, a more effective implementation process (but see Chapters 8 and 9).

A third factor behind the shift to the 'new' approach was the subsidiarity principle. As we have seen, this principle was established by the SEA and the Treaty of Maastricht not only as a guiding principle for environmental policy, but as a general basis for action for the EU. The subsidiarity principle – which is ultimately a reaction to the increasing criticism of the bureaucratic culture in Brussels – emphasizes forms of governance which 'protect autonomy and are compatible with the Community objectives' (Scharpf 1993) to the greatest possible extent. Thus, interventionist types of regulation which encroached upon the member states' room to manoeuvre were no longer as politically legitimate as in the past. According to this line of argument, the subsidiarity principle facilitated the development of new patterns of governance, as they merely allotted the member states a framework of objectives, but not the means to reach these objectives (Knill and Héritier 1996, 227).

Fourthly, the changes in the governance modes in EU environmental policy were rooted in a global wave of reforms characterized by catchwords such as privatization, liberalization, deregulation, withdrawal of the state, and the emergence of New Public Management (Wright 1994; Benz and Goetz 1996; Kickert 1997). They all shared a focus on more flexible and effective governance concepts and facilitated and legitimized the creation of context-oriented governance approaches at the European level. Thus, the transformation of environmental policy governance must be viewed not only as the result of internal, policy-specific factors, but also as an expression of reform discussions at the global level (Lenschow 1999a, 40–1).

Policy instruments

We have now discussed the various substantive principles as well as the different regulatory paradigms underlying EU environmental policy. The general principles constitute a rich and multifarious basis, allowing for the development of a wide variety of policy measures. We have seen, moreover, that the regulatory character of environmental policies endorsed by the EU has changed considerably over the years. In order to cast these principles and paradigms into a concrete form, a well-equipped 'toolbox' of environmental policy instruments has been developed. In this context, we frequently find a distinction in the literature between substantial and procedural instruments. Substantial instruments are characterized by the fact that they specify concrete demands in terms of policy substance. Procedural instruments, on the other hand, do not lay down concrete policy goals and restrict themselves to the definition of certain rules of procedure, with which the member states must comply (Heinelt et al. 2000).

As far as substantial instruments are concerned, two basic subcategories can be distinguished, which have already been mentioned several times in the previous sections: the regulation of emissions at their source and the regulation of the quality of the environment.

The discharge of harmful substances into the environment is generally regulated on the basis of so-called emission standards. Such standards define maximum levels for the discharge of individual pollutants into different sectors or compartments of the environment (air, water, earth). For example, the Directive on Large Combustion Plants sets such limits on the emission of sulphur dioxide, nitrogen oxides and dust into the air. Besides concrete numerical standards, other forms of regulating emissions

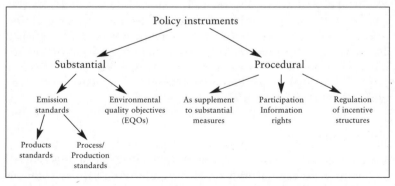

Figure 2.1   *Basic categories of instruments used in EU environmental policy*

are also conceivable. The Framework Directive on the Combating of Air Pollution from Industrial Plants, passed in 1984, for instance, stipulates that an operating licence may only be issued to a company if it uses the best available technology to reduce pollutant emissions.

As regards the regulation of emissions, a further distinction between production and product standards is useful. While production standards define technical features which must be taken into account when designing production facilities and operating the production process (e.g. limits on emissions from power plants or waste incineration plants), product standards apply to the composition and quality of finished products (e.g. exhaust emissions from motor vehicles, noise emissions from lawn mowers).

The regulation of emissions should be distinguished from the regulation of immissions on the basis of so-called environmental quality objectives (EQOs), which define limits on the maximum or minimum concentration of certain substances in specific sectors of the environment. An example of this is the series of air quality directives, which lay down an array of legally binding standards for ambient air quality.

While substantial measures set concrete goals with respect to the improvement of the quality of the environment or the prevention of emissions, procedural instruments are limited to the definition of procedural rules. They stipulate certain administrative and legal courses of action, without prescribing the actual result of such courses of action. Although a few policies of this type were passed before the 1990s (e.g. the Directive on EIA in 1985, as the most prominent example), this category clearly brings us within the realm of the 'new' approach to environmental regulation, introduced in the previous section.

At the European level, a broad spectrum of procedural rules can be identified (Heinelt et al. 2000). As a start, substantial measures frequently entail supplemental procedural provisions regarding the course of action to be taken when implementing and monitoring the substantial requirements. Such provisions typically pertain to authorization and/or monitoring procedures.

Secondly and in particular since the beginning of the 1990s in the context of the 'new' approach, procedural measures have been passed which regulate opportunities to obtain information and to participate in decision-making processes. In this context, we should underline the 1990 Directive on Access to Environmental Information. It entails a passive right to information, which means that upon request each person must be granted free access to all environmentally relevant information from national authorities without evidence of a particular interest in the matter (Kimber 2000). The Framework Directive on Air Quality, passed in 1996, expanded the participation of the public by granting active rights to information. Along these lines, when limits are exceeded, national authorities must publish action plans specifying how they intend to improve the air quality in the regions concerned. Moreover, if the measured values reach a certain alarm threshold, defined in a so-called 'daughter directive', the member states are obligated to inform the public about this by means of the press and broadcasting services (Knill and Héritier 1996, 226).

A third form of 'new' procedural governance concerns the establishment of incentive structures for environmentally friendly behaviour. On the one hand, such measures may be geared towards producers and consumers. An example of this is the EMAS-Regulation. It defines the procedural rules for the voluntary establishment and certification of environmental management systems in companies. As long as a firm fulfils the conditions of the regulation, it is authorized to use a statement of participation for marketing purposes (Bouma 2000). The eco-label is based on a similar voluntary incentive structure for the marketing of individual products (Wright 2000). The recent scheme establishing a market for permits for the emission of greenhouse gases (emissions trading) also fits into this category. Increased scarcity of emission rights will increase their price and thus stimulate technological development (see also Chapter 6).

On the other hand, there are incentive structures which seek to stimulate environmentally friendly behaviour by the member state authorities. These include the strategies of information exchange and publication of the results of the implementation of EU policies, proposed in the Sixth Environmental Action Programme. By these means, the member states have an incentive to perform as well as possible, so that their reputation at the European level is not damaged (Héritier 2002).

Policies and fields of activity: an overview

So far, this chapter has attempted to come to a better understanding of the character of EU environmental policy by employing general and fairly abstract concepts and categories. The different types of policy instruments presented in the previous section as well as the regulatory approaches discussed earlier are analytical tools, invented by political scientists in order to get a better grip on reality. The policy principles, in contrast, can be found in policy documents such as the environmental action programmes or in the EU Treaty. In the latter case, they have a legally binding status and must be taken into account when policies are designed. What ultimately counts in terms of environmental protection, however, are the concrete measures and policies which have been passed to reach a wide range of specific environmental goals and in which those abstract principles, paradigms and instruments have materialized.

In view of the number and variety of individual measures passed since the beginning of the 1970s, our objective here cannot be to list and present all regulations individually.[7] Instead, this section serves to convey a general overview of the EU's central fields of action and main activities with regard to the environment. In this context, a distinction will be made between policies that focus on distinct sectors or compartments of the environment and those which are more cross-sectoral. Furthermore, it is useful to be aware of the different legal forms employed in EU environmental policy. This aspect will be elaborated on first.

Forms of legislation for the common environmental policy

According to Article 249 (ex-Article 189) of the TEU, five different forms of legislation are available in the EU: directives, regulations, decisions, recommendations and opinions. Of particular significance here are the first two.

In practice, the most important form of legislation in the environmental policy field is the directive. As pointed out earlier, directives are binding for the member states as regards their objectives, but they leave it up to them to decide which means are most adequate to reach those objectives. Along with that, directives as a rule must be transposed into national legislation in order to take legal effect. In that sense, they should be distinguished from regulations, which are completely binding as 'European law' and apply immediately in all member states, without the necessity of their being put into national law. Thus, regulations generally allow the member states less leeway in terms of their practical implementation than directives, as they make both the objective and the selection of instruments mandatory. In the area of environmental policy, regulations are particularly significant when it comes to the ratification of international agreements and in the implementation of institutional, organizational and financial measures (Knill 2003, 53).

In practice, however, the boundaries between directives and regulations are blurred. As pointed out earlier, some directives contain very detailed requirements, which allot the member states very little room for manoeuvre when implementing them. Conversely, there are regulations which are formulated in a relatively flexible manner and thus imply a great degree of leeway in the implementation phase. For example, it is possible for so-called framework directives to initially allow for a very broad framework for action, which is narrowed down later by highly specific 'daughter directives', which are quite similar to regulations in terms of content (Rehbinder and Stewart 1985, 35). With respect to their immediate applicability, the differences between directives and regulations have also been reduced by the jurisdiction of the ECJ: if directives are not implemented properly or not implemented in due time, they have immediate legal effect at the national level.

In contrast to the generic character of directives and regulations, decisions serve to regulate individual cases; they are of an individual nature and are only binding for those that they refer to. For EU environmental policy, they are only of limited relevance. The same holds for recommendations and opinions which are legally unbinding forms of action. However, the latter might gain in significance in the future due to the Commission's increased interest in cooperative strategies.

Overarching measures

In contrast to the somewhat rhetoric emphasis placed on integrated, overarching environmental protection in documents such as the environmental action programmes, concrete measures have restricted themselves for a long time to the conventional, sectoral regulation of individual problems. Thus, up to now only a comparatively small number of overarching policies have been adopted. These have posed considerable demands for the adaptation of national regulatory patterns, however, which also tend to be structured according to the different sectors or compartments of the environment. Hence, the adoption of these measures is frequently met with great resistance in the member states, resulting in far-reaching implementation problems (see Chapters 7–9). Of particular significance are the measures listed in Table 2.2.

Table 2.2 *Major overarching measures in EU environmental policy*

Directive on Environmental Impact Assessment (EIA)	1985, 1997
Directive on Access to Environmental Information	1990
Regulation establishing a Community eco-label	1992, 2000
EMAS-Regulation	1993, 2001
Directive on Integrated Pollution Prevention and Control (IPPC)	1996
Decision on a European Pollutant Emissions Register	2000

The EIA Directive explicitly aims at an integrated approach to environmental problems. When projects with a significant impact on the environment are authorized, their environmental compatibility should be assessed not only in terms of the distinct sectors of the environment (soil, water, air, etc.), but also in terms of their mutual, cross-sectoral effects. The main focus of the Information Directive, on the other hand, is greater transparency in the regulation of environmental policy and greater participation of the public in the process (Kimber 2000). The European Pollutant Emissions Register serves a similar goal by collecting, storing and disseminating emissions data from industrial facilities. The EMAS-Regulation grants industries the possibility of setting up an environmental management system on a voluntary basis and having its quality validated by external experts. While the EMAS can be characterized as a production-related concept, the eco-label is geared towards individual products, indicating their environmentally-friendly production and composition (Bouma 2000; Wright 2000). The IPPC Directive, finally, establishes an integrated approach for the authorization of industrial facilities. It seeks to take into account the full range of sectoral effects on the environment as well as their mutual interactions. If functioning well, such an approach serves both the environment and the companies involved, as they need to apply for only one instead of several permits.

Sector-specific measures
As pointed out, however, the majority of environmental policy activities in the EU are still focused at individual sectors of the environment. Here we can distinguish, in particular, between the areas of water protection, air pollution control, noise control, waste management, chemicals control, and nature protection.

In the area of water protection (Table 2.3), extensive regulatory activities were developed in the 1970s. For an array of different types of water (such as bathing water, shellfish waters and drinking water) relatively strict quality standards were adopted. In addition to that, a framework directive was passed in 1976 which regulated the discharge of hazardous substances into surface water. On the basis of this directive, more concrete 'daughter directives' were enacted, which defined emission limits for individual harmful substances. Further important measures are the Directive on the Management of Urban Waste Water, passed in 1991, and a new and more encompassing framework directive in 2000. The latter requires the member states to organize water management around river basins

Table 2.3   *Major measures in the area of water protection*

Water quality	
Bathing water	1975
Shellfish waters	1979
Drinking water	1980, 1998
Discharge of hazardous substances	
Framework Directive on the Discharge of Dangerous Substances into the Aquatic Environment	1976
Ground water	1979
Urban waste water	1991
Nitrate from diffuse sources	1991
Water Framework Directive	2000

Important measures dealing with air pollution control were not passed until the 1980s (Table 2.4). These entailed, firstly, air quality limits for a number of individual substances, followed in 1996 by a comprehensive Framework Directive on Air Quality. This framework directive, in turn, was followed by a series of 'daughter directives' updating the existing limits for individual pollutants as well as setting some additional ones. Second, the regulation of emissions, in particular the authorization of industrial facilities, was dealt with initially by means of a framework directive. It was subsequently concretized by a number of 'daughter directives' setting emission limits for specific sources and pollutants. Of particular significance here is the 1988 Directive on Large Combustion Plants, a major effort instigated above all by Germany to combat acidification and forest dieback. The provisions of the directive were tightened in 2001. In addition to that, nationwide emission ceilings for a number of acidifying substances were set in 2001. Since the late 1990s the EU has also entered the field of climate change, not least due to the need to implement the 1997 Kyoto Protocol, which had been endorsed jointly by the EU and the member states. Most notably, a key was developed to distribute the 'burden' of the single, EU-wide reduction target for greenhouse gases over the individual member states. In a second step, a system for trading the emissions of greenhouse gases among companies was established. Finally, the EU boasts a series of product standards relating to air pollution. Since the 1970s, numerous standards for automobile emissions have been passed and continually adapted to technological development. For CO_2, moreover, voluntary agreements with the automobile industry were concluded in 1999 and 2000 and confirmed by the Commission by way of recommendations. In addition to that, several product standards concerning the quality of liquid fuels are worthy of mention (see Haigh 2000).

In the area of noise control too, a wide array of directives has been adopted since the 1970s. These measures primarily entail product standards, setting limits for the noise emissions of certain products. The spectrum ranges from automobiles, motorcycles, tractors, construction machinery, lawn mowers and home appliances to concrete breakers and subsonic jet aeroplanes.

As with noise and water control, many regulations in the field of waste management emerged during the 1970s (Table 2.5).

Table 2.4   *Major measures in the area of air pollution control*

Air quality	
Sulphur dioxide and dust	1980, 1999
Lead	1982, 1999
Nitrogen oxides	1985, 1999
Ozone	1992, 2002
Framework Directive	1996
Benzene and carbon monoxide	2000
Arsenic, cadmium, mercury, nickel and polycyclic	
aromatic hydrocarbons	2004
Emission limits	
Framework Directive	1984
Large combustion plants	1988, 2001
Municipal and hazardous waste incineration	1989, 1994, 2000
Volatile organic compounds (VOC)	1994, 1999, 2004
Burden sharing agreement	1998
National emission ceilings	2001
Greenhouse gas emissions trading	2003
Product standards	
Automobile exhaust	1970–99
Particle emissions from diesel vehicles	1988, 2001
Voluntary agreements and Recommendation on	
CO_2 emissions from cars	1999, 2000
Sulphur content of liquid fuels	1975, 1993, 1999
Lead content of petrol	1985, 1987
Petrol and diesel quality	1998

Notably, a framework directive was enacted in 1975 and subsequently amended by 'daughter directives' for various specific waste problems. A particularly far-reaching one among these was the Directive on Packaging and Packaging Waste (Haverland 1998). All in all, the strategies pursued by the EU with regard to the prevention and re-utilization of waste material had a long-lasting influence on the legal and political development in the member states.

Primarily for reasons of consumer protection and health, important regulations in the area of chemical control have been passed since the 1960s. They were amended and updated several times over the past decades. The diverse measures pertain, in particular, to the regulation of chemical additives in foods, the

Table 2.5 *Important measures concerning waste management*

Framework Directive	1975
Waste oil	1975
Sewage sludge	1986
Hazardous waste	1991
Batteries	1991, 1993
Cross-border shipment of waste	1993
Packaging and packaging waste	1994
PCBs and PCTs	1996
Landfill of waste	1999
Incineration of waste (see also air pollution control, Table 2.4)	2000
Waste from ships	2000
End-of-life vehicles	2000
Waste electric and electronic equipment	2002

categorization, packaging and labelling of hazardous substances, restrictions in the usage and spread of hazardous substances, and the prevention of accidents caused by hazardous substances. Along with that, the regulation of genetically modified products is a relatively new area. Table 2.6 summarizes those measures which are relevant in particular to preventing harm to the environment.

Table 2.6 *Important measures in the area of chemical control*

Framework Directive (Categorization, Packaging and Labelling of Hazardous Substances)	1967–2001
Major-accident hazards (Seveso Directive)	1982, 1996, 2003
Genetically modified organisms	1990, 2001
Regulation on persistent organic substances (POPs)	2004

EU activities concerning nature protection focus on the protection of species and, more recently, habitats. They frequently entail the implementation of international agreements, including measures to conserve wild birds (1979), whales (1981) and young seals (1983), and to monitor trade in wild animals and plants (1997). A major step in this field was taken with the Habitats Directive of 1992, which demands the comprehensive protection of the living areas of wild animals and plants.

All in all, this overview demonstrates that the development and scope of EU environmental policy vary to a great degree depending on the issue at hand. For example, with regard to waste management, water protection and chemical control, far-reaching framework directives and supplemental measures were passed at a relatively early point in time. As for air pollution control, in contrast, the EU did not press ahead with decisive measures until the middle of the 1980s. Notable activity in the field of nature protection only started in the 1990s.

The reasons for this unbalanced development include, firstly, the extent to which the different fields of activity affect the Common Market. The more relevant the harmonization of divergent national regulations was for the realization of the Common Market, the greater the chances were for legislation at the European level. This made the adoption of product standards for noise emissions or air pollution from cars much easier than the establishment of policies in the area of nature protection. The link with the functioning of the Common Market was particularly relevant in the early years, since no explicit legal basis existed for an independent environmental policy until the mid-1980s (see Chapter 1).

The different degree of politicization and the different perception of political problems in various fields of activity can be regarded as a second factor. Along these lines, individual events and problems such as the major chemical accident in Seveso or acidification and forest dieback had a decisive influence on the reactions at the EU level.

Thirdly, for the 'Europeanization' of a certain policy area, it makes a difference whether the problems it entails are of a cross-border character and thus cannot be effectively solved by the individual states. Many problems associated with water protection, air pollution control, waste transport, but also the authorization of hazardous chemicals and genetically modified products, possess such a cross-border character. In the area of nature protection, in contrast, cross-border problem structures are less obvious.

Fourthly, international agreements can play an important role in initiating EU activities. This holds, in particular, for the areas of climate change and nature protection, where most of the EU's activities are ultimately based on the application of international agreements that were jointly signed by the EU and the member states (Sbragia 1998).

The transformation of environmental policy governance in the EU?

The previous sections have made it clear that the EU environmental policy area has matured over the years at least in terms of its substance. It has incorporated an encompassing set of environmental policy principles, several of which have found their way into the EU Treaty. While certain gaps still existed in the 1970s and 1980s, moreover, EU environmental legislation now covers all major areas and issues of the policy field. Today it is not easy to find aspects of environmental policy in the member states which have not at least to some extent been affected by the EU (see Jordan and Liefferink 2004).

While the institutionalization of the policy field in terms of substance (environmental policy principles, issues and issues areas) has largely been a matter of steady evolution, a more dynamic pattern could be observed with regard to governance patterns. Generally speaking, a shift seems to have taken place over the past ten to fifteen years from technology-based intervention to more cost-oriented, contextual forms of steering, characterised by 'new', often procedural policy instruments.

To what extent does this shift actually constitute a general trend, a veritable 'transformation in European environmental governance' (Lenschow 1999a)? And what do these changes signify in terms of the success of environmental policy governance in the EU?

If we begin by analysing the political opinions and declarations of the EU Commission as laid down in the Fifth and Sixth Environmental Action Programmes or the White Paper on *Governance in the European Union* (European Commission 2001), we wind up with the impression that a fundamental change in European environmental governance has indeed materialized. However, if one examines more closely the actual contribution of 'new' instruments to the entire corpus of EU environmental legislation, this first impression is clearly put back into perspective.

For example, Hey (2000, 85) ascertains that no general renunciation of typical governance instruments for the sake of purely procedural regulation can be observed in the EU of the 1990s despite such widespread perceptions. Thus, standards and technical norms for products and facilities still play a crucial role in EU environmental policy. Legally unbinding forms of regulation, such as negotiated agreements of private self-regulation, are still of minimal importance as compared to classical forms of interventionist regulation (Héritier 2002).

In light of this fairly marginal quantitative shift, it is difficult to judge whether the described developments actually evoke a comprehensive re-orientation of environmental governance in the EU. Despite the political rhetoric by the Commission, it remains to be seen whether the current initiatives are symptomatic of a new trend or merely a complement to the existing spectrum of environmental policy instruments.

Regardless of its quantitative relevance, questions also arise as to the extent to which these new developments have actually led to improvements in the EU's governance capacity in the environmental field. After all, the development of 'new' forms of governance was a reaction to the EU's weak decision-making capacity and the ineffective implementation of European environmental policies. In light of the sparse empirical data available up to now, no conclusive answer can be given. However, there are many indications that the new developments with regard to environmental policy governance have yet to fulfil the expectations associated with them.

As far as decision-making is concerned, it appears that resorting to voluntary or purely procedural agreements by no means necessarily results in an acceleration of the process. Empirical analysis shows that policies of the 'new' generation (Directive on Access to Environmental Information, Regulations on EMAS and Eco-label) were generally not agreed more easily than measures which define concrete targets (Héritier, Knill and Mingers 1996; Wright 2000).

Héritier (2002) and Hey (2000) come to the same conclusion with regard to the concretization of objectives in voluntary agreements. While the willingness of industries to cooperate is contingent on the use of relatively flexible and 'soft' wording in such agreements, the Commission is pressing for more ambitious and clearly defined demands. Moreover, the Council (i.e. the member states) does not want to lose control over the process (see

Mol, Liefferink and Lauber 2000, 223) and press for voluntary agreements being formulated only in combination with interventionist measures or 'in the shadow of the hierarchy'. Thus, voluntary models are seldom used in their purest form, but rather as a hybrid of voluntary cooperation and hierarchical intervention.

Also with respect to implementation, comparative studies indicate that the application of 'new' context-oriented concepts by no means produces better results than the 'old' instruments (Knill and Lenschow 2000b). On the one hand, as just pointed out, it appears that 'new' instruments can hardly ever be found in their ideal form, but rather as hybrids of traditional and 'new' components of governance. As a result, they in part demonstrate similar implementation problems to those of traditional approaches. On top of that, it turns out that the use of 'new' instruments frequently leads to additional problems. These are associated, among other things, with too flexible and vague objectives, which fail to provide sufficiently specific incentives to polluters and national authorities alike (see further Chapters 7–9).

Notes

1 It should be emphasized that the allocation of individual principles to the various categories leads to a certain analytical simplification and does not take potential overlappings into account. For instance, the polluter pays principle is not only an important concept in terms of the internalization and integration of environmental policy goals into other policy areas, but can also be regarded as an environmental policy management principle.

2 Of particular significance in this regard is the so-called 'Seveso-Directive' (82/501/EEC), which was passed in reaction to the poisonous gas catastrophe in Seveso (Italy) in 1976.

3 However, in political practice this in no way means that the adoption of quality standards is of secondary importance as compared to emission limits. For one thing, this has to do with the fact that the principle of action at the source cannot be applied in equal measure to all types of damage to the environment. On the other hand, it is generally easier to adopt quality standards within the framework of the European decision-making process, because they allow the member states to decide themselves on the measures with which they would like to reach the targets set by the EU (see also the section on Regulatory approaches).

4 For a thorough introduction into the concept of 'regulatory competition' see Chapter 5.

5 Due to European policies and the demands for adaptation which they pose at the national level, there has been at least a partial approximation of German and British regulatory concepts in the past few years. However, this has not fundamentally reduced the contrast between both countries (Knill 2001; Jordan 2004; Wurzel 2004).

6 It must be noted that the explicit restriction to encompassing goals by way of framework directives and environmental quality objectives was by no means entirely new as such. Already in the late 1970s and early 1980s a number of environmental quality standards in the fields of water and air protection had been adopted. Due to serious implementation problems (Rehbinder and Stewart 1985, 137; Bennett, G. 1991), however, these policies have always led a relatively marginal existence.

7 Such a list can be found at the Internet site of the EU Commission: http://europa.eu.int/eur-lex/lex/en/repert/1510.htm (accessed 9 September 2005).

3
Central institutions and actors

The previous overview of the historical development, policy orientations and governance patterns of EU environmental policy can only be understood and explained when we take a closer look at how this policy is actually made. What are the general institutional and procedural conditions for the design of European environmental policies? Who are the important actors? What are their respective responsibilities? What general interest constellations and patterns of interaction can be observed?

Our starting point for answering these questions is an overview of the main actors and institutions active in the formulation of the EU environmental policy. Here we initially focus on the different European institutions: the Commission, the Council of Ministers, the EP, the ECJ and the EEA. Subsequently, emphasis will be placed on private actors who aim to exert influence on the formation of European environmental policies. Finally, we have a closer look at the role of the EU in international environmental institutions. Decisions and policy developments at the international level may have important repercussions for environmental policy-making in the EU.

The EU Commission

The Commission plays a crucial role in the institutional system of the EU. This is due to the diverse powers of the Commission which range from agenda-setting to monitoring functions on to executive tasks.

For the phase of environmental policy formulation, which we

are interested in here, the agenda-setting tasks are of great significance, as they entail the planning and elaboration of proposals for Council decisions. Only the Commission has the right to initiate legislation. Without a proposal from the Commission, the Council of Ministers cannot preside over legislative acts (with a few exceptions). Along with that, it is important to note that the Commission can withdraw its proposals and stop the process at any time during the legislative process.

However, in practice this formal monopoly on agenda-setting is subject to certain restrictions. For example, both the EP and the Council can request the Commission to draw up certain proposals and to bring them into the legislative process. Furthermore, as a rule the chances of a Commission proposal being implemented increase when the member state governments are consulted before a formal proposal is made (Christiansen 2006, 108ff.).

Despite these practical limitations, the Commission does retain diverse means of initiating joint policies and steering them in its desired direction. Even if Commission proposals are extensively modified and reformulated during the negotiations in the Council of Ministers, fundamental changes to the regulatory concepts put forward by the Commission are very rare:

> The Commission ... is the key player at the stage of policy formulation, since the regulatory approach that it adopts can be very difficult to change completely. Commission proposals tend to define the ground on which governments negotiate. (Sbragia 2000, 298)

In the area of environmental policy in particular, the Commission has made ample use of the agenda-setting powers granted to it. This was especially evident in the 1970s when the Commission triggered many successful initiatives for a common environmental policy (Holzinger 1994, 94). Against the background of increasing environmental problems and greater environmental awareness, it was often difficult for national governments to oppose the transfer of environmental policy responsibilities to the Community in areas in which joint activities appeared reasonable (Rehbinder and Stewart 1985, 258). In the course of time, however, a greater influence over the initiation of Community environmental policy activities on behalf of the member states can be observed. On the one hand, environmental policy initiatives were increasingly based on requests by the Council of Ministers. On the other hand, the member states increasingly attempted to influence environmental policy initiatives in an informal manner.[1]

Decisions on political initiatives and proposals are currently made by the college of the twenty-five members of the Commission (i.e. the Commissioners), who are each in charge of a certain field of functions. Although the resolutions are formally reached with a majority of members, the Commission seldom makes use of this rule in practice. In most cases, its members attempt to balance out diverging interests and forge a consensus.

The proposals are prepared in the responsible DGs and units, which are under the authority of the Commission. As for the elaboration and management of environmental policy measures, the DG Environment generally bears responsibility. Among its areas of authority are radiation protection, disaster prevention, environmental chemicals, biotechnology, waste management, soil protection, noise, water pollution control, air pollution control, nature conservation, environmental information and international matters concerning the environment.

However, this does not imply that the DG Environment is solely responsible for all environmental protection issues. Instead, many environmental problems can be traced back to activities in other areas, such as energy, transport, agriculture, public investments, infrastructural measures and the liberalization of the Common Market. The result is that when drawing up environmental policy initiatives the DG Environment frequently relies on the cooperation of other DGs who are in charge of these areas and for whom environmental protection issues are generally a smaller political priority (Sbragia 2000, 299; Weale et al. 2000, 89).

Due to this crossover effect in the character of environmental policies, attempts have increasingly been made in past years to integrate environmental concerns into the activities of other DGs. For example, in 1993 a separate unit within the DG Environment dealing with the incorporation of environmental policy into other policy areas was established. In the other DGs so-called 'integration correspondents' were designated to ensure that environmental policy concerns are taken into consideration in the elaboration of proposals in other policy areas in close coordination with the DG Environment. All DGs were also supposed to carry out a yearly evaluation of their environmental policy activities. However, despite the continuing efforts to increase the observance of environmental policy concerns in other policy areas at the Commission level, studies on the implementation of these reforms only point to relatively marginal progress (see Lenschow 1997, 1999; Wilkinson 1997).

These problems are due, on the one hand, to the fact that many of the larger DGs (such as agriculture and industry) had already created their own environmental departments before the reforms. These departments continued to work according to set routines and patterns, without taking the concerns of the DG Environment into consideration to any great extent, or coordinating activities with it (Favoino, Knill and Lenschow 2000). On the other hand, the other DGs do not necessarily interpret the integration principle to the extent that environmental policy concerns should be given more attention in their activities. Instead they see a possibility of 'turning the tables' and having their own sectoral concerns increasingly integrated into the policies of DG Environment (Wilkinson 1997, 162).

In this context, a further problem emerges from the fact that despite the continuous expansion of its fields of activity, DG Environment is among the smaller DGs. The number of permanent posts for qualified technical personal (so-called A-positions) has indeed multiplied ten times since the 1980s (from forty to sixty employees in the middle of the 1980s to currently around 500). However, measured proportionately to the entire staff of the Commission and compared to the workforce of similar agencies elsewhere (for example the USA's Environmental Protection Agency), the workforce of DG Environment can be viewed as relatively small (Weale et al. 2000, 89).[2] Its comparatively weak position vis-à-vis other DGs is also demonstrated by the fact – similar to the personnel situation – that the percentage of the overall budget allocated to the DG Environment is far behind that of other areas, although it has indeed increased in the course of time (Knill 2003, 92).

Among the core executive tasks of the Commission is the obligation to create the conditions for the implementation of Community legal acts and take the necessary measures for doing so. For example, these entail guidelines for the concrete design and application of authorization specifications, which are stipulated in a directive in general terms. In fulfilling these tasks, which have as a rule to be delegated to it by the Council, the Commission in turn relies on the collaboration of special committees which consist of representatives of the national governments. The composition and tasks of these committees vary depending on the type. This system of committees, known as 'Comitology', was institutionalized in 1987 and serves to monitor and, ultimately, to restrict the Commission's activities. In the area of environmental policy there are over thirty such committees that advise and monitor the DG Environment while drawing up implementation instructions for directives (Demmke 1997; Weale et al. 2000, 90).[3]

The monitoring tasks of the Commission primarily involve the phase of implementation of European policies: as the 'guardian of the treaties', the Commission is obligated to watch over the application of and compliance with primary and secondary Community law. The former entails the treaties that the Community is based on; the secondary Community law is the law created by the legislative bodies of the Community, such as directives or regulations on environmental policy. In order to carry out its monitoring functions, the Commission can gather all required information in the member states and conduct investigations. The member states have extensive obligations to provide information to the Commission. If the Commission determines that a violation against Community law has been made, it can start a formal infringement procedure with the ECJ against individual member states or other EU institutions (see Chapter 7).

The Council of Ministers

Although a stepwise expansion of the authority of the EP has taken place since the middle of the 1980s, the Council of Ministers still is the most important institution in the decision-making structure of the EU. Decisions on the adoption of European legislative measures, such as directives and regulations on environmental policy, are essentially made by the Council of Ministers.[4]

From a purely legal standpoint, the Council of Ministers is a uniform institution, although it does convene in different formations. Currently there are approximately twenty Councils with different areas of responsibility, such as the Council of Foreign

Ministers (or 'General Council'), the Council of Agriculture Ministers, the Council of Finance Ministers or the Council of Environment Ministers responsible for environmental policy measures. The members of the Council are thus the respective national ministers for different areas of expertise, which are determined by the national governments and bound by their instructions and mandates (Hayes-Renshaw and Wallace 1997).

In the Council of Ministers the interests of the member states are represented at the European level. The goal of the individual members of the Council is to assert their respective national interests at the European level to the greatest possible extent, in order to avoid criticism from their own government, the affected societal interest groups, and voters. At the same time, it is in the common interest of all members to reach an agreement. Nevertheless, the definition of national interests and policy positions in individual cases is often disputed at the member state level. For example, environment ministers from member states, in which environmental protection is a comparatively minor priority, have frequently used the negotiations at the European level as a means of strengthening environmental policy concerns at the national level (Collier and Golub 1997, 237).

> The fact that the environment ministers have usually deliberated amongst themselves in Brussels should not be underestimated. They have acquired an autonomy of action that they often lack at the national level, although how much varies depending on how national policy is coordinated in each member government. Environment ministers have undoubtedly been able to approve some legislation in Brussels for which they would have been unable to win support in their national cabinets. (Sbragia 2000, 300)

Although the Council of Environment Ministers is generally responsible for decisions over environmental policy manners, decisions made by other Councils (such as the energy, transport or agriculture ministers) frequently have direct implications for environmental policy. This can be traced back to the cross-sectoral nature of environmental policy. Similar to the development of policy proposals within the Commission, at the level of the Council of Ministers we also detect a sectoral fragmentation of responsibilities, which generally works against the effective integration of environmental policy concerns into other policy areas. In order to enable a certain degree of coordination in policy-making against this backdrop, joint Council sessions are sometimes held (for example environment and transport ministers). However, such joint consultations take place relatively seldom (Weale et al. 2000, 100).

The most important task of the Council of Ministers is its role as a legislator in the area of secondary Community law according to the decision-making procedures stipulated in the treaties. Typically, the Commission presents a proposal to the Council of Ministers, which in turn discusses, modifies, or amends it. The EP's involvement in this process varies according to the issue. However, it is also plausible that no agreement is reached between the national representatives during the negotiations and that no decision is made. In the area of environmental policy there are several examples of the complete failure of negotiations. The failed attempt to pass legislation on an energy tax is a notable example (Héritier, Knill and Mingers 1996, 314).

Depending on the policy area under contention, decisions are taken in the Council of Ministers on the basis of a simple majority, qualified majority, or unanimity. However, voting with a special majority requirement (qualified majority or unanimity) is the norm (Hayes-Renshaw and Wallace 1997). As set out in the previous chapter, the decision-making procedures in the Council of Ministers were modified a number of times over the 1980s and 1990s. In the SEA the original unanimity requirement for all decisions on environmental measures relevant to the Common Market was replaced with QMV. In the Treaty of Maastricht, the use of the qualified majority rule was extended to most areas of the joint environmental policy (see Chapter 4 for a more detailed presentation of decision-making procedures).

During preparations for Council summits, particular significance can be attached to the Committee of Permanent Representatives (COREPER).[5] The members of the COREPER are bound to the instructions of both the Council and the member states. Before certain measures are discussed in the COREPER, questions on technical details are smoothed out in various working groups, which primarily consist of national officials. The fact that the national officials sitting in these working groups are usually the same as those participating in the committees consulted by the Commission when preparing for decisions, demonstrates how tightly knit national and European bureaucracies are (Wessels and Rometsch 1996). Along with that, representatives of the Commission also take part in the meetings of the Council of Ministers.

As a rule, issues are only passed on to the Council of Ministers for deliberation if no agreement could be reached in the subordinate negotiation committee (COREPER and working groups) and a political solution to the problem appears necessary. In all other cases, the members of the Council formally confirm the agreements drawn up at the lower levels. The ultimate decision, however, is always that of the Council of Ministers (Hayes-Renshaw and Wallace 1997). Up to now, though, there are no thorough scientific analyses on the effects of the informal coordination between national officials at the COREPER level and the close bonds between national and supranational administrations and experts on European environmental policy-making (see Weale et al. 2000, 99).

Besides the COREPER and the subordinate working groups, the Presidency of the Council of Ministers plays an important role in the decision-making process. The Council Presidency rotates from one member state to the next every six months. The Presidency leads the negotiations in the Council of Ministers and the subordinate committees and working groups. By these means, it can set political priorities and – with certain restrictions – determine the agenda of negotiations. It thus plays an important role and at the same time assumes political responsibility for the activities and decisions of the Council (Kirchner 1992, 90; Wurzel 1996).

The European Parliament

The powers of the EP can hardly be compared with those of national parliaments, because at EU level there is no government which can be installed or controlled by the parliament. In general, a distinction is made between two fields of responsibility of the EP: besides parliamentary monitoring authority, which primarily entails the possibility of giving the Commission a vote of no-confidence with a two-thirds majority as well as appointing Commission Members, the participation of the EP in the legislative process is particularly worthy of mention.

Internally, the EP is basically organized according to the same pattern as national parliaments. The directly elected representatives form several parliamentary parties which are not organized by nationality, but by party affiliation. Similar to national parliaments, the technical details of decisions are smoothed out in various committees, whose responsibilities are basically oriented towards the DGs of the Commission. The Committee on the Environment, Public Health and Consumer Protection, which has existed since 1973, is responsible for environmental policy issues (see Hix 1999, 74–83).

As for the participation of the EP in the legislative process, we can distinguish between three main co-existing decision-making procedures: consultation, cooperation and co-decision.[6] For each area of legislation, it is specified which procedure applies. According to the consultation procedure, the EP is only granted an advisory function, i.e. it has the right to offer its opinion on the proposals of the Commission, but this opinion is not binding for the decision of the Council of Ministers. The introduction of the cooperation procedure in the SEA in 1987 led to an extension of the until then very limited decision-making powers of the EP for all decisions relevant to the Common Market and thus all environmental policy measures which fall into this category. While under the cooperation procedure the ultimate decision-making authority was still reserved for the Council of Ministers, according to the co-decision procedure introduced with the Maastricht Treaty the EP can now make decisions on equal footing with the Council. With regard to environmental policy, this procedure initially applied to all decisions relevant to the Common Market as well as decisions on environmental action programmes. In the Treaty of Amsterdam, the co-decision procedure was then expanded to all areas of environmental policy.

From the beginning, the EP played a very active role in EU environmental policy. Since the end of the 1960s it has continually requested the Commission to become environmentally active. Moreover, in its opinions during the legislative procedure it has continually advocated stricter and more extensive measures, which frequently went beyond the positions of the Commission and the Council of Ministers.

Despite its relatively weak legislative authority, in particular before the SEA was passed, the interventions on behalf of the EP are frequently well reflected in policy outcomes. Besides the formal amendments to the decision-making procedure since the end of the 1980s, an additional factor which explains the EP's considerable influence on environmental policy is that the environmental committee of the EP was able to establish informal relations relatively early with other institutions participating in the decision-making process, in particular the DG Environment. For instance, Judge, Earnshaw and Cowan (1994, 33) point out that 'a shared inter-institutional ethos between Committee members and Commission staff has served to enhance the informal exercise of parliamentary influence over EC environmental legislation'. Other observers also emphasize the political leadership of the chairman of the Committee for many years, the Scottish Labour representative Ken Collins (Weale et al. 2000, 92).

In light of the active role of the EP in environmental policy, one might assume that strengthening the powers of the EP would facilitate the further development of the EU's environmental policy. However, it is highly questionable whether a parliament with considerably enhanced legislative authority would still be the same parliament from an environmental standpoint. National environmental policy differences would most likely become more pronounced in the Parliament, leading to a partial shift of conflicts from the Council of Ministers to the Parliament. This could lead to more 'political realism' on behalf of the parliamentarians and thus to more moderate environmental protection demands. However, the effects of the EP's increased legislative competences in the field of environmental protection are still difficult to estimate at present.

The European Court of Justice

The ECJ is responsible for the interpretation of and compliance with primary and secondary community law. Among its powers, which are precisely stipulated in the TEU, two procedures are of particular importance with regard to the elaboration of policies. The first entails procedures against individual member states who have not properly complied with the legal obligations associated with primary and secondary Community law. Both the Commission and other member states can bring such procedures to the ECJ. The second procedure entails the power of the ECJ to review the constitutionality of the executive and legislative actions of the Community institutions (McCown 2006).

In contrast to the Commission, the Council of Ministers, and the EP, the ECJ is thus not directly involved in EU environmental policy-making. However, this does not change the fact that it has decisive influence over the regulation of the environmental policy in the EU:

> the Court is one of the most important institutions in European environmental governance. It is the Court that sets the limits within which policy is made and, in conforming or rejecting the legality of European-level legislation, affects or even alters the focus and priorities of environmental policy. (Weale et al. 2000, 102)

As for the design of European environmental policy, we can highlight several factors that illustrate the ECJ's power and influence. Firstly, the Court has decisively contributed to the formation and development of the EU's environmental policy, particularly in the period of a failing treaty basis (see Chapter 1). In several decisions it affirmed the possibility that environmental measures could be upheld by Article 94 of the TEU or, if they were not relevant to the Common Market, by the general clause of Article 308. The Court also facilitated the development of the environmental policy by accentuating the significance of environmental protection as an essential objective of the Community, regardless of the absence of treaty foundations (Sbragia 2000, 302).

Secondly, once environmental protection was incorporated into the Treaty by the SEA, the ECJ played an important role in developing criteria for balancing economic and environmental policy goals. In various decisions the ECJ basically affirmed that environmental protection concerns – including those that go beyond the exceptional cases stipulated in Article 30 TEU[7] – can substantiate import restrictions and are thus to be regarded as more significant than the objective of the free movement of goods. However, a prerequisite for this is that the restrictions are actually suitable and necessary for reaching the targeted environmental policy objectives (Koppen 1993).[8]

Thirdly, the various decisions of the ECJ on how to interpret the Treaties had important ramifications for the development of new legal measures because they changed the possibilities for action of the actors participating in the decision-making process (Alter and Meunier-Aitsahalia 1994; McCown 2006). Thus, the threat of a complaint to the ECJ may constitute an important political resource in the European decision-making process for both the Commission and individual member states. For example, while attempting to introduce stricter emissions limits for auto-mobiles in the 1980s, the German Federal Government was faced with harsh resistance by the other member states and thus threat-ened to unilaterally enforce its position under reference to Article 30. Consequently several member states announced that they would initiate a Treaty violation procedure against Germany if this were the case. Another example is when the Commission threatened to open up a Treaty violation procedure against Germany in 1991 due to the tax relief for diesel automobiles that met stricter standards than the planned European limits. It is interesting to note that this took place at a point in time in which the corresponding European regulation had yet to be definitively passed (Holzinger 1994, 119–21).

Fourthly, the existence and the decisions of the ECJ had rami-fications not only for the design of European environmental policies. The Court also played an important role in the imple-mentation and application of European legal acts in the member states – an increasingly explosive political issue that we will deal with more thoroughly in Chapters 7–9.

The European Environment Agency

The essential task of the EEA, which was established in 1994, is to gather and process information on the state of the environment in the Community. This information is supposed to allow for a comparative analysis of the state of the environment in the member states and provide empirical indicators which can be referred to as a basis for the design of environmental policy meas-ures at the level of the member states and the EU (Dilling 2000).

The EEA thus does not have any regulatory authority in terms of the development of policy or the implementation of European legislation in the member states. On these grounds, it differs significantly from comparable agencies such as the Environmental Protection Agency in the USA (Sbragia 2000, 202). However, this by no means implies that the current role of the Agency in the distribution and collection of environmentally relevant data and statistics is of little political significance. For example, Majone (1997) points out that the compilation of such information can have regulatory effects, because it demonstrates implementation deficits and thus triggers the necessary pressure for political action.

Despite the independent position of the Agency, which is in no way subject to the instructions of the other European institutions or national governments when fulfilling its tasks, it appears to cooperate very closely with the national environmental administrations in its daily work. These national environmental institutions are incorporated into the European Information and Observation Network (EIONET), on the basis of which the EEA collects its information. A frequent criticism is that the close bonds between the Agency and the national administrations have enabled the network to seal itself off from other actors, such as environmental organizations or local agencies (Wynne and Waterton 1998, 128).

> Critics fear that NGOs and local governments, for example, can easily become marginalized given the centrality of national ministerial officials. The issue of whose data is transmitted to Copenhagen has potentially far-reaching impacts on both the type and quality of data gathered by the EEA, one reason why the seeming monopoly of national administrations in the network has raised considerable concern. (Sbragia 2000, 303–4)

Interest groups

In particular since the adoption of the SEA and the realization of the Common Market programme, we have been witness to a dramatic increase in the number of societal actors and organizations at the European level. The primary goals of the European interest groups are gathering information for their members on the developments in Brussels, the bundling of the interests of their members, and the representation of these interests vis-à-vis the Community institutions in the policy-making process (Greenwood 1997; Aspinwall and Greenwood 1998; Mazey and Richardson 2006).

As for their respective organizational structures, there is a great degree of variation. However, the European interest groups are mostly organized as federations – so-called Euro-feds: their members are national associations representing a branch or a societal interest. More recently, an increasing number of interest associations has emerged which call for the direct membership of individual actors (e.g. individual firms). Moreover, the interest associations differ with respect to the array of interests which they represent. This spectrum ranges from cross-sectoral umbrella organizations to sector-specific trade associations on to single-issue networks and round tables (see Aspinwall and Greenwood 1998; Green Cowles 1998; Pijnenburg 1998).

Their informal contacts with the European institutions, in particular, allow the interest groups significant means of influence which are generally used in parallel. The most important contact and channel of influence in the process of policy-making is the Commission. In light of its comparatively weak personnel resources in the elaboration of its proposals, the Commission relies to a great extent on the know-how and expertise of the interest groups. By incorporating the interest associations, the Commission equally aims to increase the societal acceptance of its proposals. In order to avoid being confronted with divergent national positions, the Commission prefers contacts with interest associations that are organized at the European level. Thanks to the gradual expansion of its decision-making powers, the EP has also increasingly come to be viewed as an important institution for European interest associations to contact. Finally, the national governments and ministerial administrations have remained very important targets of lobbying activities due to the central position of the Council of Ministers in the European decision-making process. Thus, the Council of Ministers is primarily influenced by means of the 'national route'. However, in this context the European associations are attributed an important function in the coordination of the national associational activities (Greenwood 1997; Knill and Lehmkuhl 1998).

Even though the various means of influence are equally open to all interest groups, regardless of their concrete focus and goals, there are large differences with respect to the representation and assertiveness of different interests at the European level. In the area of environmental policy, this unequal distribution of influence capacities is demonstrated by the overrepresentation of economic interests. Business interest groups clearly outweigh environmental interests not only in terms of numbers, but they are also generally better equipped financially and in terms of staff (Hey and Brendle 1994, 331–87; Mazey and Richardson 2006).

On the one hand, the causes of this disequilibrium can be traced back to the original construction of the EU as an economic community. Accordingly, economic interest groups established themselves relatively early at that European level. As for environmental interests, the necessary incentives to organize at the European level did not emerge until the EU's environmental policy authority was developed and expanded, in particular through the SEA and the Treaty of Maastricht.

On the other hand, it is safe to say that environmental interests are more difficult to organize than economic interests. While the benefits resulting from the realization of environmental policy goals are distributed relatively diffusely across numerous relevant parties, the potential costs of environmental measures tend to be concentrated on a comparatively small number of concerned companies. In the organization of environmental interests, this leads to a 'free-rider' problem: the concerned parties indeed profit from the activities of the environmental associations (e.g. in the form of a higher level of environmental protection), but do not contribute accordingly to their activities (Olson 1965). Furthermore, such constellations are promoted by the fact that the quality of the environment is generally not regarded as a primary aspect of life. The primary focus of people's lives is their career: people's individual interests as an employee or entrepreneur usually outweigh their interest in environmental protection (Holzinger 1994, 128).

Against this background, the slow development and comparatively weak representation of environmental interest groups at the European level hardly comes as a surprise. For example, for a long time the European Environmental Bureau (EEB) was the only large environmental association that was active in Brussels. The EEB was founded in 1974 and with well over 100 member associations it still is the most comprehensive environmental interest association. Not until the middle of the 1980s were additional European unions of environmental organizations established (e.g. Friends of the Earth, Greenpeace, and the Worldwide Fund for Nature), which were joined by three organizations with a more specific focus in the 1990s (BirdLife

International, Climate Network Europe, Transport and Environment Federation) (Hey and Brendle 1994; Webster 1998). The personnel and financial resources of these associations are however relatively weak (Long 1998, 107–15; Sbragia 2000, 304).

In contrast, many of the European business associations existing today originated in the early years after the creation of the EEC. One example is the umbrella organization of private industry and employers (UNICE), which was founded in 1958 and represents more than ten million businesses. Along with that, there are European trade associations for almost every single branch, some of which are highly influential. This holds, for example, for the representation of agricultural interests as well as the automobile, chemical, pharmaceutical and bio-technological industries. Multinational firms and large businesses, in particular, limit themselves not only to influencing European policies by means of national and European associations, but also attempt to bring their interests into European policy-making by means of direct lobbying (Coen 1997; Green Cowles 1998).

In light of the dominant position of economic interests at the European level the Commission attempts to compensate for the structural inferiority of environmental associations in particular by means of supporting them financially. For example, the funds from the Commission are the most important source of income of the EEB (Webster 1998). Above all, DG Environment tries to strengthen the influence of environmental interests vis-à-vis other interests by granting them privileged means of access to the policy process (Hix 1999, 197). However, these measures only do little to change the overall constellation which remains characterized by the prevalence of economic interests. It is also a frequent criticism that the interest groups that are given privileges and supported financially could wind up in a state of dependence, which could have effects on the substance of their political activities (Knill 2003, 103).

International environmental regimes

The number of actors in the field of international environmental protection is vast: governments, agencies, national and international non-governmental organizations (NGOs), interest groups, lobbyists and scientists form a dense and complex network. The UN provides them with a forum for global negotiations and consequently, the most important and influential international environmental regimes have developed within and around this framework. In general, the EU has played a rather influential role within these regimes. At the same time, EU environmental policy was driven and influenced by the developments at the international level.

In the 1970s issues of environmental protection reached the top of the international political agenda. The first global conference on environmental issues took place in Stockholm in 1972. This UN Conference on the Human Environment resulted in the founding of the United Nations Environmental Program (UNEP) by the UN General Assembly (see for example Bauer and Biermann 2004). For the EU the conference became a catalyst for the development of environmental activities (see Chapter 1). With the approval of the First Environmental Action Programme and its successors and by giving environmental issues a legal base with the SEA, the EU took the first steps on the way to becoming one of the driving forces behind global environmental protection (Collier 1996; Sjöstedt 1998).

Eleven years after the Stockholm Conference, an international commission was set up by the UN to work out strategies for 'sustainable development'. It was chaired by the then Norwegian Prime Minister Gro-Harlem Brundtland who gave her name to the 'Brundtland-Report' published in 1987. 'Our Common Future', as the report was officially named, became the base line for the following UN actions.

By that time, the EU had become involved in several fields of global environmental policy, including air pollution, water pollution and nature protection. Among other things, it had developed into the second leading force next to the USA in protecting the ozone layer. However, its efforts were – and in fact often still are – hampered by the difficult inner-European decision-making process. First, the EU has to solve the question of who should represent the Union in international negotiations. Sometimes it is the European Commission acting on behalf of the Council; sometimes the Union is represented by the Council Presidency. No matter which option is being chosen, the decisive institution is always the Council, meaning that the member states have to agree on a common position prior to any international negotiation. This constraint poses the second problem: limited flexibility for the negotiator and thus strategic disadvantages in order to not depart from the internal agreement. The process is further complicated by the fact that most competences in the environmental field are divided between the EU and the member states (Sjöstedt 1998; Oberthür 1999). Given this division of competences, member states in most cases also take part in international negotiations on an individual basis, parallel to being represented by the EU. This often gives rise to confusion, both internally and to the outside world. Legally speaking, this constellation is reflected in so-called mixed agreements which are signed and ratified both by the EU and by the member states individually (Sbragia 1998).

The next important international conference, the UN Conference on Environment and Development (UNCED) or 'Earth Summit' took place in Rio de Janeiro in 1992. It resulted in the Agenda 21 which called for action to achieve sustainable development worldwide. The most important achievement of the UNCED was, however, the foundation of the United Nations Framework Convention on Climate Change (UNFCCC), the first international treaty exclusively dealing with climate issues. Even though it was ratified by 154 states, the UNFCCC did not become a success. This was mainly due to the fact that it contained no legally binding commitments, not least because the USA, the world's largest producer of greenhouse gases, wanted as vague formulations as possible, while the EU and other states demanded concrete aims. Yet, the Convention came into force in 1994 after the required number of fifty ratifications was reached. The EU joined the convention in 1993 after approval by the Council (Sjöstedt 1998).

The Kyoto Protocol to the UNFCCC was developed on and between the annual meetings of the Conference of the Parties (COP) to the Framework Convention and was adopted in 1997. It defines clear objectives with regard to the emissions reduction of six greenhouse gases, including carbon dioxide (CO_2), by at least five per cent per developed country. The reduction can be measured by taking either 1990 or 1995 as a base line and the target must be reached by the period 2008–12. In addition to adopting measures of emission reduction, the involved countries are allowed to trade emission credits thus establishing an international 'emission trading' regime.[9] They can also obtain 'emission reduction units' by financing projects in other participating countries known as Joint Implementation, or in developing countries (Clean Development Mechanism).

Once again, the EU had been one of the driving forces behind the Protocol. Initially, it pressed for an emission reduction of up to fifteen per cent by all parties. The final agreement was much lower due to the firm position of the USA and the lack of flexibility on the part of the EU, as mentioned above. Also in Kyoto, the Union was plagued by the complex internal decision-making process, although some progress has been made in that area. As a consequence of a growing body of European legislation concerning environmental issues, increasing harmonization of member state interests can be detected, facilitating the agreement on a common position (Sjöstedt 1998; Oberthür 1999).

Following the scheme of the 'mixed agreement', not only all of its member states as well as the Central and Eastern European accession countries became parties, but also the EU itself signed the Kyoto Protocol. To emphasize its stand on the issue of climate change, Brussels signed the Protocol as early as 29 April 1998. The Protocol was simultaneously ratified by the EU and its member states in May 2002, thus entering the Kyoto Protocol into force. In addition to that, Brussels has continuously tried to speed up ratification processes in other states, most notably in the USA (Brauch 1996; Ott and Oberthür 1999).

The EU's ambitions in the global environmental arena are further illustrated by its role at the 2002 World Summit on Sustainable Development in Johannesburg. On that occasion, an 'Action Plan' was negotiated on, containing concrete actions, measures and timetables for achieving sustainable development in developed and developing countries alike. The plan, which builds on the agreements of the first Earth Summit, covers a wide range of issues all connected with environmental protection, such as the fight against poverty, energy policy, the sound management of natural resources, globalization, chemical safety and good governance. It reconfirms the importance of the UNFCCC as the key instrument to fight global warming and the commitment to the Kyoto Protocol's aims. Apart from that, at the Summit the EU launched an initiative to increase the use of renewable energies.

Notes

1 See Chapter 4.

2 In this regard one should stress, however, that DG Environment partially compensates for its relatively weak personnel resources by falling back on external associates, who are sent and paid by the member states. In practice, the number of such 'national experts' was frequently nearly as high as the number of EU officials (Holzinger 1994, 100).

3 Besides that, the Commission's executive tasks include the external representation of the Community during negotiations concerning matters of private and international law (see section on International environmental regimes below) and the administration of the EU budget and various funds.

4 Only in exceptional cases (e.g. on the occasion of the Dublin Summit in 1990) is environmental policy attributed such a high political priority that it becomes an issue during consultations in the European Council. The European Council is the highest decision-making body of the EU in which the Heads of State and Government of the member states and the President of the Commission, supported by the foreign ministers and an additional member of the Commission, meet at least twice annually. As a rule, 'high politics' issues, such as foreign policy and economic policy as well as matters concerning the further constitutional and institutional development of the EU dominate the agenda of the European Council.

5 It convenes at two different levels: at that of the national ambassadors (COREPER II) and that of their representatives (COREPER I). While for the most part less politically explosive issues are deliberated in COREPER I, COREPER II deals with matters of greater political significance.

6 Only an overview of the different types of procedures is given here. A more elaborate illustration follows in Chapter 4. There is additionally a separate procedure for resolutions on the EU budget.

7 According to Article 30, trade restrictions which are justified to protect the health and life of humans, animals and plants are exempted (see Chapter 1).

8 With this view, developed among other things in a case against Denmark about a national ban on disposable beverage containers such as beer cans (Koppen 1993, 140–1), the ECJ deviated from its previous decisions in which it generally decided in favour of the Common Market objectives when they contradicted environmental protection objectives.

9 For a detailed discussion of the introduction of emissions trading in the EU, see Chapter 6.

4

Political processes and decision-making procedures

For a full understanding of the factors and conditions shaping EU environmental policy, the analysis of central actors and institutions in the previous chapter constitutes an important, but not a sufficient starting point. In this chapter, we will complement this picture by focusing upon the characteristic processes and decision-making procedures in the development and design of EU environmental policies. Of particular significance here are not only formal decision-making rules and procedures, but also informal patterns of interaction and the relationships between the involved actors and institutions.

These patterns are marked by tensions between Community and national interests, which are typical for the EU. In other words, the relationships between actors and institutions which are primarily committed to the interests of the Community as a whole (in particular the Commission, the EP and the ECJ) and those marked above all by individual national interests (in particular the member states gathered in the European Council and the Council of Ministers) have important ramifications for policy-making. The actual balance between supranational and intergovernmental elements cannot be defined exactly. There are fluctuations not only between and within individual policy areas, but also with respect to the concrete stage of the policy process.

Against this background, the following sections aim to analytically distinguish between different phases of European policy-making. These comprise the problem definition and agenda-setting phase, the elaboration of policy proposals at the level of the Commission and the phase of decision-making through the European legislative process. As for decision-making in particular, we will see that the respective means of influence of the participating actors and institutions can vary considerably depending on the procedural rules on which they are based.

Problem definition and agenda-setting

Environmental measures in the EU do not come from a vacuum. Instead, they should be regarded as reactions to problems which have been perceived by actors in different ways, defined accordingly and viewed as sufficiently politically relevant. In other words, the question whether and to what extent the Community becomes politically active depends on two prerequisites: the perception of a problem (such as global warming) as well as the will of the involved actors to actually deal with this problem and hence put it on the political agenda (agenda-setting).

Both the definition of the problem and agenda-setting are ultimately the result of a normative selection process which is determined to a great extent by those actors that are able to assert their ideas in the political process. Depending on how different actors are affected by the issue, these ideas can vary significantly. This holds not only for the question whether and to what extent a certain situation is perceived as problematic at all, but also for the selection of politically relevant aspects of the problem, which are to be dealt with on the basis of appropriate measures (Howlett and Ramesh 2003, chapter 5).

For example, the acid rain problem in the 1980s shows that the member states can have highly diverse perceptions of a given policy problem. In the UK, which was hardly affected by the negative effects of its own emissions into the air due to its position as an island and the favourable west wind, the problem was hardly sensed. Accordingly, the British were critical of activities on behalf of the EU. They feared competitive disadvantages for their industries, which at that point in time were confronted with comparatively lenient emission regulations. The circumstances were totally different for countries such as Germany, which were much more affected by the negative impact of cross-border air pollution. In particular in response to the forest dieback (*Waldsterben*), the problem was politicized to a greater extent than elsewhere. Thus, Germany had a strong interest in putting the topic on the EU agenda. In doing so, it focused not only on ecological, but also economic interests: in order to avoid competitive disadvantages for German industries which were subject to strict emission regulations, there was a strong interest in making these standards binding for the other member states as well by means of European regulations (see Boehmer-Christiansen and Skea 1991; Héritier, Knill and Mingers 1996, 179ff.).

The question of which actors assert their ideas in defining a political problem and during the agenda-setting process can be of utmost significance for the further decision-making process. The manner in which a problem is specifically defined has direct ramifications for the potential measures, upon the basis of which the problem is supposed to be solved.

> As the questions asked invariably colour the answers received, it is important to consider who is asking the questions, and who (or what) causes environmental issues to be placed on the European agenda. The questions themselves, or rather the assumptions underpinning the questions, often determine the shape of a particular policy. For example, is the function of European environment policy to the best of one's ability, given the present technological (and cost) limits, or is environmental problem-solving worthwhile only when scientific research offers 'objective' answers about the most effective policy avenue? (Weale et al. 2000, 114)

In this regard, the Commission with its exclusive right of initiative has a particularly important resource to influence the orientation and political priorities of EU environmental policy in individual cases as well as in the long term. Due to it is formal position as a monopolist in initiating joint measures, the Commission may generally be supposed to be able to shape the agenda largely according to its own preferences and priorities.

Even though the Commission can formally be viewed as the initiator of Community policy, however, we cannot automatically conclude that all environmental policy measures in the EU can be traced back to the activities of the Commission. For example, many Commission proposals can be attributed to initiatives of other actors who approach the Commission and request it to draw up certain policies. Besides the Council of Ministers and the EP, which formally have the possibility of demanding that the Commission draw up a certain proposal, the informal activities of the member states play a particularly important role in this regard. Most notably in the area of environmental policy, it appears that the Commission is frequently more preoccupied with reacting to the initiatives of individual states than playing an active role on its own. The member states frequently take advantage of opportunities to favourably influence the definition of problems and the agenda-setting process at the European level by seconding national officials to the Commission (Knill 1995, 124).

The responsiveness of the Commission to member state initiatives depends on various factors. Firstly, the Commission is interested in developing proposals and strategies which generally are in line with the interests of the member states, because this increases the chances of their initiatives being translated into policy (Weale et al. 2000, 114). Secondly, the relatively scarce personnel resources of the Commission play an important role here. Sending national experts is particularly welcomed by the Commission because they are an important source of information. For example, about half of the employees of the DG Environment are sent from the member states for a restricted period of time. 'We address member states and ask for people who have expertise in a specific field. Personnel all in all is very scarce' (Employee of the DG Environment, quoted in Knill 1995, 125). Thirdly, the influence of the member states on the definition of problems and shaping the agenda is facilitated by a 1973 agreement between the member states and the Commission.[1] It stipulates that each member state must inform the Commission about national legislative initiatives in the environmental policy field and suspend the national decision-making process until the Commission communicates within an arranged time limit that it does not wish to become active in this area. If the Commission declares its intention to draw up its own regulations, it must present a corresponding draft within five months. As the member states usually present very precise and detailed legislative proposals, however, it is difficult for the Commission to draw up a consensual Community-wide solution within a reasonable timeframe. Thus, in such cases it is by all means possible that the national proposal is simply copied by the Commission or that a uniform EU-wide regulation is not proposed at all due to the lack of Commission resources (Rehbinder and Stewart 1985, 259).

The question whether or how the Commission exercises its right of initiative is not influenced by the member states alone, though. There are often societal interest groups and associations as well who attempt to influence the initiatives and proposals of the Commission to their benefit by providing information and expertise. As we have seen in Chapter 3, economic interests are at a fundamental structural advantage vis-à-vis environmental interest groups. This is only insufficiently balanced out through the support of environmental associations on behalf of the Commission. Moreover, in the past the Commission did not always consequently live up to its general aspiration to equally consult environmental associations and economic interest groups in the conceptualization of policy proposals (Mazey and Richardson 2006, 247ff.).

Along with that, environmental initiatives by the EU are subject to the influence of external developments. In this regard, we should especially note international treaties and agreements signed by the EU (see Chapter 3). For example, many EU activities in the area of nature protection originated in broader international cooperation. External shocking events and catastrophes (such as the poisonous gas catastrophe of Seveso), which are typically characterized by an intense politicization of environmental problems, can also trigger environmental policy activities.

Altogether, it is evident that the decision on whether a common societal problem needs to be dealt with at the European level, as well as the perception of this problem, are influenced by numerous factors. Besides the interests of the Commission, other European institutions and the member states, national and European interest associations also play an important role in defining problems and setting the agenda for European environmental policies. The perceptions, interests and options for action of these actors can in turn be strongly influenced by external events. The consequence of the complexity of the environmental policy process is that in many cases it is hardly possible to exactly reconstruct the definition of problems and the shaping of the environmental policy agenda at the European level (Peterson 1995, 77; Weale et al. 2000, 115).

Against the backdrop of this constellation, questions about the actual influence of the Commission arise. To what extent does the Commission's formal right of initiative enable it to decisively affect the definition of problems and shape the agenda for European environmental policy despite the array of involved actors? We may actually gain the impression that the Commission can be attributed no more than secondary importance here, regardless of its formal resources. Along these lines, observers have pointed out that the openness and responsiveness towards external initiatives makes the Commission highly dependent on national and societal interests. In extreme cases, the result is that the Commission is dominated by influential interests and thus no longer able to effectively pursue its role as an independent intermediary between a large array of interests, a phenomenon known as regulatory capture (see Hix 1999, 53; Weale et al. 2000, 116).

Even if we cannot completely rule out individual DGs of the Commission being taken advantage of by particularistic interests, this description of an actor entirely dependent on external expertise conveys a highly distorted picture of the Commission's potential for influence. The Commission should rather be characterized as a corporative actor capable of acting on its own because the member states have delegated authority and resources to it. In contrast to intergovernmental actors such as the Council of Ministers, whose interests coincide with aggregate individual interests, the Commission not only pursues Community goals, but also its own institutional interests, which can run counter to the views and preferences of individual member states (Kenis and Schneider 1987).

Due to its relatively limited room to manoeuvre in terms of financial resources, which are used for the most part for agriculture and structural policy activities, it stands to reason that the Commission aims to uphold its institutional *raison d'être* by expanding its regulatory authority. Majone emphasizes along these lines (1996, 65) that 'the utility function of the Commission is positively related to the scope of its activities rather than to the scale of the services provided or the size of its budget'. Clear evidence of this is offered by the constantly increasing regulatory activities of the EU in environmental policy, a policy area which to a certain extent has been created by the Commission (Majone 1989, 167; see also Chapter 1).

The main resource with which the Commission pursues its goal of expanding its authority is its right to initiate EU measures and thus to influence the course of the decision-making process. Against this background, the Commission has been conceptualized as a 'political entrepreneur' (Majone 1996; Cram 1997;

Pollack 1997) which is able to shape the political agenda according to its own interests through clever manoeuvring and taking advantage of the informational advantage vis-à-vis other actors gained through extensive consultations (Fairbrass and Jordan 2001, 2):

> The Commission does not have a monopoly on information and expertise. However, the Commission can drive the policy agenda by manipulating asymmetries between the member states and different private interests. (Hix 1999, 53)

This holds in particular when information is dispersed unequally among actors, when the preferences of the involved actors are not sufficiently defined and access to the political process is relatively open (with fluctuations in the number of participating actors) (Kingdon 1984). These conditions frequently exist especially in the European context in light of the great complexity and the low degree of legal institutionalisation of political networks (see Héritier 1993).

If a certain environmental problem is defined as such and put on the political agenda, this creates important foundations for passing joint measures. However, by no means may we infer that this leads to actual decisions on those policies. This demands two further steps. First, a policy proposal has to be drawn up. Subsequently, this has to pass through the European legislative process as a Community legal act (e.g. in the form of a directive or regulation). Both aspects will be examined more closely below.

Programme formulation: the drafting of policy proposals

The actors involved in the drafting of EU policy proposals are broadly the same as those in the phase of problem definition and agenda-setting. Having the right of initiative, the Commission is solely responsible for the development of programme concepts: 'Only the Commission staff draft legislative proposals that form the basis of eventual regulations, directives, and decisions' (Weale et al. 2000, 117). Despite the fact that policy proposals are developed within the Commission, however, close cooperation with national administrations, interest groups and experts can be observed in this phase as well.

Within the Commission, the development of programmes

demands extensive coordination and consultations between different levels and concerned DGs. On the one hand, a draft directive or regulation is coordinated among different hierarchical levels of the DG in charge. On the other hand, other DGs, who might be affected by the planned measure, are consulted about the proposal. In this regard, the trans-sectoral character of environmental protection implies that DG Environment is to a great extent dependent on the cooperation with other DGs when elaborating measures (such as agriculture, transport or competition, for instance) (see Chapter 3). Because the latter generally do not regard environmental protection as a main priority, this can lead to a considerable 'watering down' of the original concept. Not until these vertical and horizontal consultation processes have been completed is the proposal presented to the College of Commissioners for decision (Christiansen 2006).

In particular the internal coordination among different DGs if often marked by significant conflicts of interests.[2] These result, on the one hand, from the high degree of fragmentation and differentiation within the Commission bureaucracy. On the other hand, this coordination is made difficult by the fact that the individual DGs are characterized by different administrative cultures, i.e. by different ways of incorporating interest associations as well as divergent interests and ideals, which are in part not easily compatible with one another (Cini 1996; Cram 1997; Page 1997). These conflicts of interest, which in some cases already emerge when specifying the responsible DG that is entrusted with the task of drawing up a proposal, can often only be reconciled through the intervention of the Commission President (Weale et al. 2000, 118).

The efforts to prepare a directive for the introduction of a European CO_2/energy tax at the beginning of the 1990s are an example of those coordination problems. The effects of such a tax were assessed very differently within the Commission. For example, the DG for Industry emphasized the potential dangers for the international competitiveness of the European economy. They asserted that a tax should only be introduced under the condition that similar measures are also taken in the USA and Japan (principle of conditionality). The Transport DG pointed out that the effectiveness of the planned tax had not been scientifically proven. In particular, it doubted the assumption that the introduction of a tax would have a decisive effect on the driving habits of motorists.

However, the DG Environment and the DG Energy played the main role in drawing up the draft for the directive. Both regarded the stabilization of CO_2 emissions as an essential prerequisite for combating the greenhouse effect. There was indeed a conflict of interest with regard to the relative weighting of the taxation of energy and CO_2. While DG Environment advocated heavier taxation of energy from all sources in order to create general incentives to reduce energy consumption, the DG Energy pressed for the heavier taxation of CO_2 components only and thus a lighter taxation of energy prices.

As a result, these different positions were incorporated into a compromise solution, which provided for an equal weighting of the taxation on energy and CO_2. Moreover, the concept took the position of the DG Industry into account by linking the introduction of a European tax to corresponding measures in other OECD countries. Even though a compromise was found within the Commission, however, the member states could not agree on the adoption of the directive in the subsequent negotiations in the Council of Ministers (see Héritier, Knill and Mingers 1996, 314–15; Jachtenfuchs 1996).

The internal coordination process at the Commission level during the elaboration of regulatory drafts is characterized by close cooperation with national bureaucracies. This primarily takes place in numerous working groups, composed of national officials, experts from the Commission, representatives of interest groups and external experts (Wessels and Rometsch 1996; Wessels 2001). While these groups constitute an important source of information for the Commission, they offer the member states the opportunity to influence policy formulation through their own experts: 'National civil servants try to influence the Commission towards their own position' (Wessels 1990, 238).

At the same time, there are some indications that the relationships and interactions at this informal level are characterized by problem-solving rather than by bargaining (Scharpf 2000). This means that the activities of the working groups are not so much about defending national policy positions, but rather about cooperation in the interest of joint solutions to problems.

This is facilitated by the fact that the activities of the working groups are not aimed at solving politically explosive issues. Instead they serve to smooth out legal and technical difficulties, which might complicate a later agreement in the Council of Ministers as well as the subsequent implementation. The task of the experts is thus 'to highlight and then iron out those elements in a proposal which will render its implementation or application in the member states difficult' (Weiler 1988, 35). Here 'expertise is what counts' (Arp 1993, 162).

This allows for the de-politicization and de-nationalization of the negotiation process to a certain extent (Bach 1992, 24). Thus, a rather cooperative atmosphere predominates to promote joint solutions to problems; the defence of national interests is not a primary focus of this phase. The working groups and committees provide arenas for the diffusion of ideas, convictions and knowledge. This in turn can have repercussions for national and supranational perceptions of a certain policy problem as well as the policy instruments applied to solve the problem.

The informal process of reaching consensus within the working groups is marked by the relatively influential position of the Commission. This is due to the fact that it can select those arguments out of the multitude of presented arguments which are consistent with its preferences. The discussions within the working groups enable the Commission to collect arguments, on the basis of which it can later substantiate its own position:

> Everything is discussed. And to each issue there are at least two opinions. The Commission officials listen to everything, but don't participate in the discussions. Finally, the Commission presents a directive proposal, and every aspect of this proposal is legitimated, since there was always someone who supported it. (Member of an expert committee, quoted by Eichener 1993, 54)

Hence, the Commission and thus the supranational point of view can be attributed a relatively important role in the phase in which EU measures are drafted. Nevertheless, national and external experts can exert decisive influence due to the scarce human and time resources of the Commission. A prerequisite for this, though, is that their ideas sit well with the arguments and proposals of the Commission (Knill 1995, 127).

The decision-making process

While the definition of the problem and agenda-setting as well as the development of policy proposals are characterized by a relatively influential, albeit not necessarily dominant role of the Commission, this scenario clearly changes as soon as a regulatory draft leaves the informal arena of the working groups at the Commission level and is passed onto the Council of Ministers and the EP as an official legislative proposal. In the Council of Ministers, which remains the most important institution in the European legislative process despite the increased authority of the EP, the negotiation climate is defined not so much by the elaboration of joint solutions to problems (problem-solving), but rather by opposed interest and distributive conflicts between national governments (bargaining).

However, this does not mean that the decision-making process can be reduced to intergovernmental negotiations in the Council of Ministers alone. Instead, this process can only be fully understood when the inter-institutional relations between the Council of Ministers, the EP, and the Commission are analysed more closely. The power of these three institutions varies depending on the procedural rules which are applied.

Negotiations in the Council of Ministers

Within the Council, national representatives who are committed to the environmental policy positions of their respective governments negotiate with one another. Thus, the conflicts are primarily centred around national rather than social conflicts. Although ultimately the focus is placed on balancing ecological with economic interests also here, the member states negotiate and make decisions on the basis of national positions. In order to reach an agreement, the differences between the member states must be overcome. The EU's environmental policy is thus to a great extent defined by balancing national interests.

This basic pattern pervades all levels of environmental policy negotiations and comprises both the discussion of technically and politically less explosive issues within the Council working groups and the COREPER as well as the ultimate decision-making process by the Environment Council. The national experts represented in the working groups are frequently the same ones who already participated in drawing up the proposal in the working groups at the Commission level. In legal terms, however, they now represent the official position of their governments in the working groups at the Council level, while when working with the Commission, they are able to express their personal opinion (Holzinger 1994, 86–7; Pellegrom 1997). In this manner,

> they will be performing a rather different function. They will be seeking to work through some of the more controversial technical questions, with an eye to the national positions likely to emerge once the proposal is sent on to COREPER. (Weale et al. 2000, 123)

In the area of environmental policy, two voting procedures come to play in the Council: decisions based on unanimity and qualified majority decisions. As outlined in Chapter 3, most environmental policy decisions today require a qualified majority in the Council, while the unanimity rule is applied in certain exceptional areas.

In practice, the transition to QMV did little to change the fact that the negotiations in the Council of Ministers are characterized by a deeply rooted culture of consensus. Even if it is theoretically possible to outvote individual states, formal voting is extremely rare. Instead the member states usually attempt to find an acceptable formula for compromise during the negotiations. However, the sheer possibility of being outvoted ('the shadow of the vote') has long-lasting effects on the negotiation process:

> The knowledge that votes may be called often makes doubting governments focus on seeking amendments to meet their concerns rather than on blocking progress altogether. Under unanimity rules reluctant governments are generally much more likely to delay or obstruct agreements. (Wallace 2000, 19)

As a rule, we would expect a more dynamic development of European environmental policy through decisions based on qualified majority, as individual member states no longer have the possibility of blocking environmental policy measures. To enforce their interests, they are instead dependent on creating coalitions with other states to form a blocking minority, and if this is not possible they must actively participate in the process of reaching a consensus.

As we saw in Chapter 1, it depends on the number and the influence of more or less environmentally ambitious member states whether and to what extent positive effects emerge for the level of environmental protection in the EU. While environmentally ambitious states were able to block European regulations at a low level during unanimous decisions, they can be outvoted by a coalition of states for whom environmental protection is a smaller political priority during qualified majority decisions (see Holzinger 1994, 1997). Against the background of Eastern enlargement, such scenarios can by no means be ruled out (Stevis and Mumme 2000, 32).

Table 4.1 *Voting weights and power distribution in the Council of Ministers after the Nice Treaty*

Country	Population		Votes		
	Million	%	Number	%	Power index
Germany	82.0	18.2	29	9.03	9.49
UK	59.2	13.2	29	9.03	9.37
France	59.0	13.1	29	9.03	9.37
Italy	57.6	12.8	29	9.03	9.37
Spain	39.4	8.8	27	8.41	8.67
Poland	38.7	8.6	27	8.41	8.67
Netherlands	15.8	3.5	13	4.05	3.95
Greece	10.5	2.3	12	3.74	3.61
Belgium	10.2	2.3	12	3.74	3.61
Portugal	10.0	2.2	12	3.74	3.61
Czech Republic	10.3	2.3	12	3.74	3.61
Hungary	10.1	2.2	12	3.74	3.61
Sweden	8.9	2.0	10	3.12	2.99
Austria	8.1	1.8	10	3.12	2.99
Denmark	5.3	1.2	7	2.18	2.06
Finland	5.2	1.2	7	2.18	2.06
Ireland	3.7	0.8	7	2.18	2.06
Slovakia	5.4	1.2	7	2.18	2.06
Lithuania	3.7	0.8	7	2.18	2.06
Luxembourg	0.4	0.1	4	1.25	1.17
Latvia	2.4	0.5	4	1.25	1.17
Slovenia	2.0	0.4	4	1.25	1.17
Estonia	1.4	0.3	4	1.25	1.17
Cyprus	0.8	0.2	4	1.25	1.17
Malta	0.4	0.1	3	0.93	0.88
Total votes			321		
Required for resolution			232	72.3	
Required to block			90	28.0	

Source: adapted from Holzinger et al. 2005, 109–15.

Table 4.1 depicts the number of votes and the relative influence of each member state in majority decisions, as agreed in the Treaty of Nice (2001). In addition to revising the voting weights for each member state in view of the Eastern enlargement, the Nice Treaty introduced the principle of 'double majority' (which is in fact a principle of triple majority). Accordingly, for the adoption of legislative acts of the Community by majority decisions, three requirements have to be fulfilled: a policy proposal requires the support of a qualified majority in the Council (i.e. a minimum of 232 votes out of a total of 321, cf. the final rows of Table 4.1) as well as a simple majority of the number of member states (i.e. a minimum of 13). In addition, individual member states can demand that a decision must have the support of at least 62 per cent of the EU population.

While each state has the same opportunity to influence the decision during unanimous decisions, votes and political influence are weighted by population in decisions based on qualified majority. Even then, however, a certain overrepresentation of the citizens of smaller member states remains (Felsenthal and Machover 1997; Holzinger and Knill 2002). This can be easily seen if one compares the voting power of, for instance, Luxembourg and Germany. While Luxembourg (with 400,000 people and 4 votes) has 1 vote per 100,000 inhabitants, Germany (with 82 million people and 29 votes) has to be content with 1 vote per approximately 2.8 million inhabitants.

Looking at it more systematically, the chance of a member state being the pivotal actor and ultimately determining the success or failure of the negotiations can be conceptualized as its voting weight. Differences in voting weight can then be depicted by power indices such as the Shapley-Shubik Index in which all possible coalitions of all members are taken into consideration (see the last column of Table 4.1). The share of a member state in all possible positions decisive for the resolution of an issue thus determines its voting power. Under unanimity, this proportion is equally high for all member states. As for qualified majority decisions, the voting power varies depending on how the votes are weighted. According to their number of votes, the member states differ in terms of their chances of being the decisive pivotal actor in reaching a qualified majority. As shown by the table, the voting power calculated according to this index varies considerably between the member states, even if this variation is significantly less than the differences in population figures (see Holzinger et al. 2005, 108ff.).[3]

However, the calculations of the share of power of the member states during qualified majority decisions are based on the assumption that all possible coalitions between member states are equally probable. In reality, however, this is not the case (Garrett and Tsebelis 1996). In particular in the area of environmental policy, we often find bilateral or multilateral alliances between member states with similar interests.[4]

For example, in the past one could frequently observe coalitions of 'green' member states, who pressed for the expansion and strengthening of the environmental policy activities of the Community. Besides the Nordic countries, this group of states comprised the Netherlands, Austria and Germany (with a certain degree of restraint as of the mid-1990s). On the other side of the table we would primarily find the Southern member countries such as Spain, Portugal, Greece and Ireland, which tended to emerge as 'laggards' in European environmental policy and frequently only voted for measures if they received financial compensation or were able to enforce exceptions. Besides these constellations there was a group of states (such as France, Belgium, Luxembourg and Italy), who did not hold a constant policy position and generally neither pushed for stricter EU environmental policies nor resisted them in every case. Depending on the concrete issue at stake, these states either sided with the advocates or the opponents of environmental policy measures. Along the same lines, it has also been difficult to clearly categorize the UK, which has evolved – at least in some areas – from a laggard to a leader in European environmental policy (Holzinger 1994; Héritier, Knill and Mingers 1996; Andersen and Liefferink 1997; see also Chapter 1).

If we take into account that the decisions of the Council of Ministers are generally made on the basis of a consensus even when the qualified majority rule is used, the question arises of which factors can contribute to a balance between different national positions. Evidently, not only the danger of being outvoted is responsible for promoting consensus. As Chapter 1 illustrated, even when the unanimity principle was applied, a substantial program of environmental policy measures was passed at the European level.

One first factor of great significance in this regard is the role of the Presidency which rotates among the member states every six months. It chairs the negotiations at all levels (working groups, COREPER, the concerned ministers) and decides on the agenda and timing of individual sessions. On the one hand, a national government which holds the Presidency can influence the negotiations according to its political priorities by these means. For example, the Presidency can postpone dealing with a proposal that opposes its interests by not putting it on the agenda of the negotiations. Conversely, the Presidency is able to advance an issue in which it is particularly interested by putting it high on the agenda, at least in as far as a Commission proposal on this topic exists on which consultations can be held. At the same time, the Presidency has the opportunity to modify the Commission's proposal according to its own interests by drawing up its own recommendations and compromise solutions (Kirchner 1992; Wurzel 1996; Wallace 2000). On the other hand, these possibilities of influencing the European decision-making process according to national interests are relatively limited. This has to do, in particular, with the Presidency's obligation to accommodate both national and Community interests. The Presidency thus must reconcile both its individual national interests and Community-wide objectives (i.e. finding a consensus in the Council of Ministers). Here the key factors linking both elements are political responsibility and the political prestige associated with a successful Presidency (Kirchner 1992; Hayes-Renshaw and Wallace 1997; Christiansen 2006a).

Second, even though the negotiations in the Council of Ministers are to a great extent dominated by national interests, the Commission's means of influence in this phase should not be underestimated. Of particular significance here is the Commission's right of initiative, with which it continues to determine the daily agenda and the content of discussions in the Council. The Commission's proposal provides a rough decision-making framework, which the member states can only completely change when they all agree to do so. However, in light of divergent national interests this is rather unlikely (Eichener 1993, 45):

> Once a directive has been proposed by the Commission it should ... be discussed and either be rejected or accepted in roughly the same form as in which it was proposed ... You can't change the

nature of it on the Council table. (Commission representative quoted in Knill 1995, 128)

The Commission can also threaten to withdraw an already proposed alternative altogether. Thus the Council of Ministers is under great pressure to reach an agreement, because in such cases the political decision-making process would be terminated. Finally, the Commission together with the Presidency plays an important role in this phase because it mediates between the interests of the individual states. Therefore, there is close cooperation between the Presidency in the Council of Ministers and the Commission as regards setting agendas and making policy proposals which working groups, COREPER and the Council of Ministers deal with (Wallace 2000; Christiansen 2006a).

A third factor which can provoke individual member states to refrain from politics of blockade in the Council of Ministers can be traced back to the particularities of the decision-making environment. It is frequently the case that the Council of Ministers deals with several measures up for decision simultaneously. Since it is seldom politically justifiable for a member state to continually say 'no', it will focus its resistance on those measures which are least compatible with its policy position and conversely no longer block policies which are less contrary to its position. In other words the member states choose the 'lesser evil' and by these means perhaps vote for measures which they would have rejected under other circumstances (Knill 1995; Schmidt 1997).

For instance, such considerations facilitated the British government's acceptance of the Directive on Air Quality Standards for NO_2 passed in 1985. At the outset the UK was very sceptical towards the draft directive. Besides being less affected by environmental pollution (which can primarily be attributed to its geographical location), the British feared extensive adaptational demands for their existing regulatory practice, which had managed up to then without legally binding standards. An important factor that enabled the British to rethink their position was the fact that at the same time two further directives were discussed at the European level which to a much greater extent catered to the British interests: the Framework Directive on Air Pollution from Industrial Plants as well as the Directive on Air Pollution from Large Combustion Plants. Both measures entailed for the British not only greater costs of legal and institutional adjustment, but also were associated with great costs for British industries raised by the installation of the required cleaning technologies (see Knill 1995, 137–40).

A fourth possibility which can sway member states to give up their resistance is (monetary) compensation for the costs which arise for them during the implementation of the planned measures (Scharpf 2000, 217). The means of doing so are limited, though, as the EU does not have any specific financial resources from which such compensatory payments could be made. However, the Cohesion Funds, established with the Treaty of Maastricht in order to promote economic development in the poorer member states, place particular emphasis on financing environmental protection measures and can be interpreted in this regard.

Fifth, one of the potentially most significant strategies to overcome negotiation impasses in the Council of Ministers is to create so-called package deals. During the negotiations various decisions are linked with one another; concessions by individual countries in one area are compensated for by the concessions of other states in other areas. This can take place within the same policy domain in the Council of Ministers, but also across different policy areas at the level of the European Council. Against the background of the given interest constellations, a compromise can frequently only be reached this way.

In practice, however, the possibilities for such issue-linkages are often limited. Within one policy area, the interest constellations for different measures are often in the same direction. In EU environmental policy there are therefore mostly only a few decisions in which 'green' member states can accommodate the 'laggards', so that the latter give up their resistance. Hence, there are not very many possibilities for reciprocal package solutions within the area of environmental policy. There is a better chance of creating package deals when problems from several policy areas with complementary interest asymmetries can be linked with one another. A prerequisite for this is that the negotiations take place at the 'summit level', i.e. at the level of the European Council rather than in 'sectoral' Councils such as the Environment Council (Scharpf 2000, 219–20). However, package deals at this level have hardly played a role up to now in environmental policy. Holzinger (1994, 92) cites several factors which explain this situation: the difficulties involved in linking highly technical and administrative issues with other policy areas, the comparatively low degree of politicization of environmental problems, and the lack of public interest and corresponding pressure on national governments.

Even though these factors and strategies can facilitate an agreement in the Council of Ministers, one must not overlook that accommodating all divergent national interests frequently leads to a large-scale 'watering down' and weakening of the proposal originally drawn up by the Commission. Besides the long duration of negotiations, the necessity of finding a compromise frequently implies typical programme deficits, such as norms with a low degree of obligation, vague legal terminology, long transition and adjustment periods and extensive exceptions to the rule.

Moreover, in many cases the member states only approve political projects at the European level because they hope to 'correct' the undesired effects of the measures by means of lax implementation. In this way, political conflicts between the member states not solved in the Council of Ministers are postponed to the phase of implementation, resulting in implementation deficits which are relatively large in the area of environmental policy (cf. Chapter 10). For example, Weiler emphasizes (1988, 355–6) that states such as Denmark, which appear to be 'tough and detail-minded negotiators' in the Council, are also intent on the implementation of EU policies in accordance with their legal and practical requirements. Conversely, we find large deficits in the implementation phase among countries which are generally very willing to compromise.

In addition, it is by no means certain that the negotiations in the Council of Ministers will lead to success every time. However, the danger of negotiations breaking down has generally decreased with the transition to decisions based on qualified majority. Finally, the quality of environmental policy decisions depends not only on the course of negotiations in the Council of Ministers, but rather is also considerably influenced by the type of participation of the Commission and the EP in the European legislative procedure, as we will see in the following section.

The legislative procedure

The respective means of influence of the Council of Ministers, the EP and the Commission on environmental policy decisions are influenced by the respective rules applied in the legislative process. Of great significance in the present context are three particular decision-making procedures, which were already briefly addressed in Chapters 1 and 3: the procedure of consultation, cooperation and co-decision.

The selection of the relevant procedure was subject to great changes in the course of time. For example, the consultation procedure which initially applied to environmental policy was replaced with the cooperation procedure in the SEA and the Treaty of Maastricht, while the Treaty of Amsterdam generally replaced the latter with the co-decision procedure. Moreover, the applied procedure can vary according to the issue at stake. This holds in particular due to the cross-sectoral character of the EU environmental policy, which results in many environmental measures being passed in other policy areas. In the agricultural sector, for example, the consultation procedure still applies (Weale et al. 2000, 125).

Box 4.1   *The consultation procedure*

(1) Commission proposal to the EP and Council of Ministers
(2) EP: Opinion to the Council of Ministers with amendment proposals where applicable
(3) The Council of Ministers adopts the law on the basis of unanimity or qualified majority (depending on the legal foundation)

According to the consultation procedure both the EP and the Commission have few possibilities of influencing the decision of the Council of Ministers (see Box 4.1). The primary decision-making authority rests with the Council of Ministers, which is not bound to the position of the EP.[5] Thus, the procedure is dominated by intergovernmental negotiations with very limited means of influence for supranational actors. The constellation of national interests determines the political output.

By contrast, the influence of the EP and Commission under the cooperation procedure are significantly increased (see Box 4.2). The Parliament has no actual right to veto under this procedure as the ultimate decision whether to accept or reject a policy is still reserved for the Council of Ministers, but in a second reading the EP can reject or amend the position of the Council. In such incidents the Council can only reject the decision of the Parliament unanimously, whereas a qualified majority is sufficient to accept the EP's amendments. Tsebelis (1994), in particular, pointed out that this grants the EP important influence capabilities as a 'conditional agenda-setter', even though it is not in a position to veto: it can select its amendments to the effect that they are more likely to be accepted than rejected by the Council of Ministers and by these means exert a lasting influence on the outcomes of European policy-making.

Box 4.2 *The cooperation procedure*

(1) Commission proposal to the EP and Council of Ministers
(2) First reading in the EP: Opinion to the Council of Ministers with amendment proposals where applicable
(3) The Council of Ministers adopts a Common Position on the basis of qualified majority (adoption or rejection of the Commission Proposal)
(4) Second reading in the EP: Approval, rejection or modification of the Common Position of the Council of Ministers on the basis of absolute majority
(5) The Commission can accept or reject amendment proposals of the EP or withdraw its proposal when rejected by the EP
(6) Council of Ministers:
  • Amendment proposals accepted by the Commission are accepted: Adoption of the law by qualified majority
  • Rejection of the EP's amendment proposals accepted by the Commission or the refusal of the EP's rejection: Adoption of the law by unanimity

---

However, the EP relies on the support of the Commission here, because passing on its amendments to the Council of Ministers is subject to one important precondition: they must be accepted by the Commission and incorporated into its (revised) draft (Steunenberg 1994; Moser 1996). As a consequence, tacit as well as 'pre-cooked' coalitions between the EP and the Commission, amounting to the Commission's acceptance of the EP's amendments, emerged very frequently in the area of environmental policy. They served the goal of pushing through stricter regulations vis-à-vis the Council (Weale et al. 2000). Thus not only the EP, but also the Commission is granted greater influence under the cooperation procedure than under consultation (Tsebelis et al. 2001).

The introduction of the co-decision procedure led to a further enhancement of the powers of the EP in the legislative process (see Box 4.3). The EP now possesses an actual right to veto and has thus become an equal partner with the Council in this regard. This means that amendment proposals can no longer be outvoted by the Council of Ministers. Instead in the case of non-agreement a conciliation committee must be convened, consisting of delegates from the Council and the EP. It can draw up a compromise proposal, which can no longer be modified by the EP and Council, rather only accepted or rejected (Earnshaw and Judge 1995; Moser 1997; Holzinger et al. 2005, 126).[6]

However, certain restrictions to this increase in power emanate from the fact that the EP – unlike under the cooperation procedure – is no longer able to influence the decision in the Council of Ministers as a 'conditional agenda-setter' as in the past (Garrett 1995; Steunenberg 1997; Tsebelis et al. 2001). Therefore, in light of the newly created option of the conciliation procedure, the Council of Ministers is under less pressure to agree with the proposals of the EP, in order to prevent the failure of the negotiations.

At the same time the position of the EP vis-à-vis the Commission is strengthened. Thus, if the EP chooses to pass on amendments to the Council of Ministers, it no longer depends on the approval of the Commission. The opinion of the Commission has ramifications for the quorum required in the Council of Ministers however: amendments rejected by the Commission can only be unanimously accepted in the Council of Ministers, while a qualified majority suffices when the Commission approves. In contrast to the cooperation procedure, the Commission therefore has much smaller capabilities of having an impact on the content of a measure during the legislative process. In the conciliation committee it also only has an advisory function (Garrett 1995).

The increased significance of the EP under the cooperation and co-decision procedures has had a great impact on environmental policy decisions in the EU. For example, the Parliament was able to achieve significant changes in some areas, which would not have been possible under the consultation procedure (Judge, Earnshaw and Cowan 1994). A frequently mentioned example, which sheds light on how the EP exerted influence under the cooperation procedure, is the introduction of catalytic converters in small cars in the 1980s, discussed in more detail in Chapter 6. Here the EP asserted the adoption of stricter emissions limits than originally planned. In later decisions on the basis of the co-decision procedure, the EP was equally able to enforce stricter measures as compared to the original position of the Council on various occasions. Furthermore, the increased political significance of the EP is illustrated by the fact that interest groups no longer restrict their lobbying activities to the Commission and the national governments, but instead increasingly attempt to establish contacts with the respective committees of the EP (Sbragia 2000, 302; Young and Wallace 2000). Against the backdrop of these developments, Weale (1999, 37) for example emphasizes that the EP 'has had more influence on environmental measures than is typically true for more well-established national Parliaments'.

At the same time, the influence of the EP in the legislative process should not be overestimated. For example, there have been numerous incidents in which the EP did not exhaust all its possibilities in the cooperation and co-decision procedures. A fundamental reason for this was that the necessary absolute majority for rejecting or changing the Common Position of the Council of Ministers could not be reached (Earnshaw and Judge 1995, 631–2). Furthermore, the EP particularly restrained itself and hence its influence when amendments did not seem enforceable due to the interest constellations in the Council of Ministers and when the planned measures threatened to fail completely – a result which the EP regarded as even worse than what it viewed as the Council of Minister's sub-optimal position (Weale et al. 2000, 128).

The observations up to now point to the great complexity of formal and informal processes, means for action and interaction patterns in the shaping of the European environmental policy. These are manifested not only by the complex rules of the game that structure the legislative procedure, but also by the mutual interaction of different actors in the various phases of the prepa-

Table 4.3   *The co-decision procedure*

(1) Commission proposal to the EP and Council of Ministers
First reading in the EP: Opinion to Council of Ministers
with amendment proposals where applicable
(2) The Council of Ministers adopts a Common Position on the
basis of qualified majority (Acceptance or amendment of the
Commission proposal)
(3) Second reading in the EP:
   • Approval by simple majority → law passes
   • Rejection by absolute majority → law fails
   • Amendment proposal by absolute majority →
     Commission
(4) Commission: Opinion: acceptance or rejection of the
proposals of the EP
(5) Council of Ministers:
   • Acceptance of the amendment proposals of the EP
     accepted by the Commission by qualified majority → law
     passes
   • Acceptance of the amendment proposals of the EP
     rejected by the Commission by unanimity → law passes
   • No required majority: Conciliation committee convened
(6) Conciliation committee (15 members of the Council of
Ministers and the EP each and 1 Member of the Commission
without the right to vote)
   • Adoption of a common draft bill (qualified majority of
     the Council of Ministers and absolute majority of the EP
     representatives)
   • No common draft bill → Law fails
(7) Third reading
   • Acceptance of the common text by qualified majority in
     the Council of Ministers and simple majority in the EP →
     Law passes
   • No sufficient majority in the Council of Ministers and
     EP → law fails

ration of decisions, such as the definition of the problem, agenda-setting the development of regulatory proposals at the Commission level and during the negotiations in the Council of Ministers.

Whereas it hardly seems possible to forecast the results and future development trends in EU environmental policy in light of the highly complex picture painted here, we can identify a number of typical patterns of interaction and interest constellations. These will be addressed in the following chapter.

Notes

1 Official Journal C 9, 15 March 1973, with an addendum in the Official Journal C 86, 20 July 1974.
2 These different interests, in particular, are responsible for the fact that previous efforts at environmental protection integration have only been marginally successful (see Chapter 3).
3 The power index takes into account that the Nice Treaty in addition to a decision with qualified majority in the Council requires the support of a majority of the member states representing at least 62 per cent of the EU's population.
4 However, the formation of such alliances can vary from case to case according to concrete national interests (Liefferink and Andersen 1998). At this point we only intend to demonstrate general tendencies.
5 When this procedure applies, the EP only has the possibility of prolonging the decision-making process by waiting to state its position.
6 The co-decision procedure was somewhat simplified by the Treaty of Amsterdam. This has led to a further slight enhancement of the position of the EP vis-à-vis the Council. The Council previously had the opportunity to present its Common Position to the EP for decision if the conciliation procedure broke down. Hence, the only possibility that remained for the EP was to accept the original position of the Council or to reject this position in its entirety, which would have implied the ultimate failure of the negotiations (see Hix 1999, 88–92).

5

Typical interest constellations and patterns of interaction

If we look back on the previous chapters, the question arises whether the concrete design of EU environmental policy can truly only be understood as the result of highly contingent processes or whether certain analytical interrelations exist after all, on the basis of which this complex overall picture can at least be partially deciphered. As the following section will show, we can indeed identify general interest constellations and interaction patterns in EU environmental policy, which enable us to explain different policy processes and outcomes.

In this respect, two different forms of regulatory competition between the member states are of particular significance. On the one hand, the environmental policy interest constellations of the member states are defined to a great extent by the 'systems competition' within the European Common Market. In this context, regulatory competition pertains to the national reactions to international or European competition for mobile production factors and mobile sources for tax revenue.[1] These constellations have significant ramifications for the possibilities and boundaries of environmental policy harmonization at the European level. On the other hand, the second form of regulatory competition pertains to the active efforts of the member states at the European level to influence the content and form of environmental policy regulations according to their interests. These interests are particularly associated with minimizing the potential costs of administrative and institutional adaptation and at the same time securing the competitiveness of national industries.

Besides the different forms and consequences of regulatory

competition between the member states it must not be underestimated that the interest constellations in EU environmental policy can change as a result of learning processes and the diffusion of ways of perceiving and solving problems between the member states. These processes, which are promoted by institutionalized forms of interaction between national and supranational actors at the European level, have significant ramifications for the concrete form and content of European environmental policies.

Regulatory competition (I): effects of market integration

As for the effects of the first form of regulatory competition outlined above on the design of European environmental policies, we can generally distinguish between two theoretical steps in the argument: in the first step we must enquire whether and to what extent the integration of markets changes the environmental policy interest constellations of the member states and facilitates certain adaptive responses at the national level. In a second step, we then examine the consequences of this development for the means and resources of environmental policy governance at the European level.

National responses to European integration

The establishment of the European Common Market had significant ramifications for the regulation of environmental policy in the economies of the member states. The consequence of the dismantling of trade barriers in the member states was that different environmental regulations in the member states had a direct impact on the economic competitiveness of a country. For example, enterprises in states with strict environmental standards are generally faced with higher production costs and are thus at a disadvantage vis-à-vis competing firms which produce in countries with less strict standards.

The result of these circumstances is that the governments of the member states find themselves in a state of regulatory competition for the most favourable production locations and competitive conditions. The core and – to a certain extent classical – research question which arises in this respect relates to the impact of this type of competition on the level of national environmental regulations. Does it lead to a so-called 'race to the bottom', in which regulatory standards are continually relaxed or even abolished? Or is it possible that the exact opposite trend sets in – that the dynamics of market integration cause the member states to collectively elevate their national standards ('race to the top') (Holzinger 2002, 62–3)?

In empirical studies in the area of international and European environmental policy we find evidence of both scenarios (Vogel 1995, 1997; Zürn 1997; Jänicke 1998; Kern 2000). This calls into question the conditions which promote the one or the other scenario. In this context, Holzinger (1991, 1994, 2002) and Scharpf (1996, 1997, 1997a) point to an important distinction between product and production standards.

As for product regulations, which pertain to the quality and characteristics of certain goods, two significant mechanisms can prevent the emergence of a 'race to the bottom' between two member states (Scharpf 1997a, 523). Firstly, it is very plausible that the competition between different products is based not only on their price, but also on their quality. If quality factors come to the fore, stricter standards can certainly imply competitive advantages, which can subsequently induce a 'race to the top'.

Secondly, a 'race to the bottom' can be prevented when it is possible for individual states – despite economic integration – to refuse domestic market access for foreign products that do not comply with national environmental standards. As a rule, the member states are entitled to this possibility of market segmentation according to Article 30 TEU. Article 30 allows for national trade restrictions to protect the health and environment under the prerequisite that these restrictions do not constitute a discrimination towards foreign products (Scharpf 1997a, Holzinger 2002).[2]

David Vogel (1995) has demonstrated that such trade restrictions can not only contribute to preventing a 'race to the bottom', but under certain conditions can also contribute to the tightening of regulations in the individual states. This applies in particular when producers in states with low product standards are highly dependent on exports to 'green' states with strict regulations. In order to avoid being confronted with different standards, those industries will press for a harmonization of the regulations, which will result in the elevation of the standards in less strictly regulated markets. Vogel describes this effect in the case of California, whose stricter emissions regulations for automobiles triggered an increase in the standards of other US states.

However, the described mechanisms are less relevant when it comes to the environmental regulation of production standards, which define the conditions and processes under which certain goods are produced. The competition over product quality has no impact on the production standards under which goods of the same quality are manufactured. For instance, a purchaser of electricity will hardly make his/her buying decision dependent on whether the electricity is produced in compliance with more or less strict environmental regulations. Nor does the possibility of market segmentation exist in this area. No member state can restrict the import of products which were produced under conditions which do not correspond with its own regulations on air quality control or water protection. With respect to process regulations, there is thus basically a greater probability that the regulatory competition between the member states will lead to a 'race to the bottom' (Scharpf 1999).

Whether and to what extent this is the case depends on additional factors, though. These include, in particular, the costs for stricter environmental regulations (impact of stricter environmental standards on production costs), the degree of international competition in a certain industrial sector, and also the political conditions. The latter pertain to factors such as the respective political influence of actors who lobby for (e.g. the concerned industry) or against (e.g. environmental interest groups) the lowering of environmental standards. Such constellations can vary from case to case and from country to country (Holzinger 2002).

Repercussions on policy formulation

Up to now, the analysis has shown that the environmental policy positions of the member states are influenced to a great extent by the consequences of economic integration. Even though the effects of the regulatory competition resulting from this are difficult to forecast, the question arises whether and to what extent at least a 'race to the bottom' can be prevented by harmonizing environmental regulations at the European level. The potential and boundaries of European regulation vary here depending on the respective constellations of member state interests. Generally, the constellation of national interests facilitates the harmonization of product standards at a high level of regulation, while the harmonization of production standards is more difficult.

To substantiate this hypothesis a distinction is usually made between poor and rich member states (Rehbinder and Stewart 1985; Holzinger 1991, 2002; Scharpf 1996, 1997a). Rich countries demonstrate a high level of economic development. Their populations attach a high priority to the quality of the environment. Accordingly, these countries are willing to bear the economic costs for a more ambitious environmental policy. In poorer, less economically developed member states, the quality of the environment is only a secondary priority. The population is less willing to bear the economic costs that are brought on by strict environmental regulations. Along these lines, these countries prefer environmental regulations at a lower level.

This fundamental conflict of interest, however, does not necessarily stand in the way of the harmonization of European product standards at a high level. This can be attributed to the fact that all member states also have a common interest in Europe-wide standards. Different national product standards and authorization procedures would pose restraints on industries in all countries and be at odds with the purpose of the Common Market. We are thus faced with a situation in which all states have a harmonization advantage and thus a common interest in European regulation (Holzinger 2002, 69). The conflict of interest primarily pertains to the level of regulation: poorer countries tend to prefer lower standards than rich countries.

Nevertheless, those states that are interested in higher standards basically enjoy a more favourable negotiation position. This can be attributed to two factors: firstly, Article 30 enables the introduction of trade restrictions for products that do not adhere to the national level of regulation. Secondly, Article 95 TEU allows for the conservation and introduction of stricter national product standards, even when standards have already been harmonized at the European level (Stewart 1993). Even though there are certain restrictions when referring to these provisions (Koppen 1993; Holzinger 1994),[3] they basically enable the rich countries to enforce stricter product standards on their own. To this extent, according to Scharpf (1996, 118), the harmonization policies of the Community actually often do reach the aspired 'high level of protection' for product-related regulations.

While both poor and rich member states prefer common standards over the continued status quo in the case of non-agreement on product-related provisions, the starting constellation is less favourable in the case of production standards. As argued above, this results in significant competitive disadvantages for rich countries, because they cannot exclude products from countries with lower production standards from the national market. They will thus attempt to assert their high regulatory level as the EU-wide standard. If they cannot achieve this objective, harmonization at a lower level would be the second-best solution from an economic standpoint, in order to improve their competitive position vis-à-vis their competitors from the poorer member states. However, in light of the high priority attached to environmental protection in the rich countries, politically asserting the second solution hardly appears to be a viable option. Thus the national governments prefer the continuation of different national standards over European regulations at a low level (Scharpf 1996, 119–20).

Albeit for different reasons, the same holds for the poor countries. In light of the lower level of economic development, harmonization at a high level would severely threaten existing industrial sectors. Harmonization at a low level would not be an attractive option either, because national industries would thus be exposed to increased competition from highly productive companies from the rich member states (Ibid.).

From this theoretical standpoint, agreements on common production standards at a high level are expected to be much less frequent than would be the case with product standards. In view of the assumptions made here, such agreements appear to be likely only when the rich countries are willing to and capable of offering the poor countries compensation payments.

Against the background of these theoretical notions, on the whole one arrives at a relatively sceptical assessment with regard to the EU's capacity for an effective environmental policy. Progress can primarily be expected in the area of product regulation, while regulations on production standards in most cases either do not come about or are agreed on only on a rather weak level.

However, this sceptical view is frequently rejected by empirical findings. For example, the EU has passed very strict production standards in important areas such as air and water pollution control, chemical control and waste policy, which indeed were not always at the level of the most ambitious member state, but in fact did go far beyond the standards of the least regulated states (Sbragia 2000). Moreover, it appears that the member states often accept measures the implementation of which are associated with significant economic and institutional costs (Héritier, Knill and Mingers 1996; Jordan 1999; Zito 1999).

Do these developments reflect isolated incidents (Golub 1996), in which the interest constellation exceptionally allowed for an agreement on high standards? Or does the distinction between product and production standards and the associated interest constellations perhaps not comprise all analytically relevant factors? In view of the fact that according to the dominant assessment in the literature, the number of exceptions clearly outweighs the theoretically forecasted cases of failure, there seems to be a great deal of support for the second alternative (see Holzinger 2002).

First of all, the fact that the distinction between product and production standards only insufficiently accounts for potential differences between various environmental policy measures is of great significance in this respect. This applies in particular to production standards and their impact on the economic competitiveness of national industries. For example, at the European level there are many measures that indeed can be interpreted as production regulations, but do not have any long-lasting impact on industrial competitiveness. This pertains, for example, to the entire area of purely procedural measures (e.g. Directives on EIA or on Access to Environmental Information). The same holds for regulations on EMAS and the eco-label, which are aimed at creating framework conditions for the voluntary self-regulation of industries. As regards the numerous environmental quality standards passed by the EU (e.g. for air pollutants, drinking water or bathing water), the question of whether and to what extent such standards affect economic competitiveness depends on the concrete means which the national governments select to implement these measures.

A second problem lies in the fact that the preferences of the member states do not necessarily reflect the asymmetries between poor and rich member states assumed in the model (Holzinger 2002, 63). There can certainly be situations in which the member states collectively attach a high political priority to environmental policy measures at the European level and are affected by the economic consequences of the proposed regulation in a similar manner (Scharpf 1996, 103).

In environmental negotiations at the European level it also appears that conflict lines usually run between a few large, economically dominant member states and more seldom between poor and rich countries. It frequently suffices when the influential states find a consensus. Smaller countries generally do not play a dominant role in this process, but rather function as coalition partners. This in turn reduces the problem of the heterogeneity of national interests and thus the complexities involved in reaching cooperative solutions (see Genschel and Plümper 1997). This effect is enhanced by the fact that often many member states assume a relatively neutral and indifferent position with respect to the measure on the agenda (Héritier, Knill and Mingers 1996).

A third factor that can explain why the EU environmental policy in reality often goes beyond the theoretically forecasted developments involves the effects of decisions on the basis of qualified majority in the Council of Ministers. Even though the member states basically strive for a consensual decision also under this decision rule, one must not underestimate the fact that the negotiations now take place in the 'shadow of the vote', which tends to facilitate cooperative negotiation strategies as described in Chapter 4.[4]

Regardless of these points of criticism the distinction between product and production standards and the associated interest constellations of the member states provide valuable first insights for understanding the patterns from which the European environmental policy has crystallized. The theoretical model contains important hypotheses which can serve as a point of departure for the analysis and can be modified and further developed according to the empirical findings. As for this analytical elaboration, not only the addressed points of criticism are of relevance, but also two further patterns that characterize the formation of European environmental policy: the regulatory competition between the member states when it comes to transferring their regulatory patterns to the European level, and institutional forms of learning and policy diffusion. We will examine these factors more closely in the following sections.

Regulatory competition (II): the advantage of the 'first move'

The fact that the net result of EU environmental policy turns out to be much better than one would generally expect it to be in view of the 'systems competition' between the member states enabled by economic integration, can also be attributed to a second form of regulatory competition, which interferes with the interest constellations presented in the previous section. Of great significance here is the observation that the member states not only pursue their interests by means of adjusting national environmental regulations, as was assumed for the first form of regulatory competition. Instead they simultaneously seek to incorporate their national regulations into the European legislative process to the greatest possible extent. Thus they find themselves in constant competition also when it comes to influencing European policies (Héritier, Knill and Mingers 1996).[5]

What brought on this phenomenon? What motivates the member states to influence European policy-making in line with their national standards and regulatory patterns? Two factors are crucial here: institutional and economic interests of the member states as well as strategic advantages which result from their 'forerunner role' in the process of European policy-making.

The interests that are pursued by the member states in the process of European policy-making are primarily concentrated on two aspects: besides safeguarding the economic competitiveness of national industries (which can entail both protection from foreign competition as well as the development of new markets for domestic industries), the member states are particularly interested in minimizing the costs which arise due to the legal and institutional adaptation of existing national regulatory concepts to European requirements (Héritier, Knill and Mingers 1996, 12).

There is frequently a tight link between European policy content and institutional preconditions required for the proper implementation of these regulations at the national level. Accordingly, European measures that are not compatible with existing regulatory patterns at the national level can result in thorough adjustments to administrative structures and regulatory styles in the member states (Knill and Lenschow 1998; Knill 2001). The main concern here is not so much the concrete level of European regulations, but rather the question of whether and to what extent European patterns of governance and regulatory instruments can be integrated into national structures and regulatory processes without great efforts.

As indicated for instance by the German Advisory Council on the Environment (*Rat von Sachverständigen für Umweltfragen*) this problem is by no means trivial. It ascertains that the more recent European environmental directives increasingly contain principles for policy design which are alien to the German environmental protection practice, but have to be integrated anyway (SRU 1998, 163). The implementation of the EIA Directive, for example, poses great problems in Germany. This directive is aimed at the integrated evaluation of environmental problems. Before authorizing projects with a significant impact on the environment, their environmental compatibility is to be assessed not only with respect to individual elements of the environment (soil, water, air), but also from a cross-media perspective. However, its implied requirement for the integration of administrative responsibilities is hardly compatible with the horizontally fragmented, media-specific administrative structure that exists in Germany (Knill 1998).

As for the form of regulatory competition described here, there also exist differences between poor and rich member states. Poor member states generally have a much lesser interest in influencing EU environmental policy with their own regulatory concepts. As demonstrated in the previous section, on the one hand this has to do with these countries basically not having an interest in unitary EU-wide environmental regulations, except when product standards are concerned. On the other hand, there is generally a smaller risk of these countries being faced with significant costs of institutional adaptation. Due to the often lacking or weakly developed administrative capacities in the area of environmental protection, there are frequently no structures or regulatory patterns to be adjusted to European guidelines at all (Börzel 2000; Knill and Lenschow 2000b). The result is that the competition for influence over EU environmental policy primarily is centred on the rich member states, who have developed a differentiated and comprehensive system of environmental policy structures and procedures (Héritier, Knill and Mingers 1996, 14–15).

One could certainly argue that the economic and institutional interests of the member states alone are not enough to explain the

phenomenon of regulatory competition over the greatest influence on European environmental policies. Why do the member
states not simply rely on national strategies for adaptation and, if
need be, block European regulations that are not consistent with
their interests?

A crucial factor that compels the member states to play an
active role in the European policy-making process is the advantage of the 'first move'. Environmental pioneer states have a
greater chance of successfully putting their interests and concepts
on the European agenda than states that tend to 'wait and see' or
block policies. This can be attributed, among other things, to the
fact that the possibilities of blocking decisions have been
restricted by the increased significance of voting on the basis of
qualified majority (Héritier, Knill and Mingers 1996; Andersen
and Liefferink 1997; Jänicke and Weidner 1997; Liefferink and
Andersen 1998). Now how do these 'first mover advantages'
manifest themselves in concrete terms?

In order to secure a good starting position, the member states
often attempt to influence the European policy-making process at
a very early stage. Since the Commission as a rule reacts very positively towards initiatives from external actors – as described in
Chapter 4 – a country with innovative policy proposals thus has
an increased chance of influencing the definition of the problem
and the agenda-setting procedure. However, a prerequisite for
this is that its concepts are constructive and compatible with the
Commission's understanding of the problem and interests.

If a member state is able to win the support of the Commission
in this phase, it can have a long-term impact on the perception
and handling of a certain problem at the European level. This
holds, in particular, for the subsequent phase in which drafts for
regulations are elaborated:

> If the proposal is compatible with the Commission's views on the
> issue and how to tackle it, the initiator country has a good chance
> of seeing its national approach become the received view of the
> issue ... for the ensuing drafting phase. (Héritier, Knill and
> Mingers 1996, 13)

Along these lines, when the Commission wants to draw on a
national proposal, it asks for experts from the country concerned,
who then collaborate during the concrete drafting process of the

Commission proposal. For instance, the Commission proposal on the Directive on the Free Access to Environmental Information passed in 1990 was essentially written by an expert from the British Environment Ministry. By these means, the UK was able to successfully transplant its extensive domestic reforms to improve public access to documents to the European level (Kimber 2000; see Chapter 6).

Whether and to what extent a strategic 'first mover advantage' thus acquired actually is reflected by concrete outcomes, greatly depends on the subsequent negotiations in the Council of Ministers. Member states who were not able to influence the early stages of policy-making will now attempt to assert their interests. The extent to which the final measure deviates from the original concept of the 'forerunner' depends on the concrete interest constellations in the Council of Ministers as well as the interests and influence of the EP, the Commission and interest associations.

In this regard, the empirical findings point to four general patterns. First of all, the 'forerunners' can indeed succeed in pushing their concept in almost original form through the European decision-making process. This holds, for instance, for the mentioned British initiative for the Information Directive or for the German initiative for the regulation of emissions from industrial plants. Second, it is possible that individual proposals from member states are further expanded by the Commission and integrated into a more comprehensive concept. Thirdly, the need to address the concerns of opposed member states can lead to a watering down and modification of the initial proposal, for example, with regard to the stringency of the limits or in the shape of exceptions. A fourth possibility is when the concept of the 'forerunner' is greatly enriched by other parties, which can lead to a situation in which different, sometimes contradictory national regulatory traditions are reflected in the very same directive (see Héritier 1996; Héritier, Knill and Mingers 1996, 332–4; Eichener 1997, 604).[6]

It appears that the 'first mover advantage' only vanishes to a great degree in the fourth constellation. In all other – empirically observed – scenarios, the 'forerunners' succeed in bringing their interests into the political process (see Liefferink and Andersen 1998; Kern, Jörgens and Jänicke 2000, 512; Börzel 2002).

What impact does this form of regulatory competition between the member states have on EU environmental policy-making and the level of regulation? Firstly, we should bear in mind that this mechanism to a considerable extent accounts for the broad spectrum of instruments and patterns of governance which can be observed in the EU environmental policy (see Chapter 2). The diversity of regulatory concepts reflects the different regulatory traditions at the national level, as it is not always the same countries that assert themselves in situations marked by regulatory competition. Furthermore, from the Commission's standpoint it would hardly be legitimate practice to exclusively fall back on the expertise of individual states during the development of policy proposals:

> European regulatory policy ... is a patchwork of regulatory traditions and approaches taken from national regulatory experience to be stitched together into European legislation ... Not only within a single policy area but sometimes within one and the same directive, divergent approaches can be on parallel offer, if it has proved impossible to negotiate a consensus. (Héritier, Knill and Mingers 1996, 21–2)

As set out in Chapter 2, the competition between German and British regulatory traditions was reflected particularly clearly in the design of European environmental policy. In the 1980s the Germans were initially able to act as 'pace setters' for EU environmental policy. In reaction to the problems of forest dieback and acid rain, Germany had enacted relatively innovative and strict regulations. These measures were based on the definition of detailed authorization requirements and uniform emission limits, which were in line with the state-of-the-art technology. The orientation of EU environmental policy towards German concepts demanded extensive changes in British regulatory traditions, which focused on environmental quality, scientific causality and economic commensurability.

These pressures for adjustment together with domestic political developments led to extensive reforms of the British environmental policy at the beginning of the 1990s, which in some areas (access to environmental information, integrated pollution control, EMAS) went beyond the European policies. In the aftermath these developments enabled the British to influence EU environmental policy with innovative proposals, which focused more on procedural guidelines, industrial self-regulation and quality standards. As a result of this new orientation in EU environmental policy the Germans were now confronted with new concepts which were hardly compatible with existing regulatory patterns (Héritier, Knill and Mingers 1996).

The frequently recurring competition between Germany and the UK is to a great extent responsible for the different and in part opposed patterns of governance and regulatory instruments in EU environmental policy. The influential role of Germany and the UK by no means rules out that other member states can act as 'forerunners', however. In particular, Denmark and the Netherlands with their various domestic innovations (energy policies in Denmark, the National Environmental Policy Plan in the Netherlands) play an important role as pioneers in European environmental policy. The same holds for Sweden, Finland and Austria since their accession to the EU in 1995 (Liefferink and Andersen 1998).

Secondly, the regulatory competition between the member states helps prevent the often-feared 'race to the bottom' in European environmental policy. This effect is enhanced by the Commission, which is inherently interested in the expansion of its regulatory authority (see Chapter 4). Along these lines, initiatives on behalf of the member states can only receive the support of the Commission when they fulfil this criterion.

Against this background, we can expect a continual expansion of more stringent environmental standards at the European level. This general trend of course does not rule out the possibility of negotiations breaking down in individual cases or European regulatory demands partially lagging behind those of individual member states. Nevertheless, the dynamics of regulatory competition enhance the scope and the regulatory level of the EU environmental policy in the long term.

Deliberation and diffusion

Up to now we have presumed that the interests of the member states are consistent and defined relatively clearly during European negotiation processes. Accordingly, an agreement can only be expected when the preferences of the national governments are generally compatible or distributional conflicts can be avoided by concessions, package deals and compensation payments (see Scharpf 1997a, 2000). In other words, a relatively static constellation of national interests is assumed, which defines the potential options for the design of environmental policy measures at the European level.

However, Joerges and Neyer (1997) have demonstrated that this form of intergovernmental bargaining by no means is the only mode of interaction at the European level. Other incidents can indeed be observed in which the patterns of interaction are influenced to a lesser extent by actors' defending and asserting national policy positions than by a collective problem-solving orientation. In such cases, national representatives develop a common understanding of problems and solutions. Viewed from this angle, national ideas and interests can by no means be regarded as static, but can indeed change or converge over time.

Such processes are facilitated by a specific form of interaction which is described by Joerges and Neyer as deliberation. The main focus is placed on discussion and reasoning on the basis of scientific and technical insights rather than on strategic bargaining to assert national interests.[7] This 'deliberative problem-solving' facilitates learning processes between the negotiating partners (Hall 1993). Transnational networks of experts or so-called 'epistemic communities' emerge (Haas 1992) in which converging ideas, assumptions and convictions develop by means of the collective professional orientation and socialization of the participating actors. This in turn improves the basis for a convergence of national interest positions.

> During the course of this collaboration, delegates not only learn to reduce differences between national legal provisions but also to develop converging definitions of problems and philosophies for their solution. They slowly proceed from being representatives of national interests to being representatives of a Europeanized inter-administrative discourse characterized by mutual learning and an understanding of each other's difficulties in the implementation of specific solutions. For the same reason, even the intergovernmental Committee of Permanent Representatives (COREPER) is jokingly referred to as the 'Committee of Permanent Traitors' in the German administration. (Joerges and Neyer 1997, 620)

However, the development of this kind of problem-solving orientation cannot be taken for granted for all negotiations at the

European level. In the working groups at the Commission level, typical patterns of interaction – as described in Chapter 4 – are in fact characterized by this form of problem-solving. What is more important for reaching a final agreement, though, is the question of whether and to what extent such processes can also be expected in the working groups under the Council of Ministers. Here we can identify two factors which can facilitate a deliberative problem-solving mode. First, the chances for problem-solving increase according to the uncertainty surrounding the possible distributive effects of a certain policy. In such constellations, national interests and problem definitions are less structured in advance and can be modified more easily. Second, institutionalized interactions between national representatives over a longer time period enhance the diffusion of scientific expertise between the member states (Haas 1992).

Deliberative problem-solving processes may not only lead to the convergence of national interest-based policy positions and henceforth an agreement at the European level. Such patterns of transnational interaction have furthermore been identified as an important mechanism facilitating the international diffusion of innovative environmental policy concepts independently of the adoption of European measures. For example, analysts frequently observe the emulation and transfer of governance patterns and regulatory instruments that have proven to be particularly successful in one country (DiMaggio and Powell 1991; Kern 2000; Kern, Jörgens and Jänicke 2000). The trend towards internationally converging structures and regulatory patterns frequently ascertained in this regard (Bennett, C. 1991; Jänicke and Weidner 1997; Holzinger and Knill 2005; Knill 2005) can in turn contribute to a decrease in national conflicts of interests over decisions on European environmental measures.

Logjam or dynamics? National conflict lines in EU environmental policy

The analysis up to now has shown that EU environmental policy-making is marked by different constellations of national interests and patterns of consensus building. Depending on the perspective of analysis, we arrive at different assessments of the possibilities for and limits to the design of EU environmental policy measures.

Nevertheless, we can conclude with a number of general observations.

As a rule, there are more favourable conditions for European harmonization at a high level in the area of product regulation than in the area of production regulation. This can be traced back to two factors: on the one hand, the harmonization of product standards facilitates market integration and thus is associated with advantages for all member states. On the other hand, those states that advocate a high level of regulation are in a better negotiation position, because they have the legal means to enforce high standards single-handedly, if need be. Both of these preconditions are not granted in the area of production regulation. Instead a fundamental conflict of interest between poor and rich countries with regard to the necessity and the level of common regulations prevails here.

However, from this we should not generally assume that production regulation issues will lead to a failure of negotiations or sub-optimal results at a low regulatory level. Depending on how the member states are affected in economic and ecological terms, the constellation of national interests can have a different impact on the capacity for action at the European level. Furthermore, whether decisions are made on the basis of unanimity or qualified majority has a decisive impact on individual states' ability to block decisions. Compensation payments, package deals or opt-out arrangements and transition periods for poor member countries can also have positive effects on their willingness to forge an agreement. Finally, it is difficult to categorize many environmental policy measures by the EU as either product or production regulations. This means that the conflict of interest between poor and rich countries assumed for production standards may not be equally relevant for an array of other environmental policy measures.

An additional factor which tends to help overcome political impasses results from the competition between the member states to assert their regulatory concepts to the greatest possible extent in European policy-making. By doing so, they seek to avoid costs of institutional adjustment resulting from European policies which are not compatible with national traditions. In the long run, this form of regulatory competition helps prevent European 'environmental dumping', as the initiatives of the member states can potentially only be successful if they are innovative and stringent enough to be considered and taken up by the Commission. The dynamics which this creates basically increase the scope and stringency of environmental powers vested at the EU level.

The interest constellation between the member states cannot always be viewed as a static factor that determines the EU's capacity for environmental policy action. Instead, environmental policy dynamics can be promoted by processes of deliberation and diffusion that may take place, under certain conditions, during the institutionalized cooperation at the European level. Such processes in turn facilitate the convergence of national understandings of problems and solutions. By these means negotiation impasses can be avoided or overcome.

Besides the already mentioned factors which exclusively relate to how the constellation of national interests influences EU environmental policy-making, one must not overlook the fact that the impact of supranational actors and institutions described in Chapter 4, in particular the Commission and the EP as well as European interest groups, can considerably contribute to increasing the dynamics described above. This interplay between national and European influences makes it clear that EU environmental policy is a form of multi-level governance. Political processes and outcomes can only be completely understood if the interactions between national and European processes are incorporated into the analysis. In the following chapter this interplay between supranational and national interests will be illustrated on the basis of selected examples.

Notes

1 This understanding of regulatory competition not only provides the basis for many analyses of the effects of the European Common Market on the competition between member state systems, but can also be found in analyses on the national effects of globalisation.

2 See Chapter 1. Article 30 thus defines exceptions to the principle of mutual recognition defined by the ECJ in its 'Cassis de Dijon' decision. This principle states that the member states mutually accept the national product regulations. A product from one country that complies with domestic standards thus automatically also fulfils the requirements of the other member states and cannot be excluded from the market. Even though it was not brewed according to the

conventional German traditions, a Belgian or Danish beer, for example, cannot be excluded from the German market on these grounds. The principle of mutual recognition facilitates the integration of the European market despite divergent product regulations in the member states.

3 Both Article 30 and Article 95 ban trade restrictions which randomly discriminate. For example, this is the case when the primary purpose of the measure is not so much environmental protection as the insulation of national markets. In individual cases, to be sure, concrete decisions on such matters can be very difficult (Koppen 1993, 114).

4 Furthermore, those factors described in Chapter 4 that can facilitate consensus in the Council of Ministers, such as compensation payments, package deals or the intermediary role of the Commission, are also significant. As for these factors though, one must state that their respective influence can vary from case to case and that it is difficult to make generalized claims about them. Thus, these factors will only be mentioned here for the sake of completeness. A reference to contextual conditions, which can differ from case to case, does not constitute a legitimate argument against a theoretical model that stresses more abstract analytical relationships.

5 This form of regulatory competition has not only been documented within the EU, but also among the OECD countries (Jänicke and Weidner 1997).

6 An example of this is the IPPC Directive (see Chapter 2), which contains elements of both the German emissions and technology orientation and the British orientation towards quality standards and economic costs (Weale et al. 2000).

7 In the relevant literature these distinct patterns of interaction are frequently referred to as 'arguing versus bargaining' (see Risse 2000).

6

Making EU environmental policy in practice: three case studies

Until now we have examined the actors, interest constellations and processes that are crucial for the design of European environmental policies. We have done so from an analytical perspective. Our objective has been to assess general interrelationships and political patterns as well as their ramifications for the shape and quality of environmental policies. It has become clear that processes and outcomes of environmental policy-making in Brussels vary greatly with the respective interests and strategic capacities for action of both national and supranational actors and institutions. EU environmental policy does not follow a uniform scheme. It rather evolves differently depending on the regulatory issue at hand (e.g. substantial versus procedural instruments), the compatibility of the institutional and economic interests of the member states, national strategies for action ('forerunners' versus 'laggards'), the goals of the Commission and the EP, and the applied decision-making procedures (consultation, cooperation, co-decision).

In view of this broad array of potentially influential factors, it is difficult to give a fully representative overview of possible patterns of development by means of case studies. Instead the case studies presented here primarily serve to give some flesh and blood to the analytical observations made in the previous chapters. To do so, we have selected three cases from three different decades, demonstrating and referring back to a wide array of processes and patterns discussed in more theoretical terms above. More specifically, the cases pertain to the introduction of catalytic converters in cars, the free access to environmentally relevant information, and the establishment of a system for emissions trading in the context of climate policy. Most of this chapter will be devoted to the description and analysis of the three individual cases. The final section will compare them and present some general conclusions.

The introduction of cars with catalytic converters: the European Parliament demonstrates its power

The introduction of cars with catalytic converters and the adoption of the so-called Small Cars Directive in 1989, which was decisive in this regard, can be viewed as one of the greatest successes of the European environmental policy.[1] This directive, also described as 'the miracle of 1989' (Dietz, van der Straaten and van der Velde 1991, 73), imposed unexpectedly strict limits on various motor vehicle emissions (carbon monoxide, hydrocarbons and nitrogen oxides), which could only be complied with by installing three-way catalytic converters. This measure marked not only a great step forward in the reduction of air pollution in the EU, but must also be regarded as a significant success for environmentally ambitious actors and institutions at both the national and the European level, who were able to enforce strict standards in the face of strong resistance from several large member states. This holds in particular for the EP, which played a crucial role in the decision-making process.

The development of EU car emission limits
The control of emissions from motor vehicles in Europe can be traced back to the regulations adopted by the UN Economic Commission for Europe (ECE) from the late 1960s. The goal of these regulations was to facilitate and enhance European trade by means of technical harmonization. Environmental policy aspects played a minor role. Emission limits were accordingly unambitious. As most EU member states were involved in developing these regulations anyway, EU legislation for more than a decade simply followed the ECE in this field.

In the early 1980s, though, the EU started to depart from the path set out by the ECE. The decisive reason for this was an initiative taken by Germany. Against the background of growing public and political concern about 'acid rain' and forest dieback

(*Waldsterben*) resulting from it, Germany pressed for a considerable tightening of the limits. Nitrogen oxides, emitted by cars in fairly high quantities, were presumed to be an important cause of the problem. The point of reference of the German demands was formed by the strict standards in the USA (the so-called US-83 standards), which could only be adhered to with a three-way catalytic converter. In order to increase pressure on the Commission and the other member states, the Germans even threatened to 'go it alone' in case the EU would not deliver. Considering that Germany is the biggest domestic market for cars in the EU, such unilateral measures, for instance in the form of an import ban on cars not complying with the higher standards, would constitute a major barrier to trade. Not least in view of this threat, the Commission reacted positively to the German request and presented a draft directive in 1984 (Holzinger 1994).

Due to the highly divergent interests of the member states, the negotiations in the Council of Ministers turned out to be extremely difficult (Corcelle 1985; Boehmer-Christiansen and Weidner 1992). Only Germany, Denmark and the Netherlands supported the introduction of the strict American standards, while most other states rejected them. This held for France, the UK, and Italy in particular, whose automobile industries feared the loss of market shares, because they – unlike the Germans – still had little experience with catalytic converter technology. The German industry had to adapt to American standards anyway due to its high level of exports to the USA and was thus basically more positive towards the proposal (Vogel 1995). With stricter limits the German industry also aimed to prevent the introduction of alternative measures, such as the (in Germany highly controversial) introduction of speed limits. The manufacturers of large and fast cars, in particular, feared a decline in sales as a result (Holzinger 1994).

After two years of negotiations a first agreement was reached in June 1985: the so-called Luxembourg compromise. The most essential elements of this arrangement were differentiation of standards depending on the engine capacity of the vehicles as well as a time schedule for gradually introducing the standards. Furthermore, a distinction was made between new cars and new models (see Table 6.1). While the limits for large cars could only be adhered to with three-way catalytic converters, the require-

ments for medium-sized cars class were less strict. Less demanding solutions from a technical perspective, such as the lean-burn
engine favoured by the British industry, were sufficient to fulfil
the requirements. The emission limits for small cars did not pose
any additional demands at all. Stricter limits for this category
were not supposed to be set until a (as yet unspecified) second
phase. It was particularly this point which made Denmark block
the formal adoption of the Luxembourg compromise in the
Council. Remember that by this time (1985), the SEA had not yet
come into force and QMV did not yet apply (see Chapter 4).
Individual member states, in other words, still had *de facto* veto
power in the Council.

Table 6.1   *Emission limits for motor vehicles after the Luxembourg
compromise of 1985*

Engine capacity	Introduction period		Emissions in grams per ECE-Test		
	New models	New cars	CO	HC + NO$_X$	NO$_X$
Over 2 litres	1 Oct 1988	1 Oct 1989	25	6.6	3.5
1.4–2 litres	1 Oct 1991	1 Oct 1993	30	8.0	–
Up to 1.4 litres					
phase 1	1 Oct 1990	1 Oct 1991	45	15.0	6.0
phase 2	1 Oct 1992	1 Oct 1993	Specification expected in 1987		

Source: Holzinger 1994, 247.

In July 1987, however, the SEA did enter into force. Since the car
directives were founded upon Article 95 of the Treaty, i.e. the
article aiming at the realization of the Common Market, the cooperation procedure now applied. This meant, among other
things, that the unanimity requirement in the Council was
replaced by qualified majority. It made the way free for adopting
the Luxembourg compromise against the will of Denmark and
Greece in December 1987 (Directive 88/76/EEC).

In early 1988, furthermore, after intense consultations with
national experts as well as industrial and environmental associations, the Commission presented a draft for the second phase for

the category of small cars. The emission limits were the same as those for the medium-sized class defined in the Luxembourg compromise, i.e. 30 g/test for carbon monoxide and 8 g/test for the combined emissions of hydrocarbons and nitrogen oxides. This proposal, referred to as '30/8', was somewhere in between the demands of the automobile industry ('38/12.8'), and the environmental organizations, notably the European Environmental Bureau (EEB) ('20/5'). It also anticipated a compromise between the positions of the member states in the Council of Ministers. Germany, Denmark, the Netherlands and Greece[2] advocated the '20/5' solution, which could only be complied with by using three-way catalytic converters. All other member states supported the British '35/12' proposal, which did not require the use of catalytic converters. In November 1988, after comparatively short negotiations, the Council reached agreement on the Commission's '30/8' proposal.

The new cooperation procedure not only replaced unanimity by QMV in the Council, but also implied a much stronger role for the EP. In its first reading in September 1988, the EP had argued for the '20/5' solution as favoured by the 'green' member states. However, as we have seen, the EP's proposal was not taken over by the Council when adopting its Common Position two months later. This decision was not taken unanimously, though. Whereas Germany eventually agreed with the Commission's '30/8' compromise (see below), Denmark, the Netherlands and Greece continued to support the '20/5' proposal of the EP and voted against. They did not however hold sufficient votes under QMV to block the compromise.

The second reading in the EP took place in April 1989. Shortly beforehand, the Environmental Commissioner at that time, Carlo Ripa di Meana, stated that the Commission would support a tightening of the emission limits by the EP. In its second reading the EP nearly unanimously confirmed its original position, i.e. the '20/5' solution. As promised, the Commission adopted these modifications in its new proposal, which was presented to the Council of Ministers for a final decision in May 1989. Following the cooperation procedure, the amendments made by the EP and supported by the Commission could now either be rejected by a unanimous Council vote, or accepted by qualified majority. In view of the positions of Denmark, Greece and the Netherlands, the former was not to be expected. Instead, the revised proposal, prescribing the '20/5' limits instead of '30/8', was adopted by qualified majority in June 1989 (Directive 89/458; cf. Holzinger 1994, 318–36; Liefferink 1996, 97–101).

Thanks to this directive and the Luxembourg compromise the introduction of a three-way catalytic converter was now legally binding for small and for large cars, but – somewhat paradoxically – not for medium-sized ones. This inconsistency was eliminated by the so-called Consolidated Directive passed in 1991 (Directive 91/441/EEC). It abolished the division into different cubic capacity classes in favour of unified emission limits, requiring three-way catalytic converters in all new vehicles as of 1993.[3]

Reasons for this unexpected success

If we consider the opposed policy positions of the member states, the far-reaching measures to regulate motor vehicle emissions which were eventually decided on at the European level are certainly surprising at first glance. How do we explain this unexpected environmental policy success? The factors responsible for this can be subdivided into three groups: institutional changes at the European level, adjustments in national policy positions and the negotiation dynamics in the Council of Ministers.

As mentioned above, the institutional modifications triggered by the SEA brought the car directives under the cooperation procedure. This development had a profound impact on the strategic options available to the EP, the Commission and the Council of Ministers. The EP could now by absolute majority either reject the Council's Common Position or modify it according to its own preferences. In the case of a rejection, the Council in its second reading could only prevent the proposal in question from failing altogether by unanimously outvoting the EP. A unanimous decision was also required if the Council wanted to assert its position against amendments proposed by the EP and supported by the Commission. A qualified majority in the Council only sufficed to reject amendments by the EP which had not been endorsed by the Commission (see also Chapter 4).

In the case of the small cars, neither the Council nor the Commission had initially expected that the necessary majority to reject or amend the Common Position of the Council would come about in the EP. However, it soon turned out that the EP wanted to seize the opportunity to demonstrate the political power it had gained with the SEA. This ambition should be seen against the background of the upcoming European elections in 1989. More substantively speaking, to be sure, the EP's position was in line with its environment-friendly reputation in general (see Chapter 3).

In order to gain the support of the Commission for tightening emission limits, the EP threatened to reject the proposal altogether, if the Commission would not support its request for amendments. This put substantial pressure on the Commission to act, unless it wanted to risk the total failure of the measure. The Commission could not be faint-hearted on this point. Considering the position of the Danes and the Dutch, in particular, the Council was highly unlikely to reach the required unanimity on adopting the directive against the EP's veto. In view of this constellation, the Commission signalled after long internal debate that it was willing to accept the amendments proposed by the EP. As a result, a unanimous vote in the Council of Ministers was now required to reject the stricter limits advocated by the EP and the Commission together, whereas a qualified majority sufficed to accept the revised proposal (Corcelle 1989).

As for the second reading by the Council of Ministers, this meant on the one hand that holding on to the original Common Position (i.e. the '30/8' limits) would be vetoed by the 'green' member states. On the other hand, the votes of the 'green' countries alone were not enough to build the qualified majority necessary to accept the amendments by the Commission and EP (i.e. the '20/5' limits). The question whether the Council of Ministers would decide on stricter limits or ultimately break down the negotiations thus decisively depended on developments during the negotiations.

If we examine the negotiations in the Council of Ministers, we must first clarify what happened during the Council's first reading of the proposal in November 1988. Why did the member states so easily accept the Commission's original '30/8' proposal as their Common Position, despite their different policy positions? What was crucial here was a package deal, by which the Small Cars Directive was linked to the negotiations on the Directive on Large Combustion Plants, which were carried on simultaneously. The deal implied that France and the UK made their consent to the Directive on Large Combustion Plants in exchange for Germany's approval of the less strict '30/8' limits for small cars. Together with Denmark, Greece and the Netherlands, Germany had initially insisted on the '20/5' solution. The Germans, who happened to hold the Council Presidency at the time, nevertheless accepted the package in order to not risk the failure of both initiatives. Thus, the Council was able to pass its Common Position by qualified majority, because the remaining 'green' states no longer had a blocking minority.

Secondly, the question arises of which factors were crucial for the Council of Ministers' acceptance of the amendments by the EP and Commission by qualified majority during the second reading in June 1989, even though the supporters of the less strict regulations would have been in a position to block the negotiations. Several factors came to play here.

For example, concessions with regard to the deadlines for implementation were instrumental in winning over the support of the states opposed to the measure. Moreover, it would have been difficult to politically justify a breakdown of the negotiations at this point in light of the immense political pressure associated with the problem as well as the time already invested in the negotiations. In addition, Germany, Denmark and the Netherlands had threatened to introduce their own stricter standards and promote the use of catalytic converters through tax incentives. Although it is questionable if such incentives, which could be seen as a form of state support, would have survived in the ECJ (a pending court case was overtaken by the final compromise of June 1989), these initiatives helped to increase the sense of urgency around the issue (Liefferink 1996, 100–11).

Apart from these factors, however, the fact that the Council of Ministers could find a consensus on the amended proposal relatively quickly was to a large extent the result of changes in the interests of the member states. Since the middle of the 1980s environmental awareness had grown in those very countries who acted as environmental policy laggards in this case (Boehmer-Christiansen and Weidner 1992). This increased pressure for political action and made those countries more willing to compromise.

Along with that, the quick agreement was facilitated by developments on the international automobile market. By the end of the 1980s, a number of European countries outside the EU, such as Switzerland, Austria, Norway and Sweden, had also started to introduce the strict American standards. The export-oriented European industry took this as an important economic impulse for the general introduction of the catalytic converter technology. This was compounded by the fact that the development of alternative technologies, such as the lean-burn engine, did not work out as positively as originally assumed. As a result, the industries in the 'laggard countries' increasingly pushed for the catalytic converter, which further increased these states' willingness to compromise (Holzinger 1994, 342).

The decision to introduce cars with catalytic converters in the EU makes it clear that different decision-making procedures have a large impact on the substance and content of environmental policy decisions. In particular the participation of the EP during the cooperation procedure played a decisive role in this decision, which is regarded as an environmental policy success story. Moreover, it appears that an agreement in the Council of Ministers was not brought about by the dynamics of the European negotiations alone, but also by parallel changes in national interest constellations as well.

The evolution of the Small Cars Directive also profited from the influence of environmental policy 'forerunners', which played a key role both in initiating the measure and in pushing for consensus in the Council of Ministers. Their most important resource in this case was not so much their appeal to 'good arguments' or innovative national examples, but rather the threat to introduce such measures on their own if need be (cf. Liefferink and Andersen 1998).

Access to environmental information: switching roles

The Directive on Freedom of Access to Information on the Environment (Directive 90/313/EEC), passed in 1990, must be viewed within the context of the strategic re-orientation of EU environmental policy in this period, aimed at the increased participation of societal actors in designing and implementing European measures. In concrete terms, the directive aims at improving the possibilities for the public to access environmentally relevant data from national authorities. This, in turn, should help to create more 'pressure from below' in the member states to achieve better implementation of European environmental regulations. After a slow start, the measure was pushed strongly by the UK, while Germany acted more like a 'brakeman'. Compared to the previous case, the roles of the 'forerunners' and 'laggards' were thus switched.[4]

The contents of the directive: regulatory transparency

The Directive on Freedom of Access to Environmental Information pursues the objective, also laid down in the Fourth Environmental Action Programme,

> to ensure freedom of access to, and dissemination of, information on the environment held by public authorities and to set out the basic terms and conditions on which such information should be made available. (Article 1)[5]

'Information on the environment' in the sense of the directive encompasses information on the state of the environment as well as on activities, policies and measures positively or negatively affecting the environment, both on paper and in electronic form. According to the directive, member states have to make sure that such information is available upon request to anybody with or without a particular interest in the matter. This obligation, however, is restricted to public authorities at national and subnational level; private actors such as companies are not addressed by the directive. The authorities, moreover, are allowed to refuse a request for information under certain conditions, not only if national security or basic privacy rights are at stake, but also in a fairly wide range of situations where business interests may be affected.

The British as surprising forerunners

Not only the objectives of the Fourth Environmental Action Programme, but above all the heightened demands by the EP and especially its Environment Committee initially provoked the Commission to address the issue of public access to environmental information. The Commission reacted very positively to those demands, but at the same time indicated that there was only a small chance that such a measure could be enacted due to different regulations and administrative traditions in the member states and the considerable political sensitivity of the matter (Knill 1995, 245).

At that point in time, formalized access to environmentally relevant information only existed in Denmark, France, the Netherlands and Luxembourg. While it was generally expected that these states would support a relevant Commission proposal, significant resistance on behalf of the other member states was feared. In most of those countries, the access to administrative data and information was traditionally very restrictive.

In Germany, the principle of free access to information stood in strong contrast with the established principle of 'restricted public access to records' (*beschränkte Aktenöffentlichkeit*). This principle provides for access to information only if the petitioner uses the data to assert his or her subjective individual rights (Winter 1996). A similar situation arose in the case of the UK. Here the Commission's plans directly collided with the legendary secrecy of the British public administration, which only granted the public and environmental interest groups very few means of gaining access to environmental policy matters (Vogel 1986; Knill 1995, 110–11).[6] Due to the large costs of legal and institutional adjustment, Germany and the UK were extremely sceptical towards the planned measure. A large majority of the other member states in which access to files was regulated in a similarly restricted manner shared this position (Kimber 2000).

However, the UK's stance changed quite surprisingly towards the end of the 1980s. A fundamental reform of the national environmental policy was the main reason for this shift. On the one hand, this reform was necessary in order to adjust more effectively to increasingly pressing European requirements, such as the recent Directives on Air Pollution by Industrial Plants and Large Combustion Plants – and thus to get rid of the reputation of being the 'dirty man of Europe'. On the other hand, however, purely domestic policy developments played an important role. Besides a heightened environmental awareness among the population and increased activity by environmental organizations, the radical reformist orientation of the Conservative government was of crucial significance. In Margaret Thatcher's view, citizens were to be seen as customers of an accountable and transparent public administration (Rhodes 1996; Jordan 2004).

Thus, the British public was granted extensive information

rights to environmentally relevant data. So-called Public Registers were created. These registers, which can be viewed by anyone, contain all authorization-relevant information including the results of emissions measurements. This gives environmental organizations the possibility to educate the public on any potential irregularities in the authorization process and launch information campaigns or exert pressure on the authorities in the case of non-compliance (Knill 1995, 229).

Against this background, the British had now become a trend-setter in the design of the EU directive. They attempted to push ahead with the policy-making process and shape the directive in line with their new preferences. For example, the draft was written by a UK official, seconded to the Commission, who had previously participated in the planning of the national reforms. The goal of the British was not just to minimize the costs of institutional adjustment, but also to safeguard the competitiveness of their national industries. With the extensive information rights at the national level, British industries were put at a disadvantage vis-à-vis their foreign competitors. After all, public files can also be viewed by other companies, which may enable them to draw useful conclusions about production and cost structures, for instance (Héritier, Knill and Mingers 1996, 237).

The decision-making process

Even if the number of opponents to the Information Directive was reduced by the changed British position, the opponents still had a blocking minority to knock down the proposal in the Council of Ministers. Not least the Germans, fearing significant costs of institutional adaptation, offered particular resistance. Nevertheless, the member states reached an agreement after relatively short negotiations. Three main factors were responsible for this.

Firstly, the specifications and requirements of the directive were worded relatively vaguely and openly. This was linked to the goal of granting the member states as much leeway as possible for national implementation and reducing the costs of institutional adaptation. Thus, there are many uncertain legal terms and a wide scope for discretion in the text. This pertains for instance to the different grounds for exceptions, which could be interpreted very broadly. In other words: the agreement reached in the Council of Ministers was at the cost of programme deficits, which were reflected by the relatively ineffective implementation of the measure.[7]

Secondly, very close cooperation between the UK and the Irish Presidency in the first half of 1990 facilitated the quick agreement. The British were in fact able to assert their influence relatively effectively because the directive proposal by the Commission had to be reworded by the Irish Presidency – more or less at the last minute – due to numerous objections from various member states: 'The final directive was written half an hour before the Council meeting broke up' (representative of the British Environmental Ministry, quoted in Knill 1995, 249).

Thirdly, by making concessions to the other member states, the British and Irish were able to isolate Germany during the negotiations. This situation had the effect that Germany ultimately gave up its resistance, above all in order to save its reputation as an environmental policy 'forerunner' (Héritier, Knill and Mingers 1996, 238).

The case of the Information Directive shows, on the one hand, that by no means the same member states always set the pace at the European level. Contrary to the previous case of the catalytic converter, the decision-making process and the content of the Information Directive were greatly influenced by the British and their successful strategy of 'uploading' innovative regulations at the national level to the European level. On the other hand, it became apparent that an agreement in the Council of Ministers was only possible at the expense of a 'watering down' of the original draft, in particular due to the resistance by the Germans. As in the case of the car directives, furthermore, one must emphasize that changes in domestic policy positions can result in lasting effects on the European decision-making process. In the present case, this pertained in particular to the British turn-around, which can only be understood against the background of domestic developments, even if these had in turn been sparked off, among other things, by demands to adapt to other EU measures.

Climate change and emissions trading: the fruit of an international commitment and competing domestic models

Climate change is one of today's major environmental issues. Since the 1980s there has been growing evidence of a gradual warming of the earth due to anthropogenic emissions into the air. Among the so-called greenhouse gases, carbon dioxide (CO_2) is the most important. Carbon dioxide is emitted whenever fossil fuels, such as coal, oil or gas, are burnt. This implies that the industrialized countries – notably the EU, the USA and Japan – are to be seen as the major causes of the problem, while the contribution of quickly developing countries such as India and China is rapidly increasing.

The effects of climate change are still widely debated among scientists, but are potentially dramatic. A rise in sea level may cause a threat to low coastal areas, increasing temperatures are likely to lead to changes in eco-systems and the agricultural use of land, and changing atmospheric dynamics will probably increase the frequency and intensity of 'extreme weather events', such as hurricanes, floods or droughts. As the problem of global warming is so directly linked to the production of energy and cannot be solved by simply installing such things as filters or catalytic converters, however, policy measures in the field encroach upon the very basis of production and consumption. This explains why so far only slow progress has been made in tackling the problem.

The EU's involvement in international climate policy
The EU's activities in relation to climate change take place largely within the context of the UNFCCC (see Chapter 3), concluded in 1992. In the context of a Protocol to the Convention signed in December 1997 in Kyoto, the EU committed itself to an overall reduction of the emission of greenhouse gases by 8 per cent in 2008–12, relative to 1990. The targets for the USA and Japan were 7 per cent and 6 per cent respectively. The Kyoto Protocol also specifies a number of instruments by which those reductions might be achieved, including (international) emissions trading.

From the beginning, the EU has attempted to take the lead in international climate policy. As Jachtenfuchs and Huber (1993) describe, the Commission was the main driving force behind these ambitions, which were motivated not only by environmental concerns, but also by a more general desire to strengthen the EU's role as a major player in world politics. These ambitions were largely shared by the member states. Thus, the EU set out for Kyoto with a proposal for no less than a 15 per cent reduction in 2008–12, provided that other industrialized countries would go for broadly equivalent targets. During the negotiations, however, considerable concessions had to be made, particularly to keep the USA on board. Nevertheless, the USA has refused to ratify the Protocol up to the time of writing and also other countries, such as Canada, Japan and Russia, showed serious hesitations. This constellation made it possible for the EU to keep up its reputation of 'climate leader', at least to the outside world (Woerdman 2004).

Notwithstanding these pronounced external ambitions, however, the EU's internal climate policy did not work out smoothly. In particular the establishment of a Europe-wide carbon tax, first discussed in the second half of the 1980s, turned into a nightmare. In this context, it should be remembered that fiscal measures required, and still require, unanimity in the Council. In other words: just one member state feeling unhappy with a given proposal has the power to block the decision. So far, continuous debates on the precise form and level of such a tax, massive protest from industry and fear for loss of competitiveness vis-à-vis countries without a carbon tax have prevented any agreement on the issue. In addition, there were concerns of a more constitutional kind about the tax possibly functioning as a precedent for a further expansion of the EU's fiscal competences. As a result, only a couple of (mainly northern) member states currently run different kinds of carbon taxes on a national basis (see further Skjaerseth 1994; Zito 1995; Grant et al. 2000; Klok 2002).

Another point of contention was the key according to which the EU-wide reduction target agreed in Kyoto, the so-called 'EU bubble', should be distributed over the individual member states. Difficult negotiations both before and after the Kyoto meeting led to the 'burden sharing agreement' of June 1998. Taking into account important differences between member states as regards the level of economic development, domestic energy structure, past reductions and so forth, national targets ranged from −28 per cent for Luxembourg and −21 per cent for Germany and Denmark, to +25 per cent for Greece and +27 per cent for Portugal. However, the 'burden sharing agreement' still did not provide for any specific measures to reduce greenhouse gas emissions within the EU.

Emissions trading entering the EU agenda

Emissions trading is a 'new' environmental policy instrument in that it makes use of the market mechanism to regulate environmental pollution. The basis of an emissions trading system is formed by a limited number of permits, initially allocated to polluters by the authorities. These permits being tradeable, polluters that emit below the quantity allocated to them may sell part of their allowance to other polluters who have more difficulties in reaching their permitted levels, or to newcomers in the market. These transactions do not affect the total emissions within the system. Newcomers will in fact increase the scarcity of permits and drive up their market price. This is in turn likely to stimulate the use of cleaner technologies.

Emissions trading had first – and quite successfully – been used in the USA in the 1980s in relation to sulphur dioxide. Not surprisingly, therefore, it was mainly the USA who promoted the inclusion of the instrument of emissions trading in the Kyoto Protocol. As Damro and Luaces Méndez (2003) point out, this reflected the USA preference for a 'free-market environmentalism'. The EU, in contrast, did not have any experience with emissions trading. Its introduction would therefore imply considerable adaptation costs. In addition, the EU doubted the fairness of a world-wide system of emissions trading, arguing that it might lead to a situation where rich, developed countries (read: the USA) simply buy large amounts of permits abroad without making any serious effort to reduce emissions themselves. On this basis, the EU defended an approach based upon quantified goals and coordinated standards, much more in line with its own established regulatory tradition (Damro and Luaces Méndez 2003).

A number of factors led the EU to giving up its resistance to emissions trading. The first reason was the strong pressure exercised by the USA during the Kyoto Conference. Without emissions trading there was a 'very real threat' of ending the meeting with no result at all (Damro and Luaces Méndez 2003, 85). The latter, of course, would have been a slap in the face for the EU, who still wanted to act as a policy leader in the field. In the light of this concession, it must be bitter for some EU negotiators that the USA has not even ratified the Protocol so far. But other authors stress that there were also European actors who had an interest in introducing the new instrument. Notably the

Commission's DG Environment increasingly perceived emissions trading as an opportunity to overcome the frustrating deadlock in establishing the carbon tax (Christiansen and Wettestad 2003, 6; Woerdman 2004). As we have seen before (Chapters 1 and 2), the supporters of emissions trading in Europe could point to a number of recent policy documents, such as the Fifth Environmental Action Programme of 1992, which stressed the need for adding 'new', more flexible, market-oriented instruments to the EU's environmental toolbox. A final important reason for the EU to take up the subject was the fact that Denmark and the UK had meanwhile started developing their own systems for emissions trading. Consequently, these two countries took the lead in developing a similar system at the EU level and it is on their efforts as 'constructive pushers' (Liefferink and Andersen 1998) that we will focus in the remainder of this section.

The policy-making phase: the UK and Denmark take the lead
Denmark was the first EU member state to establish emissions trading at the national level. Legislation was drafted in 1998 and passed Parliament in 1999. The system took effect in 2001. It was mandatory but applied to electricity generators and carbon dioxide only. Participants were companies, eight in total, not individual sites or plants. Initial permits were allocated on the basis of past emissions (so-called 'grandfathering') (Johnson and Heinen 2004).

The UK system was designed from 1999 in close collaboration with industry in the context of a newly established Emissions Trading Group. It started working in 2002. In contrast with the Danish system, the UK scheme was on a voluntary basis. Its scope was much wider, however, as some 6,000 energy-intensive companies from various industrial sectors were eligible for participation. Interestingly, and again in contrast with Denmark, about the only sector not included – at least not directly – was electricity generation. Instead, emissions associated with electricity generation were addressed via (industrial) electricity consumption (Oshitani 2005). In addition, the UK scheme covered not only carbon dioxide but also five other greenhouse gases. A final important difference with the Danish scheme entailed the initial distribution of allowances. In the UK, a 'subsidy auction' was held among thirty-eight large emitters, most prominently chemical companies, who could 'sell' plans to reduce emissions to the state. Further companies could join in at a later stage and thus obtain exemptions from the national carbon tax, introduced in 2001. The total financial incentives involved in setting off the emissions trading scheme amounted to 215 million pounds (see further Boemare, Quirion and Sorrell 2003; Johnson and Heinen 2004).

Parallel to Denmark and the UK, some other countries, including France, the Netherlands and Sweden, were moving in a similar direction (see Boemare, Quirion and Sorrell 2003; Christiansen and Wettestad 2003; Woerdman 2004). Although their plans and projections had not yet materialized by the end of the 1990s, the risk of an outburst of different national schemes, potentially distorting the conditions of competition within the Internal Market, was now becoming too big to be neglected. By the time the Commission started to seriously take up the issue, however, the UK and Denmark still had a clear 'first-mover' advantage vis-à-vis the other member states.

In the preparatory phase for the EU policy, the Commission actively sought the advice of the two forerunners. It did so both in expert meetings and in bilateral contacts. Denmark and the UK, in turn, were both basically in favour of EU-wide emissions trading, but at the same time attempted to 'upload' crucial elements of their national systems to the EU level in order to create room for maintaining as much as possible of those systems under the upcoming EU legislation (Veenman and Liefferink 2005).

In March 2000, a Green Paper was published by the Commission, outlining the main features of the EU system, followed by a draft directive in October 2001.[8] For a pilot period from 2005 to 2007, the Commission proposal entailed a mandatory scheme, focusing on carbon dioxide only and distributing initial permits by a system of 'grandfathering', the details of which had to be worked out by the member states. A limited number of industrial sectors were covered, including electricity generation and oil refinery, as well as the steel, cement, glass, and pulp and paper industries. Although some of these features may come to be revised for the next programme period (2008–12), the proposal reflected the Danish rather than the UK system. For one part, this can be explained by the Commission's obvious wish not to make the pilot phase overly complex. For another part, however, it was due to a successful Danish strategy convincing the Commission that the reduction of complexity should take this particular form. For this purpose, the Danes maintained a close relationship with the Commission throughout the process, based on a domestically well prepared and well coordinated input. Perhaps even more importantly, they worked from a keen understanding of the Commission's need to come to a draft acceptable to a large majority of the member states. All in all, the Danish approach on this issue may be characterized as 'constructive pushing' (Liefferink and Andersen 1998; Veenman and Liefferink 2005).

After the draft directive had been formally submitted by the Commission, negotiations moved on to the Council, where under the co-decision procedure only a qualified majority was required. During this phase, Denmark did not fundamentally change its constructive approach. In a sense, Denmark's hand was forced, as the country held the Council Presidency in the second half of 2002, i.e. exactly when the Council finished its first reading of the proposal. A member state holding the Presidency is supposed to help in facilitating the decision-making and, therefore, to avoid positions obstructing the process (Wurzel 1996). The UK was now in a more difficult position, as most of its preferences had not made it into the draft legislation. In the Council, the British initially took a fairly tough stance in a last attempt to save their domestic policy. They for instance pleaded once more for including all six major greenhouse gases, instead of just carbon dioxide. However, as it appeared that support from the other member states was limited, the UK turned to a more pragmatic negotiation style. In fact the only alternative left to the British would have been to try to forge a qualified minority blocking the entire proposal. But in the end having an EU-wide scheme was considered more important than preserving the national system at any price (Veenman and Liefferink 2005).

After the Council's first reading, the proposal continued its way through the co-decision procedure quite smoothly. In a form essentially similar to what had been originally proposed by the Commission, the final text was adopted in July 2003.[9]

Conclusions: environmental policy-making in the European multi-level system

This final section will briefly compare the three cases discussed in this chapter. It will do so, first, by pointing out a number of differences and similarities between them. Second, and on the basis of that, some more general analytical observations will be made.

What all measures have in common is their far-reaching consequences at the level of the member states, either in terms of the strictness of standards or in terms of adaptations to existing regulatory practice. In all three cases, therefore, the initial positions of the member states did not appear particularly favourable for an agreement at the European level. Nevertheless, the programmes eventually agreed on went far beyond the level of regulation that one would expect in view of this.

With respect to a number of other important factors, however, the selected cases clearly differ. Firstly, this is evident when we take the type of policy – or more precisely: the type of policy instrument – into account. While the introduction of the catalytic converter was basically a matter of defining product standards, i.e. a 'classical' substantial instrument, the two other cases were examples of the 'new', more procedural approach in EU environmental policy. Within the latter category, the Information Directive focused on improving the conditions for participation of the general public, while emissions trading amounted to the regulation of incentive structures for companies (see Chapter 2).

A second difference concerns the origin of the measures. Formally, as we have seen, the Commission has the exclusive right of initiative for European policies (see Chapter 3). In practice, however, the Commission's proposals may be inspired in various ways. Thus, the catalytic converter was put on the EU agenda by the initiative of one single member state, i.e. Germany, which – not least by its threat of unilateral action – strongly pressed the Commission to come up with a draft directive. The Emissions Trading Directive, in contrast, was essentially motivated by international commitments in the framework of the Kyoto Protocol and only later endorsed by an increasing number of member states. Among our cases, the only policy primarily originating from the EU institutions themselves was the Information Directive. It may be seen as the combined fruit of the Commission's philosophy set out in the Fourth Environmental Action Programme and additional pressure from the EP, although strongly supported later on by the UK.

Thirdly, the respective measures were passed on the basis of different procedural rules. The decision on the introduction of cars with catalytic converters is particularly interesting in this context. Here the procedural rule changed during the decision-making process from consultation (requiring unanimity in the Council) to cooperation (requiring qualified majority in the Council). This shift, as we have seen, had a direct effect on the level of regulation. The EP in particular used its new powers stemming from the cooperation procedure to push through standards that were more stringent than those initially envisioned by the Council of Ministers. The Information Directive was also passed on the basis of the cooperation procedure. The Directive on Emissions Trading, finally, was adopted by co-decision (see Chapter 4).

A fourth difference between the examined cases pertains to the interest constellations and the negotiation strategies of the member states. Most notably, we could observe a clear shift of 'forerunner' and 'laggard' roles. While the regulation of catalytic converters, taking place in the 1980s, was characterized by a very active role of the Germans and a highly reluctant one of the British, we found the exact opposite allocation of roles in the more recent cases of free access to information and emissions trading. In addition to that, different strategies by the 'forerunners' and 'laggards' could be observed. For example in the case of the catalytic converter, the threat by the 'green' member states to 'go it alone' and to introduce stricter emission limits on their own, if necessary, played a crucial role in the decision-making process. In the other two cases, national policies preceding EU negotiations made it possible for the UK (in the case of emissions trading joined by Denmark) to successfully act as a 'pacemaker' at the European level (see Chapter 5).

A final aspect involves the mechanisms of reaching final agreement. In the case of the catalytic converter, a package deal was drawn up involving also the Directive on Large Combustion Plants, which happened to be negotiated simultaneously in the Council of Ministers. In the case of free access to information, the consensus was based to an important extent on the relative vagueness of the wording of the directive. For emissions trading, successful 'constructive pushing' by the UK and Denmark, in particular, turned out to be crucial.

In a more general sense, the case studies make clear that the design of European environmental policies is greatly dependent on the interplay between national, European and international developments. In order to understand the substance and outcomes of the decision-making process, it does not suffice to concentrate only on the institutions and patterns of interaction in Brussels. Instead, the strategies and interests of the member states can only be adequately understood when the economic, social, political and institutional background conditions at the national level are equally incorporated into the analysis. For example, whether a member state emerges as a 'forerunner' or 'laggard' with respect to a given initiative is highly contingent on these national circumstances and the way they develop over time. In an increasing number of issues, moreover, including climate change but also for instance biodiversity or marine pollution, the broader international context is crucial for understanding the steps taken by the EU.

However, the relevance of national developments for EU policy-making is only one side of the close interrelationship between the national and the European level. EU policy-making is not only influenced by national developments and interests, but in turn has ramifications for the national level. After all, it is the exception rather than the rule that European measures are fully compatible with pre-existing regulations at the national level.

On the one hand, this can be traced back to the fact that the roles of 'forerunners' and 'laggards' in EU environmental policy frequently change among the member states. It is not always the same states that succeed in gaining the support of the Commission for a certain initiative. Thus, all member states run the risk of being confronted with European measures that run counter to national regulatory patterns and require considerable institutional adaptation 'at home'.

On the other hand, the dynamics of the negotiations at the European level imply that the 'laggards' do not always succeed in reducing the demands for adaptation during the negotiations in the Council of Ministers. This has to do for instance with the influence of the EP in combination with majority voting in the Council, which can have the effect that some member states are actually forced to accept measures that they initially did not want. This is what happened in the case of the catalytic converter. Apart from that, it must be noted that there are often few chances of completely revising the general regulatory approach and direction of a Commission proposal, that is, as long as the Council of Ministers does not want to take the risk that the Commission withdraws its proposal altogether. Finally one should not under-estimate that majority conditions and negotiation strategies in the Council of Ministers (isolation of individual countries, package deals, etc.) in practice often force states to choose 'the lesser of two evils' and thus accept concessions that stand at least partly in contrast with national interests.

As a result, and even though finding a consensus in the Council of Ministers often leads to a watering down and weakening of the original objectives of a particular measure, member states are frequently confronted with significant costs of institutional adap-tation when implementing EU regulations. From this point of view, it should not come as a surprise that full and successful implementation can by no means be taken for granted. The member states generally seek to implement European measures in such ways that their economic and institutional impact is mini-mized. In fact, one may sometimes be left with the impression that they try to compensate for the concessions that were 'wrested' from them by subsequently implementing the measure more laxly. As we will discuss in detail in the following chapters, this strategy is not seldom at the expense of the effectiveness of EU environ-mental policy.

Notes

1 The description of the case study is essentially based on Holzinger (1994) and Liefferink (1996).
2 Greece, having no domestic car industry, hoped to alleviate the smog problems in Athens by means of stricter emissions regulations.
3 Further steps towards tightening car emission limits were taken after 1991, to be sure, but these are not part of the present case study (see for instance Wurzel 2002).
4 The following description falls back on the studies by Héritier, Knill and Mingers (1996) and Knill (1995), in particular.

5 Official Journal L 158, 23 June 1990, pp. 56–8.
6 According to the 1911 Official Secrets Act, the British public administration was even prohibited from passing on authorization-relevant data to the public or other agencies without the permission of the industrial firm concerned (Knill 1995, 228).
7 On the implementation of the Information Directive, see Chapter 9. As will be seen there, however, the room to manoeuvre at least on some aspects of the directive was much narrower than the member states initially assumed.
8 See documents COM(2000)87 and COM(2001)581, respectively.
9 Directive 2003/87/EC, Official Journal L275, 25 October 2003, pp. 32–46.

7

Implementation effectiveness of EU environmental policy

What happens to an environmental law or programme after its official passing by the EU? How do the formal transposition and the practical application of legal acts take shape at the national level? Which problems and deviations from the European objectives can be observed? At first glance, it could be assumed that questions like these are relatively trivial. Why should there subsequently emerge problems in the execution of an apparently well-devised measure that was accepted by the Council of Ministers? The fact that political reality presents itself more complex, not exclusively becomes apparent in the far-reaching implementation deficits that are generally observed for European policies. Implementation research also demonstrated in the 1970s and 1980s that even with national programmes, great deviations and shifts in objectives can occur during the execution phase.

In their classical study on policy implementation, Pressman and Wildavsky (1973), for instance, analysed why a labour-market programme of the American federal government, which received broad political support, was not duly implemented at the level of the constituent states. The subtitle of their book concisely summarizes the central message of the analysis: 'How great expectations in Washington are dashed in Oakland; or, why it's amazing that federal programs work at all'. Pressman and Wildavsky argued that the effective implementation of political programmes is rather an exception than the rule because the cooperation of a vast number of actors involved inside the implementation chain is necessary (including political decision-makers, responsible administrative agencies at different institutional levels and various societal interest groups and policy addressees), all trying to influence the execution according to their interests.

The general finding that shifts in policy objectives and deviations from the original political intentions are frequently observed during the implementation stage can be expected to be of particular relevance when it comes to the implementation of EU policies. This arises primarily from the fact that in executing EU measures a vast number of actors at different institutional levels are involved. Additionally, the Commission monitors the transposition of the Community law in the member states, but possesses comparatively few resources to hierarchically ensure the cooperation of the public and private actors participating in the implementation process. Therefore, a systematic implementation problem is multiply imputed on the EU (Krislov, Ehlermann and Weiler 1986; Weiler 1988; Snyder 1993; Mendrinou 1996; Tallberg 1999).

In recent years, there has been an increased scholarly interest in the study of implementation and compliance with EU law (see Mbaye 2001; Tallberg 2002; Börzel and Risse 2003; Mastenbroek 2003, 2005; Knill and Lenschow 2004; Sverdrup 2004; Haverland 2005; Steunenberg 2005). Notwithstanding the growing number of studies, our understanding of the size of the actual implementation deficit as well as the central factors affecting implementation effectiveness is still rather limited.

How do problems of implementation work out in the environmental field? To what extent are environmental measures of the EU actually implemented effectively at the domestic level? If we have a closer look at the current political and scientific discussion on these questions, there emerge especially two aspects which will be addressed in closer detail in the following sections. First, we have to account for the fact that the perception of problems of ineffective implementation of EU environmental policy markedly increased from the early 1990s onwards. Does this imply that implementation effectiveness was actually much better during earlier periods or are stronger concerns with implementation failures triggered by other factors? In a second step, we will investigate more closely the problems of measuring implementation effectiveness. As we will see, our evaluations in that respect are not only dependent on the underlying definition of effective implementation, but also on the concrete data and information on which we make our judgements. Before dealing with these questions, however, we briefly present the institutional framework in which the implementation of European policies takes place.

Institutional framework

In the EU, there is a clear-cut distribution of competence concerning the implementation of common policies in the member states. Responsibility for the execution of Community law generally lies with the member states (Article 10 [ex-Article 5] TEC):

> Member states shall take all appropriate measures, whether general or particular, to ensure fulfilment of the obligations arising out of this Treaty or resulting from action taken by the institutions of the Community. They shall facilitate the achievement of the Community's tasks.

The Commission as the 'guardian of the treaties' is responsible for controlling the transposition and application of Community law in the member states. For ensuring the correct implementation of European measures, the Commission, in accordance with Article 226 (ex-Article 169) TEC, can instruct an infringement procedure against member states that did not fulfil the commitments resulting from Community law. But before such a procedure is instructed, the Commission takes various informal and formal steps to warrant proper transposition. In this respect, the following steps can be distinguished.

If the Commission believes that there is an infringement against Community law in a member state, it first takes up informal contacts with the competent national authorities in order to discuss the details and possible problems at stake (Collins and Earnshaw 1992; Krämer 1996). Depending on the results of these informal discussions, the Commission can instruct the second step of the procedure, which consists of a formal reminder letter from the Commission to the member state (Holzinger 1994, 102; Jordan 1999, 74). In this way, the member state shall be given the opportunity to clarify potential obscurities and problems within the implementation process and eliminate them if necessary. If a consensual solution is not found even at this level, in a third step, the Commission gives a so-called 'reasoned opinion' explaining to what extent the affected member state has infringed the Community law. Beyond that, the state will be given a time limit within which the detected implementation deficits have to be redressed.

If the member state does not comply with the obligations resulting from the reasoned opinion within the given time limit, the Commission can appeal to the ECJ. The Court finally decides whether a member state has infringed an obligation of the Treaty. The member state is then obliged to take the requisite steps resulting from the sentence of the ECJ. But the EU only has humble sanctioning measures at its disposal for pushing through such obligations.

> Although the European Court of Justice can rule that member states are in breach of EU environmental law it has virtually no power to enforce its decisions, being, for instance, unable to send erring ministers to prison. There are member states who still have not complied with environmental rulings issued by the Court in the early 1990s. (Jordan 1999, 78)

The sanctioning potential has been somewhat widened with the Maastricht Treaty which allows for the imposition of a fine on member states not fulfilling their obligations emerging from European law. In practice, however, this option is used only reluctantly.

Before appealing to the ECJ, moreover, in many instances bilateral negotiations between the Commission and the member state in question take place with the objective of finding a consensual solution 'at the last minute'. Consequently, the number of commencements of proceedings before the ECJ is very low in relation to reminder letters and reasoned opinions:

> Even when formal proceedings are initiated, something like 80 per cent are settled before they go to court [...] Court cases tend to be long-winded, extremely complicated, stretch the Commission's meagre resources and endanger the goodwill of states. Decisions to take cases to the Court are not taken lightly; they must be sanctioned by the Commission's Legal Services and receive the support of the College of Commissioners. Being so political, recourse to court proceedings is therefore considered as a very last resort. (Jordan 1999, 81)

For instructing infringement proceedings, three constituent facts are to be distinguished: (1) the non-communication of transposition measures in the member states; (2) the incorrect or incomplete transposition; and (3) the incorrect application of Community law. While the first two aspects refer to the formal transposition, the third factor relates to the practical application of Community law.

Table 7.1 *Investigative criteria for the introduction of infringement proceedings*

	Focus	Criteria
Formal Transposition	• Legal and administrative provisions for the transposition of European law into the national legal and administrative system	• Time frame (Commission notification) • Completeness • Correct integration into the regulative context
Practical Transposition	• National regulation practice (regulatory style, organisational and administrative structures)	• Correct application and adherence to legal requirements

With regard to the formal transposition, the focus is on the respective legal and administrative provisions aimed at incorporating the legal and institutional requirements resulting from European policies into the national legal order. In this context, effective implementation not only implies the timely and complete adaptation to European requirements, but also requires the integration of these rules into the existing regulatory context. When it comes to the practical transposition of European policies, the activities of implementers and policy addressees are at the centre of attention. To what extent did the legal modifications indeed result in corresponding adjustments in national regulation practice? Are the European requirements (e.g. threshold values, the foundation of new administrative agencies or the modification of existing administrative procedures) actually complied with (Table 7.1; cf. Knill and Lenschow 2000a, 9–14; Weale et al. 2000, 297)?

Politicization of implementation problems

Until the mid-1980s, problems of implementation of Community law played a minor role on the political agenda. The rather late politicization of implementation deficits does not mean, however, that such deficits have been absent in the previous decades (Jordan 1999, 73). It has rather been in the interest of the Commission and the member states to neglect implementation problems with regard to Community law.

The Commission as well as the member states for a long time primarily concentrated their activities on policy-making. The focal point of European integration was rather on the formulation of common policies and less on their implementation. On the side of the Commission, this orientation was favoured by its own institutional interests in expanding its political authority. Enhanced interventions by the Commission in order to control and monitor the implementation effectiveness of EU policies would have endangered the political support of the member states for the expansion of political competence at the European level (Jordan 1999, 74). The Commission's position was broadly congruent with the objectives of the member states that were, for obvious reasons, hardly interested in exposing their respective problems and failures in the transposition of European policies.

This initial constellation of interests, which favoured the depoliticization of implementation problems, changed from the mid-1980s onwards. The implementation effectiveness of European policies increasingly moved to the centre of political and scientific attention. First, the objective of completing the Common Market until 1992, as defined by the SEA, implied that questions about the effective transposition of Community law gained political significance (Weiler 1988). Beyond this, the increasing politicization of implementation problems was facilitated by various judgements of the ECJ. In this context, the principles of supremacy and direct effect of Community law have to be stressed in particular. These principles were not mentioned in the original Treaties, but developed in the ECJ's case law. The ECJ not only clarified that Community law is to be regarded as superior in case of a collision between European and national rules. It also stated that European legal acts – independent of their national implementation – are directly effective at the national level (Alter and Meunier-Aitsahalia 1994).

As a result of these developments, the implementation effectiveness of European policies became a central issue on the political agenda during the 1990s. However, the mere observation that the implementation of EU policies became an increasingly politicized issue does not allow us to draw conclusions on the actual size of the European implementation deficit. This question as well as the related problems in measuring and judging will be analysed in the following section.

How big is the implementation deficit? Problems of measurement and data

If we want to judge the effectiveness of EU environmental policy, we first have to clarify the criteria on which our assessment is based. When can we judge implementation as effective or ineffective? In the literature, there is no consensus on these questions. Rather we can identify different approaches which imply different evaluations of implementation effectiveness. To be sure, these problems of interpretation could be avoided by simply relying on the statistics compiled by the EU Commission. These data indeed reveal far-reaching implementation problems in the environmental field which have substantially increased over time. However, the reliability of these data is restricted by several factors, implying that clear statements on the actual implementation deficit in EU environmental policy are rather difficult to make.

Different concepts of effective implementation
To answer the question whether a measure was implemented successfully or not, it is of crucial importance how effective implementation is operationalized (Hill 1997). Generally, the concepts that are conceivable in this context can be divided along two dimensions that refer to the analytical focus and the underlying perspective of research (Weale 1992, 45ff.).

The first dimension refers to the distinction between policy output and policy outcome. With a focus on policy output, effective implementation is already assumed if the legal transposition and the practical application correspond to the objectives defined by the policy under investigation. Yet it remains excluded, if, and to what extent, the objectives of a policy are actually achieved.

		Analytical Focus	
		Output	Outcome
Research Perspective	Target-oriented	1	2
	Process-oriented	3	4

Figure 7.1   *Different concepts of effective implementation*

Source: adapted from Weale 1992, 45.

Did the introduction of limits for automobile emissions, for instance, indeed lead to the intended improvement of the air quality? Hence, the orientation on concrete outcome implies a substantially more ambitious definition of effective implementation.

In addition to the distinction between output and outcome, a second dimension relates to different research perspectives on the implementation process (Peters 1993). These perspectives are often referred to as 'top-down' and 'bottom-up' views on the implementation process. Analysing the implementation of political programmes in a 'top-down' manner, implementation success is judged on the basis of a comparison between the intended and actually achieved outcome. The degree of goal attainment serves as an indicator for the implementation success. Effective implementation implies a match between objectives and output or outcome. If the objective of European legislation is, for instance, to set a certain standard for industrial emissions into the air, effective implementation is achieved as soon as the prescribed level is complied with throughout the Community.

This perspective is however grounded on a simplified model of political steering. Governments and legislators are assumed to have homogeneous preferences, implying clear and unambiguous standards and guidelines for administrative authorities responsible for implementation and enforcement. From analysing implementation deficits, conclusions on an improved design of future policies shall be drawn (concerning, for instance, policy objectives, the allocation of resources or the structures of the coordination and control of subordinate administrative agencies).

By contrast, the 'bottom-up' conception of effective implementation is primarily process-oriented. Policy objectives and instruments are no longer defined as benchmarks to be reached. Instead it is expected that they may undergo modifications during the process of policy implementation. Implementers should have flexibility and autonomy to adjust the policy in the light of particular local requirements, changes in the perception or constellation of policy problems, or new scientific evidence on causal relationships between means and ends. Hence, effective implementation is not measured by the attainment of certain centrally-defined objectives, but judged by the extent to which the perceived outcomes correspond with the preferences of the actors involved in the implementation process. The crucial question for evaluating implementation success is to what extent a certain policy did allow for processes of learning, capacity-building and support-building in order to address policy problems in a decentralized way consistent with the interests of the actors involved (Ingram and Schneider 1990).

This conception challenges the simplifying assumptions of the 'top-down' perspective and tries to take into account the complexity of implementation processes. Thus, it is emphasized that the formulation of clear-cut objectives often contrasts with the interests of politicians who have a preference for vague and ambiguous rather than clear-cut objectives in order to make detection and evaluation of potential failures more difficult. In addition, the 'bottom-up' perspective takes account of the fact that implementation processes are hardly characterized by a clear delineation of competencies between the involved political and administrative actors at different institutional levels. Implementation rather often implies complex interactions between public and private actors and organizations at the national, regional and local level with potentially diverging interests, beliefs and perceptions with regard to the underlying policy problem. From this perspective, implementation is to a lesser extent based on hierarchically defined and controlled requirements, but understood as a bargaining process between a great number of organizations and administrative agencies. Bargaining at the same time implies that during the implementation phase, initial policy objectives might undergo significant modifications.

The analysis of the implementation of European policies

mostly employs a target-oriented perspective, evaluating implementation performance by comparing policy objectives and policy output (box 1 in Figure 7.1). It is asked to what extent the necessary legal and administrative conditions were created in order to meet the objectives of European measures. Thus, the manner of the legal and practical implementation of European policies rather than the evaluation of policy impacts serves as an indicator for assessing implementation effectiveness (Collins and Earnshaw 1992; Jordan 1999; Knill and Lenschow 2000a; Weale et al. 2000). Although this perspective implies a somewhat restricted focus, as explained, it bears several analytical advantages.

First, in this way, a number of conceptual problems associated with alternative definitions are avoided. A focus on policy outcome (boxes 2 and 4) is analytically problematic as the actual link between policy instruments and their effects is often obscure. Whether policy objectives are achieved or not depends on contingencies of the political, economic, and social policy context beside the deliberate choice of policy instruments. Hence, this perspective is confronted with important questions such as: 'How do we know whether air or water quality has improved as a result of European legislation rather than as the consequence of other factors completely independent from European developments, such as modified weather conditions, privatisation, or economic decline?' In other words, the success of policy implementation in terms of policy outcomes is difficult to predict given the scientific uncertainties and socio-economic complexities underlying a given problem constellation (Baier, March and Sætren 1990). The application of a process-oriented 'bottom-up' perspective (boxes 3 and 4), by contrast, is characterized by the absence of a baseline for evaluating implementation results. It fails to offer a measuring rod for learning, capacity or support. When do these processes actually occur and work successfully? Moreover, and maybe even more significantly from the perspective of evaluating the impact of different policy instruments, this approach is faced with the serious difficulty of establishing a causal link between the original (EU) policy and local process of learning and problem-solving. After all, local processes could have entirely different origins. In order to assess whether the EU policy has had any impact on these local processes, in sum, we need to observe whether its 'instructions' – however open they might be – have been complied with (Knill and Lenschow 2000a, 9–14).

Second, a focus on policy output, the formal and practical implementation of EU policies, provides the opportunity to compare implementation results even of widely different measures. By contrast, it would be problematic to measure and hence compare the contributions of different policies (e.g. the Directive for Free Access to Environmental Information and the Large Combustion Plant Directive) with respect to their achievement in terms of policy outcome (such as the number of successful requests for information and air quality) (Knill and Lenschow 2000a, 13). Against this background, a focus on the legal and administrative output of EU policies in the member states generally appears to be an appropriate measuring rod for judging their implementation effectiveness.

Empirical findings
Although there is no solid data basis yet that allows for a comprehensive assessment of the implementation effectiveness of EU policies on the basis of the target- and output-oriented perspective as outlined above, it is nevertheless possible to identify certain general patterns. They can be derived not only from a careful interpretation of the Commission's data, but also from the results of various research projects on the implementation of EU policies in different policy fields (Siedentopf and Ziller 1988; Collins and Earnshaw 1992; Macrory 1992; Krämer 1996; Lübbe-Wolff 1996; Jordan 1999; Börzel 2000; Knill and Lenschow 2000; Mastenbroek 2003).

A first striking observation is that the implementation effectiveness of EU policies strongly varies across policy sectors. Comparative data reveal that implementation problems are much more pronounced for policies directed at environmental protection, the integration of the Common Market, consumer protection and social policy than for other policy fields of the Community (cf. Mastenbroek 2005). At the top of the 'list of sins' is, as Figure 7.2 shows, the environment.

Secondly, and in contrast with the pattern observed across policy areas, differences in the implementation performance of the member states are by far less pronounced than one might have expected. In particular, the often stated hypothesis of the so-

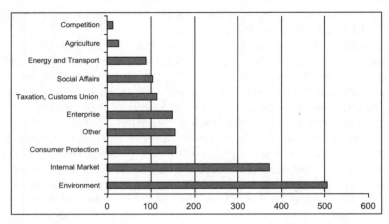

Figure 7.2 *Complaints under investigation (end of 2002, by sector)*

Source: adapted from European Commission 2004.

called 'Mediterranean syndrome' (La Spina and Sciortino 1993), which expects that Southern member states implement EU policies less effectively as a result of lacking administrative resources, is not confirmed (Börzel 2000). Implementation deficits rather vary among countries regardless of their geographic location (Knill and Lenschow 2000a). This holds true, in particular, if implementation effectiveness is not only measured by focusing on the formal transposition of EU policies, but also by considering the dimension of practical application.

Third, different studies indicate that there is not necessarily a causal linkage between the implementation performance and the choice of policy instruments at the European level. This aspect has been identified especially in the field of environmental policy. As set out in Chapter 2, in particular, EU environmental policy traditionally relied on instruments associated with hierarchical intervention and command-and-control regulation. Typical for this approach were highly detailed legal rules and standards. These had to be complied with by the member states, regardless of potentially differing environmental conditions and problems at the domestic level. The lack of room for national and local discretion was held at least partly accountable for the implementation deficit in the environmental field. In response to these problems, the Commission strongly promoted the development of so-called 'new' instruments from the early 1990s onwards. New instruments were expected to improve the implementation effectiveness of environmental policy in basically two ways. First, they purportedly left member states more leeway to comply with EU requirements by taking account of domestic context conditions. They did so by focusing on basic procedures for improving environmental awareness and behaviour rather than on concrete environmental targets. Secondly, new instruments also target the policy context directly and aim to change context factors in order to facilitate the formal and practical implementation of environmental policy in general. Here we can distinguish two strategies: the mobilization of society through more transparent processes and participatory opportunities as well as the provision of incentives for industrial self-regulation (Lenschow 1999; Mol, Lauber and Liefferink 2000; Knill and Lenschow 2000a, 4). Comparative research, however, shows that successes and failures vary across policies and countries without indicating a direct causal linkage between instrument type and implementation performance. The formal and practical transposition of new instruments poses by no means fewer problems than is the case for 'old' instruments (Knill 1998; Knill and Lenschow 1998, 2000a; Börzel 2000). Chapter 8 will go into this matter in more detail.

Problems in data and methodology

Although it is possible to identify broad tendencies with respect to the implementation effectiveness of EU environmental policy, existing empirical data hardly allow for a comprehensive assessment. This holds true not only for the environmental field, but for EU policies in general. Two sets of reasons are relevant in this respect.

First, although the data compiled by the Commission are currently the only comprehensive source for judging the implementation effectiveness of European policies, they allow only to a very limited extent for reliable statements about general tendencies (Macrory and Purdy 1997, 39). This can be traced to several problems that result from the interpretation of the data.

- It is asserted that from the observed increase in the number of introduced infringement proceedings, reasoned opinions and reminder letters, a rise in implementation deficits cannot be concluded. Hence, Jordan (1999, 81), for instance, stresses that 'the recent rise in complaints and infringement proceedings may simply reflect the Commission's determination to tighten up on enforcement rather than increasing lawlessness among member states'. From this perspective, the augmenting implementation deficits rather reflect modified political priorities of the Commission than an aggravation of actual implementation problems.

- The data published by the Commission is partially inconsistent. For example, over the years the Commission has changed the basis for the collection and assignment of implementation failures (such as the amount of infringement proceedings). The frequent modifications of the basis for the data collection severely restrict the opportunities to make valid statements with regard to the development of the European implementation deficit over time and across countries and policies (Börzel 2001, 810–11).

- The data from the Commission is incomplete in various regards. On the one hand, it only includes those violations against Community law which the Commission has either discovered itself or to which it turned its attention after complaints by domestic interest groups or citizens. On the other hand, the 'discovery rate' of the Commission concerning problems in formal versus practical implementation is unevenly distributed. Deficits in the formal transposition of European requirements into national law can still be ascertained quite easily. The detection of implementation deficits is much more difficult, however, when it comes to the practical application of the Community law. In view of its limited financial and personal resources the Commission is hardly able to monitor and control the implementation of EU policies in day-to-day practice in the member states. Instead, it has to rely on the information provided by national authorities or complaints. As a result, the number of infringement proceedings originating from complaints is much higher than the cases detected by the Commission. The implementation statistics of the Commission therefore primarily refer to problems of formal transposition; the probably more severe problems of practical application are not sufficiently captured (Jordan

1999; Weale et al. 2000, 299).

- The comparative interpretation of the Commission data is difficult. These data often tell more about the political and administrative differences between the member states than about possible domestic differences in the quality of the implementation of Community law (Jordan 1999, 82; Krämer 2000, 143). Member states with a federal structure, for instance, typically have greater problems with the formal implementation than unitary states. This results from the fact that legal transposition generally entails comprehensive coordination with individual states or regions that are responsible for the practical implementation (Toonen 1992).
- The amount of implementation failures per member state can be strongly affected by existing administrative capacities for controlling and monitoring the enforcement of EU policies. Problems of practical implementation in particular can be identified only if domestic administrations have sufficient resources to measure and control the compliance with European requirements. As a consequence, the implementation performance of member states with a low administrative capacity might be less successful than suggested by the Commission data. So, the implementation of the 1980 Drinking Water Directive at first glance seemed to be very successful in Spain, simply because of the fact that the national water authorities did not possess the technical equipment necessary to detect the strict limit values for nitrates and pesticides as defined by the directive. In Germany, by contrast, where the necessary measurement technology was available, non-compliance with the strict European standards resulted in infringement proceedings initiated by the Commission (Knill 2001, 153–4).

Second, existing studies on the implementation of EU policies suffer from certain methodological weaknesses which make general statements about factors affecting the implementation effectiveness of EU policies rather difficult. On the one hand, such studies tend to be based on the analysis of few countries and policies. The findings from these studies provide important insights, but provide no basis for the development of general statements. Moreover, there is a disproportionate attention towards certain

policy sectors (environmental policy and social policy) and countries (the UK and Germany). On the other hand, quantitative
studies that allow for more general statements typically suffer
from the problem that they rely on variables that are easy to
measure, but are maybe not the theoretically most interesting
ones (Mastenbroek 2005, 1113). These variables include, for
instance, failures of notification or formal transposition or the
initiation of infringement proceedings. This way, the question of
practical application and potential problems emerging during this
stage are systematically excluded.

Implementation as empirical and political problem

How can we assess the implementation effectiveness of EU environmental policy in light of the above considerations? To answer
this question, it is important to differentiate between two dimensions: the actual degree of implementation problems and the
extent to which these problems are actually politicized.

With regard to the first dimension, we have seen that the existing empirical data and findings allow for a comprehensive and
general assessment only to a certain extent. Nevertheless, we are
able to identify some broad trends over time (Macrory 1992).
First, there is evidence that implementation deficits in the environmental field are more pronounced than in other policy fields
of the EU. Second, the large problems in terms of formal transposition suggest that also the practical application of EU
environmental policy suffers from severe deficits. Third, empirical
findings indicate big differences with respect to the implementation effectiveness across member states which does not fully
correspond with the observed patterns of 'leaders' and 'laggards'
during the stage of policy formulation.

Apart from the actual scope of the implementation deficit,
however, the extent to which these deficits actually have a high
priority on the political agenda is important. As we have seen,
the actual existence of implementation deficits need not automatically imply their perception as fundamental political
problem. Hence, in order to analyse different concepts that have
been proposed to address implementation problems in EU environmental policy – as we will do in the following chapter – it is
not essential to know the level of existing implementation

deficits. Rather, it is sufficient to know that these deficits obviously have been perceived as sufficiently severe to trigger political responses.

8

Strategies to improve implementation effectiveness: 'new' environmental policy instruments as a panacea?

The increased politicization of implementation problems in EU environmental policy was not without practical consequences. From the early 1990s, we can observe a certain reorientation in dominant governance patterns. With a shift from interventionist instruments to so-called 'new' instruments emphasizing public participation, transparency, economic incentives and self-regulation, the EU Commission especially hoped to improve domestic compliance with EU environmental policies.

However, a closer look at the effects of these changes reveals that the expectations of the Commission were not fulfilled. Several studies indicate that there is not necessarily a causal linkage between the implementation performance and the choice of policy instruments at the European level. Instead, successes and failures vary across policies and countries. The formal and practical transposition of 'new' instruments is not on average better than that of 'old' instruments. These results are reported in comparative studies (Knill 1998; Knill and Lenschow 1998, 2000; Börzel 2000) as well as in different investigations that are restricted to individual policies or individual member states (Bouma 2000; Kimber 2000; Wright 2000; Mastenbroek 2003).

Against the backdrop of these rather surprising findings at first glance, two central questions arise that will be addressed in the following section. First, we will have a closer look at the factors that can account for the fact that neither the type of countries nor the type of policy instruments seems to have a clear impact on the implementation effectiveness of EU policies. Second and closely related to the first aspect, alternative concepts to improve the implementation performance of EU policies will be discussed. Before addressing these two questions, we will first have a short look at the characteristics and effects of the 'new' environmental policy instruments.

The limited implementation success of 'new' environmental policy instruments

The above-mentioned shift in governance patterns underlying EU environmental policy became apparent in particular with the Fifth Environmental Action Programme. The ideas developed in this programme reflect a major departure from approaches propagated in earlier programmes. Previously dominant concepts, which essentially were based on forms of hierarchical intervention, were to be replaced or complemented with 'new' forms of context-oriented governance (Knill and Lenschow 2000; Holzinger, Knill and Schäfer 2006). This comprehensive change in the dominant governance ideas is characterized by various components.

First, effective governance is to be guaranteed by the comprehensive collaboration between public and private actors at the various institutional levels during policy formulation and implementation. The focus is not so much on developing regulative measures as on integrating and consulting with the actors concerned. The 'shared responsibility' of all actors is in the foreground; this ought to be achieved by intensive dialogue with the addressees and the responsible authorities.

Second, achieving this requires that the involved actors have enough discretion to optimally align their activities with the specific political, social and economic contexts existing at the national, regional or local levels. Thereby, the Fifth Action Programme stands in contrast to the orientation emphasized in the Third Action Programme, in accord with which environmental policy problems were to be primarily surmounted with uniform measures leaving little room for the accommodation of nationally varying conditions (Johnson and Corcelle 1989, 17; Knill and Lenschow 2000b, 4).

A third characteristic of the governance change implied by the

Fifth Action Programme is the development of 'new' instruments to achieve the above-mentioned goals. The instruments proposed in this context all aim to leave responsible authorities and addressees broad discretion for practical implementation. This ought to be reached by forgoing detailed requirements, such as emission standards. Instead, the emphasis is on defining broad objectives, e.g. environmental quality objectives, in order to grant the member states greater scope of action in choosing the means to reach these objectives. Beyond this, environmental instruments shall be largely limited to procedural guidelines, without providing substantial objectives regarding the results of these procedures (Héritier, Knill and Mingers 1996, 293ff.).

Apart from this, the objective of the 'new' instruments is to directly change the national contextual conditions so as to achieve a more effective implementation of regulatory goals. The instruments are supposed to create positive incentives for societal actors to voluntarily cooperate and participate in formulating and implementing European environmental policy. In this context, two lines of argument can be distinguished. For one, the Commission emphasizes the development of instruments to improve rights to information and participation of a large group of different public and private actors. Through wide-reaching information and the use of publicity, moreover, the general environmental consciousness and the acceptance of the required environmental measures could be rigorously supported.[1] On the other hand, traditional forms of hierarchical intervention ought to be increasingly complemented with cooperative arrangements and legally non-binding agreements between public and private actors. This applies especially to the reduction of industrially caused pollution, where voluntary agreements with industry and forms of private self-regulation should play a major role (Mol, Lauber and Liefferink 2000).

The endeavour of the EU Commission to provide for more transparency as well as greater involvement of the public is visible in the Directive on the Free Access to Environmental Information. As discussed in Chapter 6, this directive establishes a passive right to information: any person may request access to most environmental information that is collected by public authorities. Similarly, the Directive on EIA makes procedures for public involvement in project authorizations with potential environmental impacts obligatory. In addition, the EIA Directive aims at an integrated approach capable of accounting for cross-media environmental effects. The provision of incentives for self-regulation on the part of industry is implicit in the EU Regulations on the EMAS and on the eco-label scheme. The EMAS-Regulation provides a framework for industry to establish on a voluntary basis an environmental management system to be accredited by external verifiers. The eco-label scheme, in turn, ties the incentive structure to product standards: the label signals to the potential consumers the environment-friendly production method and quality of the product.

What is the impact of these innovations in EU environmental governance on implementation effectiveness? Although this question is difficult to answer in view of the rather limited number of 'new' instruments adopted so far (Héritier 2002; Holzinger, Knill and Schäfer 2006), empirical evidence indicates a rather surprising pattern. So far, the changes in governance have not led to better implementation results. As pointed out above, several comparative studies demonstrate that the choice between different governance patterns ('old' versus 'new' instruments) has little or no impact on the implementation effectiveness of the respective measures. Table 8.1 gives an example of such findings.

Table 8.1   *Implementation effectiveness of 'old' and 'new' instruments (+ = effective, − = ineffective, +/− = delayed formal and/or practical transposition)*

		D	E	F	UK	I
'old'	Large combustion plants	+	+	+	+	−
	Drinking water	+/−	−	−	+/−	+/−
'new'	EIA	−	−	−	−	−
	Information access	−	−	+	+	−
	EMAS	+	+	−	+	+

Source: Knill 2003, 184.

Also country-specific factors provide no satisfactory explanation for the rather unsystematic picture of ineffective and effective implementation across 'old' and 'new' instruments. For instance, it is often argued that implementation effectiveness varies with different constellations of domestic factors, such as the environmental awareness of the public or the existence and political influence of environmental organizations and interest groups. On the basis of these differences, some authors have tried to explain differences in environmental performance between Germany (at the time environmental pioneer) and the UK (at the time environmental laggard) during the 1980s (Boehmer-Christiansen and Skea 1991; Weale 1992). Empirical evidence shows, however, that these explanations can hardly be generalized, at least with regard to the implementation of EU policies. These results hence confirm the analysis in the previous chapter, where we mentioned the limited explanatory relevance of the distinction between environmental 'leaders' and 'laggards' for the implementation performance of these countries.

Explanation: deficits in theory and practice

The above overview makes clear that 'new' approaches directed towards horizontal governance, regulatory transparency, procedural regulation or self-regulation do not automatically imply effective implementation. In order to explain these implementation failures, that seem puzzling considering the theoretical and political rhetoric surrounding their application, one could either question the validity of implementation theory or the correct application of the theory. There is a grain of truth in both explanations. In this section we advance three arguments explaining the weak performance of the 'new' approach. First, the theoretical literature on implementation and on the use of bottom-up policy instruments, in particular, suffers from inconsistencies and ambiguities in its argumentation and hence, its implications for actual policy-making. Second, political practice hardly reflects the 'pure' application of theoretical insights. In many instances 'new' concepts are actually hybrids containing elements of both 'old' and 'new' approaches. Third, it is often overlooked in theory and practice that the 'new' approach suffers from its own typical weaknesses which might lead to additional implementation problems. In particular, the factor usually viewed as the basic advantage of 'new' concepts, namely their context-orientation, remains a theoretically diffuse and practically complex category.

Theoretical ambiguity

The central analytical interest of implementation studies that focus on a comparison of policy objectives and policy output is placed on the factors influencing the extent to which the formal and practical implementation actually corresponds with the aims defined in the policy. How can the implementation effectiveness be improved? Which instruments (e.g. 'old' versus 'new' instruments) are appropriate in that respect? Such considerations were, as depicted above, of decisive relevance for the development of 'new' instruments in EU environmental policy. The Commission in particular assumed that the implementation effectiveness in that policy field could be notably improved by relying on less interventionist approaches. How can it be explained that the expectations of the Commission were not fulfilled?

A closer look at the theoretical arguments developed in implementation research suggests that the 'new' instruments as promoted by the Commission by no means are to be regarded as a superior form of governance. To be sure, in the implementation literature many arguments can be found that assume less implementation problems with 'new' instruments in comparison to interventionist approaches. However, such arguments can hardly claim universal validity. A more detailed analysis reveals that implementation theory suffers from inconsistencies and ambiguities in its argumentation and hence, in its implications for actual policy-making.

On the one hand, studies pointing at the advantages of 'new' instruments and indicating the need to consider the specific context constellation in which a certain policy is implemented (Berman 1980; Lipsky 1980) cannot be regarded as representative for the whole field of implementation research. On the other hand, there are many studies that emphasize the need for classical forms of interventionist regulation, particularly because of the clear-cut objectives and requirements for implementation and enforcement to be complied with by both implementers and addressees (Lübbe-Wolf 1996; Krämer 2000). Between these two extremes, other analyses suggest a mix of interventionist and context-oriented elements as the perfect solution (see Sabatier 1986, 23–5) or advocate a contingent approach to the choice of policy instruments (Hanf and Scharpf 1978; Linder and Peters 1989; Ingram and Schneider 1990; Peters 1993).

The empirical richness of the implementation case studies of the 1980s, in particular, contributed to scholars increasingly shying away from seeking a universal model (Mayntz 1983; Windhoff-Héritier 1987). Instead the focus moved to mid-level conclusions (e.g. on the appropriateness of certain policy instruments in light of distinctive policy problems and context characteristics), in the best case amounting to general contingency models.

But even these less abstract contingency models, identifying different problem constellations in which either 'old' or 'new' instruments are expected to be more successful, ended up contradicting one another. For instance, Ingram and Schneider (1990) argue that in constellations of low support for a policy, 'new' instruments emphasizing learning and support-building will lead to better implementation performance than detailed intervention. This view contrasts with an argument advanced by Cerych and Sabatier (1986), stating that clear and specific objectives might enhance learning by lower level agents because they provide clear and unambiguous performance indicators.

Another example is the recommendation to apply 'new' instruments in constellations characterized by high uncertainty and complexity in order to allow for sufficient flexibility to react to new developments in the light of specific context conditions and the generation of ideas useful for the further evolution of a policy (Ingram and Schneider 1990). Again, however, there are also good arguments to justify detailed intervention in such constellations. First, too much discretion for subordinate agents might imply that nothing happens at all (Lane 1995, 112; Lübbe-Wolff 1996). Second, also an interventionist policy that takes little account of the given complexity might succeed in stimulating learning processes by trial and error.

While by no means exhaustive, this short record of contradictory advice illustrates the general ambiguity of implementation theory. Even attempts to classify contingencies by identifying particular problem or context constellations, fail to establish convincing causal linkages between policy choice and implementation effectiveness.

Thus, regardless of the political factors eventually responsible for the shift in the use of policy instruments at the European level, implementation research hardly provides a sufficient theoretical basis to justify such a step. Obviously, there is no simple causal relation between policy instruments and implementation effectiveness.

Common problems of 'old' and 'new' instruments

Implicit in the controversial discussion of the potential of the 'new' approach is the assumption that 'new' policy instruments as well as the corresponding institutional innovations are distinct from traditional, top-down instruments and structures. Empirical evidence suggests that this distinctiveness is a myth, at least on the level of actual application. Most 'new' instruments and institutions are hybrids, combining deliberative and discretionary with hierarchical and inflexible characteristics. As a consequence, they share many problems with traditional tools, during the decision-making process as well as at the implementation stage.

To elaborate, it is often argued that 'new' instruments are preferable as they render greater political acceptability in both the decision-making and the implementation process. Their flexibility and responsiveness to local framework conditions suggest that 'new' policy designs are less prone to invite political conflict. Consequently, decision-making is expected to be relatively smooth. Equally, given the context orientation and discretionary structure, 'new' instruments imply a lesser imposition on implementing actors than classical regulation, hence favouring acceptance and compliance also on the ground. Political acceptance is expected to increase even more smoothly if deliberative institutional structures are developed in addition. The reality however looks less rosy.

Several studies of environmental policy-making show that political conflict does not stop, or even diminish, at the issue of 'new' instruments. The work by Héritier, Knill and Mingers (1996) for instance investigates in some detail the conflicts around the adoption of the EMAS-Regulation and the Information and EIA Directives. These experiences show that measures of the 'new' approach are not free from competency conflicts nor do they 'fit' every regulatory system. Quite on the contrary, because 'new' instruments typically focus on the procedural level – e.g. establishing channels for awareness raising and learning – they may impose quite significant reform pressures for national and local administrations. Hence, it is questionable if 'new' instruments really do reduce the adaptation challenge for decision-makers and implementers.

Take for example the EIA Directive. In administrative terms the directive assumes horizontally integrated structures that enable a comprehensive assessment of any public or private project across environmental media, such as water or air as well as across geographical areas (regardless of political or adminis-trative boundaries). Both administrative requisites violate the federal and hierarchical structures in Germany which therefore fought the directive in the decision-making process and now stands out with a minimalist approach to implementation (Knill 2001, 143ff.). It seems doubtful that the substantive objectives of the directive will be reached this way. Similarly, Wright (2000) elaborates on the political fights affecting the decision of the eco-label scheme as well as the procedural challenges implied in the application of this – after all voluntary – instrument.

The hybrid character of many 'new' instruments, furthermore, may imply ineffective implementation not only as a result of demanding procedural requirements which may be in conflict with already existing structures, trigger administrative opposition or simply exceed administrative capacities. In addition, imple-mentation of 'new' instruments may suffer from the consequences of the – after all – conflictual decision-making process. A typical result of political conflict is the adoption of a compromise cater-ing for a multitude of often incompatible interest, thereby losing clarity and cohesion. These weaknesses were mentioned in a number of studies on 'new' instruments as the cause for imple-mentation problems on the ground. Kimber (2000), for instance, mentions the ambiguities in the Information Directive as a primary reason why some member states either misunderstood or wilfully escaped their obligations under the directive (see also Chapter 9).

Hence, are 'new' instruments and structures really 'new'? Do they really escape some of the problems usually attributed to traditional regulatory measures? The answer to these questions seems to be a rather unambiguous no. Most 'new' instruments are in fact hybrid solutions, implying, usually on the procedural dimension, considerable adaptation pressure for at least some EU member states. From this follows political conflict in the policy formulation and decision-making stages, deficits in the resulting compromise solutions, and an often problematic acceptance on the part of the policy implementers as their discretion to mould the instrument according to local needs and facilities turns out in fact more limited than expected.

Specific implementation problems of 'new' instruments
The previous discussion was not supposed to imply that so-called 'new' instruments are in fact no different at all from traditional approaches. The intention was to show that the contrast is less encompassing than often thought and that both approaches share some characteristics, and hence problems. The main difference between 'old' and 'new' policies remains the more procedural emphasis of the latter, going hand in hand with more flexible and open-ended implications on the substantive side. This openness to context factors of the 'new' approach may have its own set of problems however.

The first question that arises is whether the open-ended nature of new instruments, as opposed to clearly specified obligations, really provides sufficient incentives for motivating and mobilizing administrative and societal support in favour of effective implementation. There is reason to doubt this. Kimber (2000) shows that ambiguities in the legal text may help local administrators to escape their legal obligations rather than induce them to fit the legislation into existing structures. Moreover, it has been pointed out in other studies that many 'new' instruments are too passive in their design to mobilize either administration or the general public (see Börzel 2000; Caddy 2000; Knill and Lenschow 2000a). They either lack the clear incentive, the general inclination or the skills and resources to actually respond to 'new' (communicative) instruments. For this reason, Bouma (2000) questions the extent to which the indirect working of many 'new' instruments, i.e. primarily via awareness raising and attitude change, is sufficient to reach the desired effect. He suggests that 'new' instruments may require a substantive counterpart that provides concrete incentives to change behaviour; he shows that the EMAS-Regulation suffers from the missing counterpart of financial instruments.

Second, notwithstanding their flexible and open-ended nature, 'new' instruments may not only trigger positive responses but also resistance or active opposition. Experiences with the adoption of the eco-label scheme indicate that the political and economic context for especially economic instruments may be highly conflictual, hindering their effective implementation (see Golub 1998; Wright 2000). Other studies show that also more 'voluntary' approaches in fact require fairly specific institutional and political conditions to be successful (Mol, Lauber and Liefferink 2000). 'New' instruments seem to overestimate the (positive) malleability of the local context.

In summary, aside from sharing some characteristics and problems with the classical regulatory approach, 'new' instruments have a number of inherent weaknesses. Flexible design and open institutional and procedural structures may create confusion rather than incentives to act. Furthermore, the often indirect signals sent by 'new' instruments presuppose favourable context factors. Hence, the context-orientation of the 'new' approach works only for a limited set of already favourable context constellations (e.g. low initial opposition, sufficient capacity and resources, some initial motivation, complementarity with regulatory and institutional structures, etc). Ambiguous theory has helped to mystify particularly the latter aspect.

Potential solutions: an institutional perspective in implementation research

If the implementation success of European policies is neither dependent on country-specific factors nor influenced by the underlying instrument type, we have to look for alternative explanations to account for variance in implementation effectiveness across policies and countries. In this context, several more recent studies focus on institutional theories. The central argument here is that implementation performance of EU policies is not affected by the choice of instruments *per se*, but by the degree of institutional adjustment pressure resulting from EU policies for national arrangements (Duina 1997; Knill 1998, 2001; Knill and Lenschow 1998, 2001, 2005; Börzel and Risse 2003). The more European measures require domestic adaptations, the higher the probability will be that institutional inertia might have a negative impact on implementation effectiveness. This is not to say that the implementation of EU policies is inevitably ineffective, as soon as adjustments of national institutions are required. Rather, institutional theories suggest that the adaptability of national arrangements is subject to certain institutional limits.

Although EU policies are primarily directed at the specification of policy content and instruments rather than institutional arrangements, it should not be overlooked that there is often a tight linkage between policy content and its institutional implications. Therefore, decisions on instruments to a certain extent always entail decisions on corresponding institutional arrangements for their proper application. While being aware of the fact that the degree to which policy content and institutional implications are coupled may vary from policy to policy and from sector to sector, it cannot be ignored that the growing importance of EU policies leaves its mark on domestic institutions (Jordan and Liefferink 2004). Consequently, implementation problems can be conceived as problems of institutional change.

It is important to emphasize that this argument, which is closely related to the 'goodness-of-fit' approach developed in Europeanization studies (e.g. Cowles, Caporaso and Risse 2001), does not entail a deterministic perspective on the explanatory value of institutional adaptation pressure. In developing our argument, we rather recognize the need to provide a more dynamic explanation which takes account of the fact that institutional stability and hence resistance to change cannot be taken for granted, but depend on the constellations of an array of mediating variables, such as the degree of institutional embeddedness, policy salience and domestic actor constellations and opportunity structures (Mastenbroek 2005, 1110).

Institutional adaptation pressure and implementation
effectiveness
It is one of the few generally accepted findings in the otherwise diverse institutionalist literature (Hall and Taylor 1996) that institutional change, regardless if required explicitly or implicitly, rarely takes place in a smooth and unproblematic way. Existing institutions 'matter' and they do so mainly by constraining the options for future changes and adaptations. The emphasis on institutional stability and continuity is not, however, synonymous

with a static understanding of institutional development. Rather institutions find themselves in a virtually permanent process of adaptation to their environment. However, the scope of these adaptations is restricted by the structuring effects of existing institutional arrangements. Institutional change is hence often limited to aspects that do not question the very identity of an institution (March and Olsen 1989; Thelen and Steinmo 1992).

This abstract argument is of limited explanatory value, however, as long as we do not have criteria in order to judge in which constellations EU requirements exceed the adaptation capacity of national institutions and when not. To cope with this problem, Knill and Lenschow (2001) suggest a distinction between three levels of adaptation pressure, each of them being linked to different expectations with regard to implementation effectiveness. This distinction is based on the understanding that institutionally grown structures and routines prevent easy adaptation to exogenous pressure (March and Olsen 1989; DiMaggio and Powell 1991). Hence, domestic adaptation appears to be more likely in cases where European policies imply incremental rather than fundamental departures from existing arrangements at the domestic level.

The first scenario refers to constellations of low adaptation pressure. In this case, the institutional implications of EU policies are completely in line with domestic arrangements, i.e. none or only marginal changes are demanded. Implementation therefore is expected to be rather effective, as institutional adjustment requirements are very limited or completely absent (see Figure 8.1).

In the second scenario of high adaptation pressure, by contrast, EU requirements exceed the adjustment capacities of national institutions. Ineffective implementation is the probable consequence. Such constellations can be expected when EU requirements are in contradiction with institutionally strongly entrenched elements of national regulatory arrangements (see Krasner 1988).[2] Such contradictions occur, for instance, if EU policies require changes in domestic regulatory styles and structures that represent general patterns of national state, legal and administrative traditions and that are strongly rooted in a country's political, administrative and legal system.

The third scenario of moderate adaptation pressure refers to constellations in which European policies require substantive adjustments of domestic institutions, but without challenging well-entrenched core patterns of the political, legal and administrative system. While in such cases there is a higher probability for an effective implementation of European policies, this cannot be taken for granted. In contrast with the two other scenarios, in these cases a mere institutional perspective is not sufficient to develop hypotheses on the expected implementation performance. To address this question we have to complement our analysis with a second explanatory step which considers the particular interest constellation and institutional opportunity structures at the domestic level. To what extent is there sufficient domestic support for adjusting to EU requirements? To what extent have domestic actors who support regulatory change sufficient powers and resources to realize their interests? Institutional adaptation and hence effective implementation in this scenario can only be expected if they are facilitated by favourable domestic conditions (Knill and Lehmkuhl 2002).

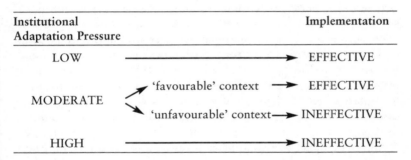

Figure 8.1 *Institutional adaptation pressure and implementation effectiveness*

Source: Knill and Lehmkuhl 2000.

Consequences for environmental governance in the EU
The institutional perspective suggests that in order to improve their implementation effectiveness, EU policy-makers face important challenges. On the one hand, imposing an allegedly 'ideal' policy design from the top while ignoring the potential impact of domestic institutions may significantly reduce the chance for

effective implementation due to institutional resistance to adapt. On the other hand, the design of policies in conformity with existing institutions may reduce the possibility to generate change and solve problems. To overcome this dilemma, policy-makers have to develop policies that require something, but not too much, from member states. In other words, there exists a curvilinear relationship between the level of adaptation pressure implied in EU policies and the effectiveness of implementation (cf. Cerych and Sabatier 1986). Only if EU legislation fits into such 'bounded space for innovation', such legislation – be it 'old' or 'new' – may contribute to problem-solving in the EU.

At the EU level, approaches that might be able to take these demands into account have been developed in recent years. They aim at minimizing as far as possible the adaptation requirements for national institutions. In so doing, they combine relatively general substantive objectives (e.g. quality objectives for air quality) with procedural regulations demanding monitoring, comparative assessment and publication of the implementation performance for each member state. In defining policy objectives that are as general as possible, the institutional adaptation costs shall be reduced to a minimum. Simultaneously, political pressure is mobilized through transparency and performance comparison.

This 'new' form of governance becomes apparent in particular in the 'Open Method of Coordination' (OMC). While certain policy benchmarks are set for the Union, national responses are formulated independently and without the threat of formal sanctions. The EU merely provides a context and enabling structures for cooperation and learning among national policy-makers. The regulatory impact of this approach rests on dissemination of best practice and the provision of incentives (peer review) rather than legal obligation and control. Hence, the level of obligation to a regulatory centre is low and a wide range of policy strategies to achieve general EU targets may be chosen (de la Porte and Pochet 2002; Scott and Trubek 2002). At present the OMC is applied to domains like information society, research and development, enterprises, economic reforms, education, employment, social inclusion, health care and pensions – i.e. flanking policies for building the economic union with an emphasis on social cohesion. The concrete design of the OMC varies from policy field to policy field. In some cases there is an emphasis on information exchange (e.g. pensions and health), while in others a stronger adaptation pressure through cross-national and Commission peer reviews is built up (e.g. employment and to a lesser extent also social inclusion).

However, even though these approaches are basically appropriate for avoiding the described problems of institutional adaptation, they are still of a limited relevance in practice. This can be traced to the fact that voluntary and self-regulatory approaches do not provide for appropriate forms of steering for all policy problems (Héritier 2002; Holzinger, Knill and Schäfer 2006). The OMC constitutes a rather unsuitable approach, for instance, if the creation of a level playing field and, hence, harmonization is one of the aims of the regulators. Such an aim would be best served through hierarchical regulatory standards. The same holds true if the decision-makers share a preference for predictable and reliable regulatory arrangements. The regulatory framework of the OMC is then likely to be too flexible, whereas hierarchical norms give clearly defined directions. It must be noted that, for these reasons, many environmental policy problems do not seem particularly suited for the OMC. Incidentally, however, OMC could be the preferable option if the maintenance of national diversity is desirable, or if this diversity is perceived as unchangeable. The same holds for constellations in which risk and insecurity are characterizing the regulatory context with the effect that no clear and generally applicable regulatory solution is in supply.

Finally, it should be emphasized that different policy designs and governance approaches should never be interpreted as a panacea to overcome all problems causing implementation deficits in the EU. None of the discussed approaches will avoid the common practice of 'creative compliance' in the member states. This practice of avoiding the intention of a law without breaking the terms of the law constitutes a common problem for all modes of regulation (see McBarnet and Whelan 1991; Cohn 2001). Moreover, it should not be overlooked that the design of a European policy is the result of often long-winded negotiations between the member states. As a result, policy proposals inevitably tend to be watered down (by making use of exception clauses or vague formulations) or enriched with elements that are in the interests of certain member states. Implementation deficits to a considerable degree are simply the result of inconsistent and ambiguous European policies. This basic deficit applies to all forms of European governance. The deliberate choice of a particular policy instrument therefore at best allows for partial improvement of the implementation performance. The design of policies for effective implementation is always constrained by the need to accommodate the diverse interests of the member states.

Notes

1 Official Journal C 328, 7 December 1987.
2 Krasner (1988) differentiates between two dimensions of institutional anchorage. Institutional depth refers to the extent to which institutional arrangements are embedded in normative orientations and dominant belief systems. Institutional breadth, in turn, refers to the extent to which institutional arrangements are interlinked with their institutional environment.

9

The implementation of EU environmental policy in the UK, France, Germany and Spain

As shown in the previous chapter, simple recipes, such as the switch to context-oriented patterns of governance, are hardly sufficient to improve the implementation effectiveness of EU environmental policy. Rather than European governance approaches or domestic factors, the institutional compatibility of EU policy requirements with national administrative traditions was identified as an important factor accounting for the varying implementation record across policies and member states.

It is the objective of this chapter to illustrate this argument empirically. To do so, we draw on recent cross-national studies on the implementation of EU environmental policy (Knill 2001; Knill and Lenschow 2001). Similar arguments, however, are also advanced by other scholars investigating the implementation of European measures in the field of social policy (Duina 1997) or health and safety at work (Eichener 1996). The following examples refer to the implementation of three environmental policies which to some extent reflect the variety of environmental governance approaches found at the European level, namely, the directives on drinking water quality, EIA and freedom of access to environmental information. The formal transposition and practical application of these policies is investigated for four member states (UK, France, Germany and Spain). These countries vary with regard to their administrative traditions and hence their institutional conditions in order to comply with EU policy requirements.

The subsequent analysis is based on three steps. First, we introduce the selected policies and the institutional implications emerging from their implementation. In a second step, we present our empirical findings: to what extent have the policies been implemented effectively (or not) in the countries under investigation? Third, we explain the observed implementation patterns on the basis of our theoretical considerations.

The selected policies and their institutional implications

The three selected policies reveal not only different characteristics with regard to their underlying governance concept (interventionist versus context-oriented, or 'old' versus 'new'), but also in terms of their institutional requirements for effective implementation at the domestic level. These institutional differences become manifest along two dimensions, namely, regulatory style and administrative structures.

The dimension of regulatory style includes patterns of state intervention as well as interest mediation. On the level of state intervention two contrasting types are often distinguished, namely a hierarchical style of intervention imposing uniform, substantive standards and a more flexible and discretionary style allowing for some level of self-regulation. Different forms of state intervention tend to go hand in hand with particular patterns of interest intermediation, ranging from formal and legalistic styles in the interaction between public authorities and the addressees of the regulation to more informal and pragmatic patterns with administrative actors playing a more mediating role between the different interests involved.

With regard to the dimension of administrative structure, by contrast, we look at the way regulatory authorities are organized within the overall state system. For instance, a regulation may call for the centralization or decentralization of regulatory processes (e.g. by requiring uniform reporting to a central authority), or demand organizational change on the horizontal level (e.g. by requiring the coordination of previously distinct administrative tasks). What are now the institutional requirements that are implied in the three selected policies?

The Drinking Water Directive is a good example of 'old' command-and-control regulation. The directive specifies quality standards for water intended for human consumption. These standards apply to a range of substances that may pose a threat to human health when present in certain levels of concentration in the water. The prescription of uniform and legally-binding standards assumes hierarchical structures of intervention and implies quite formal and legalistic patterns of administrative interest intermediation at the domestic level. The substantive standards defined in the directive are not negotiable and apply uniformly to all water providers. In view of these detailed specifications, national regulatory authorities have limited discretion and flexibility. In other words, there is a close link between policy content (uniform standards) and corresponding institutional arrangements for domestic compliance (formalist and legalist patterns of intervention).

The prescription of concrete regulatory arrangements for the domestic implementation of European requirements is not restricted to substantive measures, but can also be observed in seemingly 'new' policies with a merely procedural focus. In this context the Directive on the Freedom of Access to Environmental Information is a good case in point. Rather than defining substantive standards the directive aims to ensure free access to the information on the environment held by public authorities. It lays down the detailed conditions for making such information accessible, including appeals procedures against refusal or failure to provide information, charges for the provision of information, and exemptions from disclosure (Winter 1996; cf. Chapter 6). In view of these detailed procedural prescriptions, the directive has important implications on national patterns of administrative interest intermediation, namely by demanding an open and transparent style of environmental regulation, with different societal interests having equal opportunities in access to administrative decision-making. In this way the scope for secretive and closed interaction patterns between regulatory authorities and the regulated industry, which may be observed in many member states, is significantly reduced.

The EIA Directive obliges developers of formally specified kinds of public and private projects to provide information regarding the environmental impact of these projects to a designated public authority. This EIA can then be taken into consideration by those public authorities that are responsible for the authorization of the project(s) in question. The EIA Directive imposes a procedural requirement on public and private investors as well as regulatory authorities. It does not impose any substantive standards (specifying under what conditions a project should be denied authorization, for instance). Hence, the directive mixes hierarchical elements, related to the requirement to carry out an EIA for a defined range of cases, with indirect procedural rules encouraging public participation. Considering institutional arrangements, the EIA Directive implies a concentration or at least coordination of administrative control responsibilities. Since an impact assessment will deal with the project's implications for air, water and soil pollution as well as the threats for flora, fauna and human health, the responsible public authorities ought to be able to evaluate these impacts in a comprehensive way – hence the need for integrating administrative structures.

Table 9.1 *Administrative implications of the policies under study*

Policy	Regulatory style	Administrative structures
Drinking water	*Intervention patterns:* hierarchical, uniform, substantive, low flexibility *Interest intermediation:* formal and legalistic	No direct organizational implications
EIA	*Intervention patterns:* hierarchical, procedural *Interest intermediation:* (limited) public participation	Concentration and coordination of administrative competencies
Information access	*Intervention patterns:* procedural *Interest intermediation:* public participation, transparency	No direct organizational implications

Empirical findings

An investigation of the domestic responses to the institutional requirements of the three policies for the UK, France, Germany and Spain reveals a great variety of implementation performance across both policies and countries, as summarized in Table 9.2.

Table 9.2   *National responses to EU policy requirements in four member states*

	UK	France	Germany	Spain
Drinking water	effective, but delayed	ineffective	effective, but delayed	ineffective
EIA	ineffective	ineffective	ineffective	ineffective
Information access	effective	effective	ineffective	ineffective

With some time delay, the UK managed to meet the requirements of the Drinking Water Directive not only through considerable investments but also by establishing new structures of hierarchical state control (Maloney and Richardson 1995). Its reaction to the Information Directive was more timely than the implementation of the Drinking Water legislation. Also it was more proactive than the EU directive explicitly called for; the UK established structures for the active provision of environmental information and departed from its formerly rather secretive administrative procedures (see Chapter 6). Only in the case of the EIA Directive does the UK continue to resist adaptation towards a more formal regulatory framework as well as increases in hierarchical forms of coordination (Knill 2003, 200).

The implementation record of France reveals two cases of ineffective implementation. Although the Drinking Water Directive was basically in line with the existing approach of hierarchical intervention, the local authorities in practice retain a great deal of discretion to negotiate with industry. Thus, they often depart from the rather strict standards defined in the European directive, resulting in corresponding implementation deficits. The same holds true for compliance with the EIA Directive. Although the directive required only small changes in existing administrative arrangements (in particular with respect to the role of the impact assessment in the authorization of industrial plants), such adjustments did not occur. It is only for the case of information access that the formal and practical compliance is fully in line with EU requirements (Bailey 1997; Knill 2003, 201).

Turning to Germany, it long resisted the implementation of the Drinking Water Directive but in the end adapted to its requirements, taking advantage of technological innovations and using complementary economic instruments to deal with the redistributive implications of the legislation. Administrative resistance persisted in the cases of the Information and the EIA Directives. In the former case, resistance became evident already on the level of formal transposition which was based on an overly narrow interpretation of the EU directive. Also on the level of practical application of the law administrative actors frequently blocked rather than facilitated public information requests. Legal proceedings brought before the ECJ provide evidence of the degree of German resistance (Bugdahn 2005). Legal proceedings are equally revealing with respect to Germany's reaction to the EIA Directive. Germany particularly resisted the integrative approach of the legislation. It would have implied changes to its authorization procedures which used to be separated by environmental media such as air or water (see Lenschow 1997a; Knill and Lenschow 2001).

In the case of Spain, implementation is ineffective for all policies under investigation. Although the interventionist approach implied by the Drinking Water Directive is basically in line with the domestic regulatory style, the European standards are often not achieved, in particular because of a lack of administrative resources and monitoring capacities. Moreover, and similar to the German case, both the EIA and the Information Directive are implemented rather ineffectively. While in the EIA case, Spain has so far resisted setting up integrated administrative structures, we observe that the persistence of rather closed and secretive patterns of interest intermediation severely restricts the free access to environmental data as required by the EU directive (see Börzel 2000).

In sum, our empirical findings illustrate that the 'new' governance approach underlying the European policy does not seem to make a crucial difference with regard to implementation effectiveness. Both interventionist and context-oriented measures reveal a more or less similar implementation record, with the EIA Directive, which combines elements of both approaches, being implemented ineffectively in all countries under investigation.

Moreover, our findings illustrate that country-specific factors (such as environmental awareness of the general public or the role and influence of environmental organizations) can hardly account for the variance of implementation records across countries. In particular, the Spanish implementation record is not fundamentally different from the French and German performance, notwithstanding differences for instance with regard to the influence of environmental interests.

Explanation: implementation from an institutionalist perspective

Against this backdrop, we have to look for other factors that might account for the varying implementation effectiveness across policies and member states. In the previous chapter, we have introduced an approach that concentrates on institutional compatibility of European requirements and domestic arrangements as the crucial explanatory variable in that respect.

According to this approach the probability of effective implementation decreases with an increasing level of institutional adaptation pressure on domestic regulatory styles and structures. If institutional implications of EU policies are in line with domestic arrangements, i.e. none or only marginal changes are demanded, implementation is expected to be rather effective. In that situation, institutional adjustment requirements are very limited or completely absent. By contrast, ineffective implementation is the likely outcome if EU policies require changes in domestic regulatory styles and structures that represent general patterns of national state, legal and administrative traditions and that are strongly rooted in a country's political, administrative and legal system. It is only for constellations between these two extreme poles, that an institutional perspective does not provide a sufficient basis to predict the implementation effectiveness of European policies. In these cases, EU policies require certain institutional adjustments, however, without challenging well-entrenched core patterns of the political, legal and administrative system. We then have to complement our analysis with a second explanatory step which considers the particular interest constellation and institutional opportunity structures at the domestic level.

Table 9.3   *European adaptation pressure and implementation effectiveness in four member states*

	UK	France	Germany	Spain
Drinking water	Change possible within administrative core (effective, but delayed)	Contradiction with administrative core (ineffective)	Change possible within administrative core (effective, but delayed)	Change possible within administrative core (ineffective)
EIA	Change possible within administrative core (ineffective)	Change possible within administrative core (ineffective)	Contradiction with administrative core (ineffective)	Change possible within administrative core (ineffective)
Information access	No changes required (effective)	No changes required (effective)	Contradiction with administrative core (ineffective)	Contradiction with administrative core (ineffective)

When this explanatory framework above is applied, the following pattern emerges (see Table 9.3). Domestic responses in six of the twelve cases can be explained on the basis of the first explanatory step, which considers the institutional compatibility of European requirements and domestic arrangements. In two cases, EU policies were in line with existing arrangements, while in four constellations strong contradiction with national administrative traditions led to ineffective implementation. For the six remaining cases of moderate adaptation pressure, we have to additionally analyse the specific domestic interest constellations in order to understand the actual occurrence or non-occurrence of institutional adjustment.

Constellations of low adaptation pressure
Beginning with the cases of high institutional compatibility, two cases (information access in the UK and France) can be explained by the fact that existing regulatory arrangements at the national level were already well in line with European requirements; there was hence no European pressure for domestic institutional adjustment.

In France, the Information Directive confirmed the existing situation. Given the fact that national arrangements went even beyond EU requirements, effective compliance was possible without any legal or practical changes. The relevant national legislation is the 1978 Act on access to administrative documents which was part of a group of laws enacted in the late 1970s designed to promote public participation in administrative decision-making. Given the French tradition of an 'enlightened bureaucracy' which is superior to society, this development might come as a surprise. However, public participation served to strengthen the position of the bureaucracy by increasing its legitimacy and authority at a time of intensified technocratic intervention (Winter 1996).

Also in the UK, existing domestic arrangements were fully in line with the European requirements. This can be traced to the fact that the European rules had been strongly influenced by the British regulations. They in fact served as a model for the EU directive. As shown in Chapter 6, this active role of the UK at the European level was made possible by far-reaching domestic policy reforms, which in turn had been triggered by a confluence of national factors, notably the Thatcher government, and European adaptation requirements (Knill 2001). Initially, the requirements of the Information Directive stood in sharp contrast to the British tradition of secrecy which almost entirely excluded access and participation opportunities for third parties with respect to environmental regulation.[1] However, from the 1980s onwards, fundamental changes in British environmental policy occurred, including the introduction of information ad participation rights that went even beyond the developments at the EU level. As a consequence, the UK complied with the directive in a highly effective way.

Constellations of high adaptation pressure

By contrast, European policies severely contradicted the core of national administrative traditions in four of our twelve empirical cases, namely information access and impact assessment in Germany, information access in Spain and drinking water in France. As argued above, the high degree of institutional 'misfit' implied by core contradictions provides a sufficient basis to expect administrative resistance.

In the German impact assessment case, institutional 'misfit' developed with respect to structural and organizational arrangements. The incompatibility of European and domestic arrangements emerged mainly from the integrated cross-media approach to environmental protection required by the directive, which is in sharp contrast to corresponding core patterns in Germany. The EIA Directive implied the concentration or at least intensified coordination of consent procedures and structures with respect to different environmental media, such as air, water and soil. By contrast, in Germany administrative processing of a project is basically medium-specific and consequently uncoordinated in both legal terms and practical performance (Knill 2001, 144). These horizontally fragmented structures and procedures, moreover, are institutionally strongly entrenched by their tight vertical linkage to a multi-tier hierarchical structure at the regional (*Länder*) level. Thus, individual consent procedures are embedded in vertically integrated, but horizontally segmented administrative arrangements, representing a rigid institutional structure (Benz and Götz 1996). Due to the resistance of the German administration to adjust to the requirements of the directive, the EIA was integrated into existing authorization procedures without adopting an integrative approach, hence avoiding an overhaul of administrative structures. As a consequence, the directive has made little difference for the German traditional authorization practice which remains based on a single-media approach (Knill and Winkler 2006).

At the same time, the requirements of the Information Directive in favour of regulatory transparency and accountability did not correspond with the German state and legal tradition, where public access to documents and information is only considered legitimate if the individual requesting it can show the 'direct effect' of the project or activity in question on the individual situation. This different notion of the role of the administration and the law in society has led to strong resistance to adjusting domestic arrangements in the light of European requirements and, hence, to substantial implementation problems (Winter 1996).

A rather similar argument applies to the implementation of the Information Directive in Spain. Spanish legal provisions and administrative practices traditionally grant access to information only in justified cases, and are therefore in strong contradiction with the European legislation. In view of these institutional incompatibilities, it is hardly surprising that Spain so far has implemented the directive rather ineffectively, both in a formal and a practical sense (see Börzel 2000, 1569).

Looking at the French implementation of the Drinking Water Directive, it is at first glance surprising that this case reflects a constellation of high adaptation pressure, given the fact that the regulatory style implied by the directive is basically well in line with the French approach. The French regulation of drinking water relies on uniform and substantive standards broadly corresponding with the European values (Bailey 1997). Hence, from a mere policy-related perspective on European adaptation pressure, one would expect effective implementation.

A closer look, however, indicates that European requirements were in contradiction with a deeply rooted core element of French administrative practice, namely the considerable autonomy of the local level to negotiate arrangements with its clientele. Although administrative activities are legally specified in a detailed way, the local services have acquired a *de facto* discretionary power, allowing for the interpretation of legal rules in light of the particular situation. These 'normes secondaires d'application', which are often defined in informal and consensual negotiations between the regulators and the regulated, 'se révèlent plus déterminantes que la législation de référence' (Lascoumes 1994, 169).[2]

The autonomous position of the local level is institutionally entrenched in the strong professional integration of the administrative elite, the *grands corps de l'état*, implying that administrative coordination occurs to a lesser extent by hierarchical means, but rather by the confidence through which the top entrusts the lower ranks. Consensual interaction between administration and industry is further facilitated by the fact that administrative and industrial top officials are often 'old boys' of the same *grande école* (de Montricher 1996, 250). Against this background, the 'appropriate' application of European standards in the context of the strongly institutionalized French practice of 'secondary norms' was not sufficient to meet the uniform and legalistic objectives defined in supranational legislation.

Constellations of moderate adaptation pressure

In the remaining six cases (drinking water in the UK, Germany and Spain as well as impact assessment in the UK, France and Spain) domestic adjustment could be considered as potentially possible from an institutional compatibility perspective; i.e. European legislation required substantive changes, but no challenges to core patterns of national administrative traditions. In these constellations the actual pattern of change or persistence cannot be inferred from a mere institutional compatibility perspective, but must also take account of the specific policy context at the national level.

With regard to the Drinking Water Directive, the UK and Germany reveal an effective, albeit delayed implementation record, while in Spain, the domestic context yielded ineffective implementation results. In the British case, the regulatory changes from industrial self-regulation towards a more interventionist regime associated with the privatization of the water industry in 1989 had significantly reduced institutional incompatibilities between European and national arrangements. Certain adjustments were nevertheless necessary, in particular with regard to the formal and practical compliance with the legally binding standards prescribed by EU legislation. These remaining adjustments were facilitated by a favourable policy context. Privatization meant that the economic costs of compliance with European standards no longer interfered with the government's objective of reducing public spending, as the costs for retrofitting existing plants had to be borne by private companies. Moreover, the regulatory regime set up in the context of privatization strengthened the voice and influence of environmental and consumer groups, thereby providing new institutional access opportunities which favoured compliance with European objectives (Maloney and Richardson 1995).

In Germany, the administrative implications of the Drinking Water Directive were basically in line with the hierarchical and interventionist regulatory style traditionally characterizing German environmental policy. Though not challenging this institutional core, the Drinking Water Directive implied some adaptational pressure in the form of stricter quality standards with regard to nitrate and pesticide pollution, and hence either the imposition of emission limits on the polluting actors (industry and agriculture) or high investments in new abatement technologies. The development of a solution took considerable time because conflicts over the distribution of the costs of compliance had to be settled. Both water providers and environmental organizations pushed for stricter emission standards for the polluting actors who naturally resented such proposals. The polluting industries, most notably agriculture, had the advantage of being politically well represented not only through their own associations, but also through the federal and regional agriculture ministries. The farmers were only willing to change their production practices if they would be compensated for their anticipated financial losses. Water providers and environmentalists argued that this solution would violate the polluter pays principle. But the government was not prepared to engage in a major conflict with agricultural interests (Rüdig and Krämer 1994, 69). In view of this constellation, reaching compliance with the European standards involved difficult and lengthy negotiations. They resulted in the introduction of consumption fees (*Wasserpfennig*) as well as voluntary agreements between the polluting industry and water providers which permitted the financing of the installation of new cleaning technologies on the one hand, and some reduction of the overall level of water pollution on the other – both at little cost for the polluters (Lenschow 1997).

Similar to Germany, in Spain only minor institutional changes in terms of adjusting existing regulatory standards were necessary in order to comply with the requirements of the Drinking Water Directive. These changes, however, were enacted only in a formal way, with practical application suffering from severe problems. The fact that many water authorities actually do not comply with EU standards can be linked to the lacking political pressure exerted by environmental interest groups or the general public, which do not consider drinking water quality to be a major issue (Börzel 2000, 150).

Although implying only moderate needs for institutional adjustment, the EIA Directive was implemented rather ineffectively in the UK, France and Spain as a consequence of missing support from national actors. In the UK, an EIA already existed, and had done since the 1970s, albeit on a legally non-binding and unsystematic basis. Nevertheless, the European directive came quite close to the British arrangements with respect to the requirements regarding public participation, the information to be supplied by the developer of a project, and the balancing of this information supplied by the developer and others by the planning authorities (Haigh 2000). The directive departed from the British practice, however, in requiring more formal procedures and centralized coordination. Rather than adjusting to these demands, the UK integrated European requirements into its existing planning procedures violating the objectives of the directive. Firstly, due to the lack of coordination between central and local authorities within the British political system, there is no linkage between the EIA (responsibility for which lies at the local level) and the industrial process authorization (which for the larger plants lies with the central EEA) (Knill and Winkler 2006). Secondly, environmental impacts are given no particular rank compared to other considerations in the planning process.

> In light of the wide discretion traditionally given to the planning authorities, the latter have broad leeway in balancing the results of the EIA against other information to be considered, such as financial and economic interests. Moreover, the balancing of competing considerations is only to a limited extent subject to court review. The quality of environmental statements in general is therefore not very satisfactory. (Alder 1993, 212)

Similar to the UK, France, too had already established the legal and administrative basis for carrying out an EIA during the 1970s. However, the objectives defined in the EIA Directive would have required certain modifications with respect to public participation and the relevance of the EIA within the authorization process. In contrast to the directive's intention, the French EIA is a pure declaration of the environmental impacts of a project rather than an instrument to stop or change projects with adverse environmental effects. Moreover, public participation generally takes place only after a decision on the project has been taken (Bailey 1997). Nevertheless, given the open texture of the directive and the fact that the basic procedures were already in place in France, effective implementation would have required only moderate institutional changes on these two points. Political support by national actors, however, was not sufficient to motivate effective adaptation. This can be traced to the fact that, in offering environmental organizations certain opportunities for 'controlled' participation, the French administration managed to strengthen its position by instrumentalizing these organizations and making use of their resources, while canalizing and marginalizing their political influence (Lascoumes 1994, 211).

Institutional adaptation requirements of the EIA Directive also remained at a moderate level in the case of Spain. Several sectoral regulations already required the assessment of environmental impacts of a planned project. However, the Spanish EIA approach still had to be adjusted in several ways in order to ensure full compliance with EU regulations. Necessary changes included a higher amount of information to be delivered by the project developer, longer periods for information and consultation, and a more systematic consideration of cross-media effects. Although these changes implied no fundamental challenges to existing arrangements, the Spanish legislation did not correctly transpose the EIA Directive. In particular, Spain refused to specify the conditions under which projects listed in the annex of the directive have to be made subject to an EIA. Deficits are also reported with respect to the practical application of the directive. Overall, administrative changes have been minimal. Similar to Germany, EU requirements were incorporated into existing arrangements, implying that the requirements of a comprehensive cross-media assessment were not achieved. Although some domestic actors have mobilized against the deficient implementation of the directive, the resulting internal pressure for adaptation has been too diffuse and weak to improve compliance with the EIA Directive (Börzel 2000, 154).

Conditions for the effective implementation of EU environmental policy

What general conclusion can be drawn from the above considerations with regard to a possible improvement in the implementation effectiveness of EU environmental policy? Which factors favour the compliance with EU requirements by the member states? Our theoretical and empirical analysis suggests two general criteria in this respect.

First, the institutional compatibility of European policy requirements with domestic regulatory styles and administrative structures constitutes an important factor affecting implementation success. The higher the European adaptation pressure, the lower the likelihood that domestic arrangements are effectively adjusted to EU requirements. This goes for 'new' context-oriented measures as much as for the 'old' command-and-control approach. Effective implementation therefore demands that EU policies do not overstretch the adjustment capacity of national institutions.

In this context, the level of European adaptation pressure basically depends on the design of the European policies in question. After all, domestic institutional arrangements, such as administrative and legal traditions, can be considered as factors that are rather stable over time. However, as shown by the British cases of drinking water and information access, this stability does not exclude that the level of European adaptation pressure might change as a result of domestic institutional reforms. In the British case, far-reaching administrative reforms initiated by the Thatcher government led to a fundamental transformation of the British state, also changing the British institutional constellation in view of compliance with EU law. This way, EU requirements in the cases of drinking water no longer implied contradictions with administrative core elements, but could be achieved by moderate adjustments within a changing core. Core changes may occur as the result of external shocks (see Krasner 1988) such as the political and economic transition we have recently witnessed in Eastern European countries. Moreover, as could be observed in the British case, core dynamics may also develop from within the system. It has to be emphasized, however, that such endogenous reforms constitute an exception rather than the rule. Their likelihood is strongly affected by a political system's reform capacity, indicating the structural potential for changes of national administrative traditions and varying from country to country.

Second, in addition to basic requirements of institutional compatibility of European and domestic arrangements, implementation effectiveness is affected by the domestic constellations of actors and interests. This holds true in particular for constellations in which EU policies require no fundamental, but still substantive institutional adjustments. In this context, effective implementation is not only dependent on the extent to which domestic actors actually support compliance with EU policies, but also on the political power and influence of these actors.

In sum, these considerations suggest that improvements in the implementation effectiveness of EU environmental policy require a highly differentiated approach to policy-making, taking account not only of the institutional compatibility of European and domestic arrangements, but also on the constellation of domestic actors and interests. It remains to be seen, if and to what extent new forms of governance at the European level, such as the OMC, will actually help to improve domestic implementation performance.

Notes

1   This tradition of secrecy can be understood against the background of the British state tradition, namely the supremacy of Parliament. Since the executive power is subject to parliamentary control, administrative accountability towards society is seen as being sufficiently guaranteed.

2   'These secondary implementation norms ... turn out to be more decisive than the legislation on which they are based' (translation by the authors).

10

Taking stock: the environmental problem-solving capacity of the EU

Since its beginnings in the 1970s, EU environmental policy has developed and expanded rapidly. This is illustrated not only by the sheer volume of EU environmental policy measures, but also by the high degree of differentiation of those measures and the governance patterns underlying them. The preceding chapters have given ample testimony of this development. Despite these achievements, however, the problems and deficits of European environmental policy are frequently the subject of political and scientific debate. How should EU environmental policy best be assessed and evaluated? How capable is the EU of actually solving environmental protection problems?

Before answering these questions, we must first evaluate the results of the EU environmental policy up to now. However, any evaluation depends to a great extent on what is used as a standard of comparison. One's judgement is likely to vary greatly depending on whether one takes, for instance, the highest level of protection worldwide or the European average as a starting point. An objective and absolute standard for the evaluation of the EU environmental policy does not exist. Instead, conclusions on the EU's capacity to solve environmental problems must be viewed within the context of the evaluation criteria which have been selected (Holzinger 1994, 35).

To evaluate EU environmental policy, this chapter will apply four different assessment criteria, which address the question of the problem-solving capacity from different perspectives and on the basis of different demands: (1) decision-making capacity, i.e. the question whether and to what extent the EU is capable of action at all in the area of environmental policy; (2) the quality of the decisions made in terms of substance, for example the level of limit values or the consistency of environmental policy programmes (i.e. the problem of programme deficits); (3) the effectiveness of the implementation of these programmes at the national level (i.e. the problem of the implementation deficit); and (4) the actual effects of policy measures in terms of improving the state of the environment in the Union.

Decision-making capacity

The theoretical debate on the EU's environmental policy performance has focused up to now on the aspect of decision-making capacity (Holzinger 1994; Scharpf 1997, 207). From this point of view, problem-solving capacity primarily depends on the question of whether a political system is capable of action at all.

This conceptualization of problem-solving capacity appears to be relatively limited at first sight. Why is it considered to be a success when a political decision is made at all? Would not the actual effect of such a decision 'on the ground' be much more important? The reason for this restricted focus can be traced back to the special features of the European decision-making process, which frequently led to impasses and blockades. Due to divergent national interests and the extensive requirements for agreement in the Council of Ministers, as we have seen in Chapters 4–6 in particular, the EU's capacity for political action is subject to comprehensive restrictions (Scharpf 1988).

If we look at EU environmental policy from this angle, we initially gain the impression that the EU has a relatively large capacity for solving problems. Observers have pointed out that the EU had passed more than 200 environmental policy acts already by the middle of the 1980s (Haigh 2000; Jordan 1999). Considering that up to that moment all measures had to be adopted on the basis of unanimity, this record suggests a high decision-making capacity. After the SEA and the Treaty of Maastricht had replaced the unanimity principle by QMV, the output of environmental policy measures increased even further.

Figure 10.1 conveys an overview of how the number of environmental policy measures has increased over the years. It takes all directives, regulations and decisions into account, regardless of

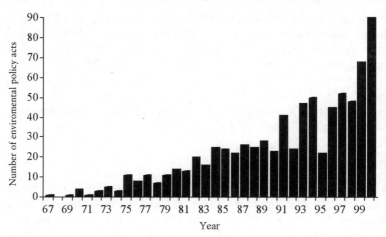

Figure 10.1   *Number of environmental policy directives, regulations and decisions passed annually*

Source: Haigh 2000, 2.1–4.

their importance and including changes to existing legislation as well as legislation which was later replaced by other measures. According to this all-inclusive count, more than 700 environmental policy measures had been passed by the EU by the year 2000. If we restrict ourselves to currently applicable directives and regulations as well as the most important amendments to them, we still arrive at around 200 legal acts.[1]

However, even if one were to agree on a unified counting procedure, these numerical data can only be drawn on as a very rough indicator of the environmental policy decision-making capacity of the EU. They do not provide any information on more sophisticated aspects of decision-making capacity such as the (often considerable) duration of the decision process or how many Commission initiatives actually led to concrete legislation (see further: Andersen and Rasmussen 1998; Jordan, Brouwer and Nobel 1999; Falkner 2000). Furthermore, they do not comprise differences between individual fields of activity in environmental policy. As discussed in Chapter 2 of this book, some areas such as water protection, air pollution control or waste management are covered by a very dense network of measures, while in the areas of nature protection, town and country planning and transport policy, a comparatively small number of legal acts were passed (see also Haigh 2000, 2.1–3).

Quality of decisions: programme deficits

A more refined assessment of the EU's decision-making capacity in the environmental field, taking into account the aspects just referred to, could doubtlessly be made by gathering and evaluating the corresponding data. However, if we were to do so, an even more important dimension of problem-solving capacity would still remain out of sight, which is the quality of the measures passed. To what extent can the legal provisions and their substance and content do justice to the environmental policy problems they seek to address? Several deficits in the environmental policy programmes of the EU can in fact be identified, i.e. weaknesses in the design of environmental measures which make it more difficult to reach the underlying policy objectives.

A first point of criticism that is often raised in this regard concerns the alleged lack of a comprehensive concept underpinning EU environmental policy (Rehbinder and Stewart 1985, 203; Lenschow 1999a; Haigh 2000, 2.1–3; Sbragia 2000). According to this line of argument, EU environmental policy has by no means been all-embracing up to now. Moreover, the depth and spectrum of regulation greatly varies between the individual fields of activities. While very detailed regulations may exist for individual problems, other environmental problems are by and large not tackled by the EU.

Holzinger (1994, 42) points out, however, that the admittedly inconsistent output of EU environmental policy cannot automatically be equated with a lack of concepts, or vision. Within the framework of the different environmental action programmes, in particular, the Commission has indeed put forward very comprehensive concepts (see Chapter 2). Yet in light of the different national interests, they could not always be implemented, or implemented the same way. Apart from that, one might raise the question of to what extent a comprehensive concept can contribute to better environmental policies at all. What seems to be considerably more important is a continuous openness to react adequately to new problems, which can never be fully anticipated even by the most comprehensive concepts.

Second, one of the most notorious standard criticisms of the EU environmental policy is the accusation that limit values are too low, or only based on the 'lowest common denominator'. This assumption is voiced in particular for environmental policy decisions which require unanimity and for which every state possesses the right to veto (Jordan 1999, 11). It is suggested that actors agree on the policy that is acceptable also to the state which is least willing to protect the environment – which may be another state for each issue at hand, to be sure. It tends to be forgotten, however, that not only those member states disinterested in environmental policy but also the environmental policy forerunners have a veto right. The latter are not automatically willing to sacrifice their more progressive environmental policy solutions. Instead, they often attempt to push through stricter limits, for instance by means of concessions in other policy areas (Holzinger 1994, 44; Liefferink and Andersen 1998). There is in fact sufficient empirical evidence which refutes the assumption that harmonization generally takes place at the level of the least progressive member state in environmental policy.

> Although opinion in other member states was often reluctant, or at least less enthusiastic, the Community began to adopt environmental legislation more stringent than many member states would have adopted unilaterally. (Sbragia 2000, 297)

Even if it is difficult to present systematic empirical evidence due to the complexity of many environmental policy measures, it appears that environmental standards were frequently passed at the EU level that constituted considerable environmental policy progress at least for several countries, even if they did not always coincide with the ideas of the environmentally most ambitious member states (Holzinger 1994; Héritier, Knill and Mingers 1996).

A third weakness of many environmental policy measures in the EU involves their overly vague and open wording. This allows the member states much leeway for 'minimalist' implementation, i.e. implementation at a lower level than originally envisioned. In this context, we can distinguish between legislation with 're-nationalisation' effects and vague legal concepts.

As regards the former category, many environmental policy

measures in the EU deliberately grant the member states a great degree of freedom when it comes to implementation. In principle this is with good reason, as it allows the member states to accommodate their specific economic and ecological interests. At the same time, however, this freedom leads to cross-country differences in the application of EU rules which were originally intended to be uniform. This, in turn, may be interpreted as a form of 're-nationalization' of European environmental policies.[2]

An important example of such regulations is formed by the series of directives on water quality, for instance for bathing water or shellfish water, where the countries themselves are free to define the bodies of water to which the directives apply. This form of self-definition, combined with the unclear wording of the classification criteria, basically leaves it open to the member states if they want to apply the directive or not, depending on their specific environmental policy goals. In the Directive on the Quality of Bathing Water, for example, bathing water is defined as a body of water, 'in which bathing is explicitly authorized by the competent authorities of each member state, or bathing is not prohibited and is traditionally practised by a large number of bathers' (Directive 76/160/EEC. Article 1[2]). This definition clearly leaves a lot of room for interpretation.

> The countries do indeed have to implement the directive, but the decision whether it is applied effectively is in practice up to the member state authorities. In extreme cases, the countries can let the directive 'run idle', by completely refraining from identifying bodies of water of the concerned type or by only designating those bodies of water that are guaranteed to comply with the quality standards anyway. (Holzinger 1994, 52–3 [our translation])

An instructive example of this is how the UK dealt with the Directive on Shellfish Water. The responsible authorities from the British environmental ministry were explicitly instructed to initially designate only a small number of bodies of water which fulfilled the European standards anyway, in order to save any potential costs for the installation of control and filter technology (Schneider 1984, 610f.; Krämer 1996).

Besides these regulations with their explicit 're-nationalization' effects, vaguely defined legal terms in the directives generally leave much room for interpretation during national implementation. Sometimes they allow the member states to 'retroactively turn the "spirit" of the regulation upside down at their own discretion' (Schneider 1984, 609).

Vague legal concepts can be of a very different calibre, such as 'a large number' of bathers in the example mentioned above, or the instruction in Article 10 of the EIA Directive that the national authorities must observe the restrictions resulting from the protection of the 'public interest' when the relevant project plans are published (Holzinger 1994, 54). We find two recurring vague legal terms when approval requirements are defined on the basis of the 'state of technology' and in line with 'economically reasonable' technical obligations. These two clauses are of great importance in many directives, such as the 1984 Framework Directive on Air Pollution from Industrial Plants or the 1996 IPPC Directive, in which the weighting of both terms was highly disputed, in particular between Germany and the UK (Héritier, Knill and Mingers 1996; Hey 2000; Sbragia 2000). Very different judgements can be made when deciding if a measure is 'economically reasonable' or if the requirements linked to the current 'state of technology' are fulfilled. The same holds for the question of whether the publication of approval data is against the 'public interest', or what should be regarded as 'a large number' of bathers.

Fourth, the transitional and adaptation phases stipulated in environmental measures often grant the member states additional leeway. Directives normally define a point in time as of which certain provisions (e.g. maximum permissible values) come into effect or by which certain quality standards must be achieved. The reason for defining transitional and adaptation phases is that burdens on the environment can often not be reduced immediately, for instance because they require far-reaching and costly technical modifications.

In some cases, however, very long transitional periods are allowed, which unnecessarily delays the environmental effects of the measures in question. For example, the 1988 Directive on Large Combustion Plants allots a time limit of fifteen years, within which the member states must reduce the emissions of air pollutants from large power plants, refineries, etc. The same holds for the directives on air quality, where transition periods of ten years are granted for areas in which the standards are particularly hard to attain (Knill 2003, 81).

Besides the possibility of temporarily exceeding deadlines, there are also indefinite exceptions to observe a deadline. For instance, the Bathing Water Directive allows member states to deviate from the generic implementation deadline of ten years in exceptional cases. In order to do so, the member states must present adequate reasons for non-compliance as well as water management plans. The Commission then decides whether to approve the exemption, and does not specify a point in time at which such exemptions expire (Holzinger 1994, 56).

Apart from the various possibilities of exceeding set deadlines, there are other exemptions defined in the directives which vary from case to case, dependent on the concrete regulatory issue at hand. These specific exemptions sometimes grant member states extensive means of deviating from European requirements in individual cases, usually resulting in the watering down of the initial common environmental goal (Krämer 1996).

The Directive on Large Combustion Plants, for example, contains various special agreements accommodating the interests of individual member states. Thus, new plants with a capacity of more than 400 megawatts are allowed to exceed twice the stipulated emission limit for sulphur dioxide, as long as they are in operation for less than 2200 hours per year. This provision was included upon pressure from France, where so-called 'peak-load plants' are used to cover peak demands which cannot be accommodated on short notice by nuclear power (Liefferink 1996, 120). Deviations from the limits imposed on large combustion plants are also allowed when energy production in a member state is based on sulphurous fuels to such an extent that the state could only comply with the limitations by using unreasonably expensive technology. This was a concession to the British, whose domestic coal has a high level of sulphur. Moreover, the member states can apply at the Commission for modifications of the reduction requirements, in case unexpected complications arise with regard to energy demands or the availability of certain fuels. Specifically for Spain, in view of its rapid economic growth at the time, it was decided that lower emission limitations hold for new plants until 2000 (Johnson and Corcelle 1989, 141; Knill 1995, 177–9; Liefferink 1996).

Another example is the EIA Directive, in which Article 2(3) grants the member states the possibility of exempting individual projects from the requirement of carrying out an EIA. The criteria for these exceptions are not specified, but the member states must instruct the Commission and the public on the reasoning for granting such exceptions (Holzinger 1994, 57).

If we look at the overall possibilities that the various exceptions, time periods, vague legal terms and regulations with 're-nationalization' effects in the European measures entail, the member states have considerable room to manoeuvre despite the seemingly 'uniform' design of most EU policies. This, in turn, results in a differentiation of environmental policy effects at the national level. In most cases, such differentiation leads to a 'watering down' of the original policy objectives. Hence, regulations allowing for deviations from the initial policy can be characterized as programme deficits. They are part of the story behind the implementation deficits of EU environmental policy which will be discussed in the upcoming section.

Quality of implementation: implementation deficits

Even if the ability to develop political programmes may be viewed as an important determinant of the EU's problem-solving capacity, one cannot neglect the fact that these programmes also must be implemented effectively in order to achieve the envisioned effect. Effective governance in the EU depends not only on the quality of decisions made in Brussels, but also on the quality of implementation 'on the ground'. In the implementation phase of European policies a shift in focus takes place from the supranational to the national level. Except for a few exceptions such as competition policy, the EU is as a rule dependent on the cooperation of the member states in the implementation of its programmes (Lübbe-Wolff 1996; Jordan 1999a; Knill and Lenschow 2000).

As discussed in detail in the previous chapters, moreover, the implementation of European policies concerns not only the formal transposition of European rules into national legal and administrative provisions, but also the practical application of those provisions in national regulatory practice.[3] Thus, the proper formal transposition by no means guarantees that European rules are actually carried out in practice. As just one example, Spain has a very favourable record when it comes to formal implementation, while great deficits can be observed during the practical implementation of measures (Börzel 2000).

As set out in Chapter 7, the Commission's own statistics actually do point out far-reaching implementational deficits for European policies. They also show that environmental policy is at the top of the 'list of sins' (European Commission 1996, 1999).[4] The deficits identified here essentially pertain to failures to observe time limits, the selection of an inadequate legal form for the implementation of measures, the incorrect or incomplete transposition or the incorrect or incomplete application of European rules (Krämer 1996). While the first three aspects concern the formal transposition of European policies, the final point relates to deficits in their practical application.

First, European directives usually define an implementation deadline within which the member states must adapt the relevant national laws to the European requirements and notify the Commission about the implementational measures. These deadlines are exceeded by the member states so often that 'the timely implementation of measures into national law is the exception, not the rule' (Krämer 1996, 14). For some directives, almost all member states exceeded the set time period. One such case is the Drinking Water Directive, for which states failed to observe the deadline for six months to four years (Knill and Lenschow 1998).

Besides the member states' sheer lack of interest in the implementation of EU measures, institutional and administrative factors can lead to the failure to observe deadlines. In Germany, for example, the individual states (*Länder*) have essential legislative authority in the area of the environment. This frequently requires extensive coordination between the Federal Government and the *Länder*. This easily leads to delays in the formal transposition of European rules (Toonen 1992; Haverland 2000).

If a member state notifies the Commission on the implementation of a directive, the Commission first examines whether the measures taken are correct in formal terms. In this context, a second type of implementation deficit may come to light if a member state does not apply European rules in the form of national laws or regulations, as prescribed, but for instance by issuing administrative decisions or circulars. According to the case law of the ECJ, mere administrative decisions or circulars are generally not accepted because they do not provide a sufficient, legally binding basis for the practical application of European rules (Schwarze 1996, 177). As a consequence, for some directives in the area of water protection and air pollution control, Germany among others has had to refrain from its national practice of setting limit values by means of administrative measures and instead pass corresponding legal regulations. The UK was faced with similar problems. Its traditional regulatory practice in the environmental field, which largely managed without legally binding limit values, had to be adapted to European requirements to a considerable extent (Knill 2001; Jordan, 2004). For the Netherlands, the use of voluntary agreements with business posed a problem in relation to the 1994 Packaging Waste Directive (Haverland 1998; Lauber and Ingram 2000, 132–3).

Thirdly, besides selecting an improper legal form, the formal transposition of EU environmental policy is frequently characterized by material legal violations. They span from the improper interpretation of vague legal terms to the incorrect allocation of exceptions or the partial or incorrect specification of limit values which are defined in the European measure.

Returning to the earlier example of the Bathing Water Directive, Ireland had interpreted the term of 'a large number' of bathers as comprising a number of at least 10,000 people per year. Subsequently it came to the conclusion that the directive did not apply in Ireland. After intervention by the Commission, Ireland corrected its initial interpretation of the criterion (Holzinger 1994, 64). Similar problems occurred when the directive was implemented in Germany and the UK (Krämer 1996, 16; Wurzel 2002). Many member states also refrained from transposing the full range of limit values which were defined in the Drinking Water Directive of 1980 into national law. This applied in particular to the parameters for pesticides and nitrate, with which it was especially difficult to comply (Breuer 1990, 86; Bodiguel 1996).

The German implementation of the 1990 Directive on Public Access to Environmental Information provides another case. The basic problems encountered by this directive in Germany were discussed in Chapter 9 (also Knill 2001; Bugdahn 2005). In order to illustrate how subtle implementation deficits may be in practice, we mention one additional example here. While the directive applies to all information that is available from administrative agencies with environmentally-related tasks, in Germany it is not possible to access information from agencies which only occasionally deal with environmental matters, such as road construction offices (Krämer 1996, 15). Germany, in other words, introduced a limitation to the principle of access of environmental information which can hardly be imagined to be in line with the directive's original intention.

Finally, even if a member state has correctly transposed European measures into national law in formal terms, this by no means rules out implementational deficits with respect to their practical application. Problems may for instance occur when the necessary administrative and organisational modifications are not made, when the compliance with limit values is not adequately monitored and/or enforced, or when certain areas or categories of sources for which limit values have been set are not designated accordingly.

For example, several member states only 'complied' with the strict limits of the Drinking Water Directive by using an insufficient measuring technique, unable to measure concentrations as low as defined by the EU (Knill and Lenschow 1998). The practices used to implement the Information Directive in many member states also show that the right to access records – regardless of legal claims – is often impeded by administrative obstacles, such as unreasonably high administrative costs (Kimber 2000). Furthermore, many problems result from the right granted by many directives to the member states themselves to designate for instance protected areas. For example, many countries did not designate the protected areas for every type of bird required under the 1979 Birds Directive. The same holds for the designation of bathing water and shellfish water (Breuer 1990; Krämer 1996).

This overview of the different implementational deficits suggests that the effects of EU environmental policy might in reality be far behind the goals formulated in the original measures. Due to the considerable room to manoeuvre available to the member states in the implementation phase, moreover, we can expect large differences across the EU. As we have seen in Chapter 7, there is only limited empirical support for the hypothesis that member states having a great interest in a strict environmental policy do a better job in applying European demands than countries which have this interest to a lesser extent. According to this line of argument, the latter would be more tempted to reduce the demands of European policies by a laxer implementation (Holzinger 1994, 66). As demonstrated in the literature and illustrated by various examples in this section, however, severe implementation problems occur also in the more environmentally progressive member states (Börzel 2000; Knill and Lenschow 2000; Jordan and Liefferink 2004).

The Commission, of course, is not unaware of these problems. As can be seen from the tables in Chapter 2 of this book, the Commission, in cooperation with the Council of Ministers and the EP, is in a constant process of revising existing directives. This is done in the first place with a view to updating the legislation to newly perceived problems, new scientific insights and new technologies. At the same time, however, these revisions provide an opportunity for removing points which are unclear and loopholes that have appeared during implementation. Thus, at least some of the programme deficits discussed above may in fact be corrected along the way.

Effects of EU environmental policy

This analysis of the environmental problem-solving capacity of the EU has up to now concentrated on policy *output*, i.e. the main focus was placed on the results of European policy-making and national implementation in the form of 'laws, regulations and institutions that governments employ in dealing with policy problems' (Weale 1992, 45). Even if this output were free of programme and implementational deficits, this alone would not yet guarantee that the achieved policy *outcome*, i.e. 'the effects of those measures upon the state of the world' (ibid.) correspond with the original policy goals (see also Chapter 7).

Thus, the ultimate yardstick for determining the problem-solving capacity of EU environmental policy is its impact on the environment. For instance, one might assess whether the quality goals or emission limits targeted in a directive were actually reached. To what extent have the measures succeeded in reducing the environmental problems for which they were originally designed? Posing the question this way, the evaluation criterion is only the effectiveness of EU environmental policy. Another criterion would be efficiency, analysing the benefits and the costs of the activities at hand. The aspect of efficiency is primarily discussed with respect to the selection of different instruments and forms of governance, e.g. as regards the advantages and disadvantages of 'command-and-control' regulation vs economic instruments such as 'green' taxes.[5] The analysis of the effectiveness of European policies may lead to the conclusion that the failure of a measure can be traced back for instance to poor implementation or rather to false assumptions on problem causes or the effects of certain instruments (Hill 1997).

If we were to attempt to pinpoint and assess the outcomes of EU environmental policy, however, we would be confronted with large problems. One of the first difficulties that arises here is the data situation. An assessment would require us to have knowledge of the quality of the environment (with regard to a certain pollutant or aspect of the environment) before and after a measure came into effect. Even though we can expect certain improvements here thanks to the establishment of the EEA, a complete and comparable compilation of all relevant parameters across Europe and over time is still far from available. The Agency has in fact thus just started to develop the necessary indicators to assess the quality of the environment in the member states (European Environment Agency 2001).

An additional problem for the assessment of the effects of EU environmental policy results from the great degree of complexity of environmental problems and their underlying causes. This complexity makes it difficult to pinpoint the specific influence of European regulations on the quality of the environment. A simple comparison between intended policy effects and actual (changes in) environmental quality is based on the assumption of a direct causal relationship between a policy and the effects it triggers. However, the problem emerges that in reality such attributions are hardly feasible in light of the broad array of other environmental, political, economic and social factors that may have an influence on the problem as well (Baier, March and Sætren 1990; Lane 1995, 110). If for example the concentration of nitrogen oxides in the air develops differently than envisioned by the EU regulation, this may also be related to climatic factors or to an increase or decrease in the volume of industrial production (Knill and Lenschow 2000a; Jänicke 2001, 20).

Against this background it is very difficult to make general statements on the effectiveness of EU environmental policy. Nevertheless, it must be reported here that the EU Commission arrived at a relatively sceptical evaluation in the Fifth Environmental Action Programme. It acknowledged 'a slow but relentless deterioration of the general state of the environment of the Community notwithstanding the measures taken over the past two decades'.[6] The EEA, based on newer data, conveys a slightly more positive assessment (European Environment Agency 2001; see Table 10.1).[7]

Table 10.1 *Development trends in environmental quality in the member states for selected areas*

	Climiate Change	Air Quality	Water Quality	Waste
Germany	Negative	Positive	Mixed	Positive
Finland	Negative	Positive	Positive	Mixed
Netherlands	Negative	Mixed	Positive	Positive
UK	Positive	Positive	Mixed	Negative
Belgium	Negative	Mixed	Positive	Mixed
Denmark	Negative	Mixed	Positive	Mixed
Luxembourg	Positive	Mixed	Mixed	Negative
Austria	Negative	Mixed	Mixed	Positive
Sweden	Negative	Mixed	Positive	Mixed
France	Negative	Mixed	Negative	Mixed
Greece	Negative	Negative	Mixed	Negative
Ireland	Negative	Negative	Negative	Mixed
Italy	Negative	Mixed	Mixed	Negative
Portugal	Negative	Negative	Mixed	Negative
Spain	Negative	Negative	Positive	Negative

Source: European Environment Agency 2001, 23.

The EEA indicators show a highly mixed picture of the development of environmental quality in the Union and suggest considerable fluctuations both between individual areas of environmental policy as well as across countries (European Environment Agency 2001, 23). The Agency emphasizes however that the selected measurement indicators are only of a preliminary nature. Thus, the data summarized in the illustration below are to be interpreted with a certain degree of caution.

The table makes it clear that the member states can be roughly divided into three categories in terms of the development of the quality of the environment. While the assessment is primarily positive for Germany, Finland, the Netherlands and the UK, developments in France, Greece, Ireland, Italy, Portugal and Spain are evaluated with a much greater degree of scepticism. As for Belgium, Denmark, Luxembourg, Austria and Sweden, a more mixed trend can be observed. Pronounced fluctuations can also be detected for individual areas. For example, the EEA findings indicate that developments regarding water quality have been relatively favourable, while the results in climate protection give reason for much greater concern.

Summary: rating European environmental policy

This chapter has shown that the assessment of the success of EU environmental policy is associated with great difficulties. This is not only due to the lack of generally valid and objective evaluation standards, which makes any assessment greatly dependent on the selection of the concrete frame of reference. As a matter of fact, even if one is perfectly explicit about the evaluation criteria employed and even if one, as proposed here, distinguishes between different yardsticks for decision-making capacity, the quality of decisions, the implementation and the substantive impact of environmental policy regulations, many serious interpretation problems remain. From this perspective, it is very difficult to generalize and classify EU environmental policy as either 'effective' or 'ineffective' or to claim that it has a 'high' or rather a 'low' problem-solving capacity.

Despite these general evaluation problems, we can detect certain trends. These are related first to the deficits frequently found in EU policy programmes and measures as such. Whereas the frequent accusations that the EU environmental policy lacks a concept and is a 'policy of the lowest common denominator' appear as questionable, the problems associated with the open wording of laws, long transition phases and various types of exceptions, which allow the member states many means of watering down the common EU regulations, have been argued to be much more severe.

This effect is then further aggravated by considerable weaknesses in the implementation of European environmental policies at the member state level. Despite different interpretations of how large the implementation deficit exactly is, there is a broad consensus that there are very significant problems. They result not only from the inadequate transposition of European policies into national legislation, but also from their inadequate and incomplete application in practice.

For the reader who has got as far as this point, the rather critical evaluation given in this chapter should not have come as a total surprise. The labyrinthic decision-making structure of the EU, the various interests competing for influence in Brussels, the high degree of diversity between the member states in many dimensions, ranging from geophysical conditions to public awareness of environmental problems and from economic structure to political culture: all those factors have been discussed in the previous chapters. They all contribute to the problems in the formulation and implementation of EU environmental policy identified here. They help to explain why such deficient programmes are in fact adopted at the European level, even though it is clear that some of the measures they entail fail to have any positive impact on the environment. And they help to explain why member states frequently do not properly implement European regulations which they helped draft themselves. At the same time, these explanations by no means justify the problems at hand. Understanding their background, however, is a first but important step towards solving them.

Notes

1 See: http://europa.eu.int/eur-lex/en/lif/ind/en_analytical_index_15. html (accessed 6 October 2005). It should be noted that there may also be differences in the definition of what constitutes an environmental

policy measure. While Haigh includes all measures 'which can reasonably be described as forming part of the Community's environmental policy' (2000, 1.3), the more restricted count is based on the official EU system used to match Community law to individual policy areas. In addition, there is of course room for interpretation when it comes to the assessment of the relevance of individual legal acts.

2 Quality standards also allow the member states much leeway for national implementation. However, they are not supposed to lead to different effects of European measures at the national level, because uniform requirements and goals are set for all member states with regard to the quality of the environment.

3 The requirement for formal transposition of European rules appears particularly virulent when these are passed in the form of directives. Directives, in contrast to regulations, demand national legislative action in order to take effect. As argued in Chapter 2, however, the difference between directives and regulations is in reality much less distinct. Many regulations are worded relatively openly and thus must be legally substantiated at the national level in order to be enforced practically despite their immediate applicability.

4 Note that these data are to be interpreted with caution. Implementation deficits are frequently clarified already in an earlier stage on the basis of informal negotiations between the Commission and national governments and an official procedure is not initiated at all (see Jordan 1999a, 81).

5 It must be noted that the criterion of efficiency, in turn, leaves out aspects of justness and acceptance of political decisions (see Jänicke 2001, 20).

6 Official Journal C 138, 28 May 1992.

7 Note that Table 10.1 only shows general trends. It should be stressed again that due to the causal complexity referred to above, it is difficult to draw conclusions on the effectiveness of EU policy measures specifically. Note also that the ten countries which entered the EU in 2004 are not included in the table. In those countries visible effects of EU measures can hardly be expected as yet.

11
Conclusions

If anything, this book has made clear that the making and implementation of EU environmental policy is a dynamic and complex process. Nevertheless, some general patterns can be discerned. First, a steady broadening of the issues covered by EU environmental policy can be observed, along with a continuous adjustment of the policy instruments used and the underlying regulatory approaches. A second feature is the close link between environmental policy on the one hand, and the regulation of the Internal Market and the integration process at large on the other. Despite the gradual recognition of environmental protection as an 'independent' policy field within the EU, this link continues to play an important role up to the present day. Thirdly, important patterns are linked to the multi-level character of the EU, such as the phenomenon of regulatory competition between the member states and the typical problems of national adaptation to European requirements in the implementation phase. Finally, the notorious implementation problems that characterize this policy field must be mentioned.

These patterns have been recurrent themes throughout the book. Their main thrust will be recaptured in the first section of this chapter. On the basis of this, the second section will explore – as far as our limited view allows us – the future perspectives of EU environmental policy. Over the past decades, in a fascinating alternation of crises and 'Europhoria', the Union and its environmental policy have dramatically expanded their scope and ambitions. At the moment of writing, however, after the recent accession of ten Central European member states and the (definitive?) failure of the Constitutional Treaty, the dynamic of European integration seems to have entered a phase of quite severe stagnation. One may wonder what the consequences will be for EU environmental policy.

Patterns of multi-level environmental governance

The first observation relates to the broad scope and steady expansion of EU environmental policy, in terms of both policy substance and prevalent regulatory approaches. As regards substance, this book has demonstrated that today's EU environmental policy is much more than an *ad hoc* collection of individual measures. Instead, it is guided by a coherent set of principles and regulatory paradigms and covers all major environmental issues, including those that have become topical only relatively recently, such as climate change or genetic modification. In addition to this, the wide variety of regulatory approaches employed in EU environmental policy is striking. From the 1990s especially, a range of 'new' environmental policy instruments was introduced alongside the existing tradition of 'command-and-control' regulation. This development should be seen not only as a strategic response to increasing problems in implementing EU environmental legislation, but also as the consequence of regulatory competition between the member states. There can be little doubt, in sum, that EU environmental policy has over the years developed into a mature, fully-fledged policy area, operating within the political framework of European integration but increasingly following its own dynamic. Understanding and explaining this dynamic has been the main objective of this book.

When considering the historical development of EU environmental policy, a second important observation is that the current, fairly mature state of the policy field has in fact hardly been reached through deliberate institutional design but rather presents itself as the sum of a large number of individual decisions. Or as Weale et al. (2000, 488) formulate it: 'The European system of environmental governance is (...) the product of political action but not of political design.'

As set out in Chapter 1, the environment was by no means referred to in the Treaties of Rome which founded the EC in the

1950s. Thus, environmental policy set off in the early 1970s without any constitutional basis. It developed as a sequence of specific measures, primarily intended to harmonize divergent policies at the national level which happened to coincide with the functioning of the Internal Market. From this point of view, the rapid evolution of the environmental policy field and the parallel build-up of the necessary institutions in Brussels, such as the DG for the Environment, can be seen as a 'spill-over' (Haas 1958) from the process of economic integration between the member states. This is not to say that deliberate institutional decisions at the level of the European Council did not play a role at all. However, these decisions were again taken only in the wake of Internal Market business and mainly served to consolidate an already existing political practice. This is true in particular for the SEA of 1987. While primarily aimed at completing the Internal Market, it was used as an opportunity to eventually provide a formal basis for EU environmental policy. Similar stories could be told for the modifications to the environmental paragraphs in the subsequent Treaty revisions of Maastricht, Amsterdam and Nice as well as for the Constitutional Treaty.

Also in a more general sense, the evolution of EU environmental policy has always been firmly bound up with the ups and downs of the process of European integration at large. In periods when the integration proceeds smoothly, such as the years following the conclusion of the SEA and dominated by the '1992' project of completing the Internal Market, there is room for progress in the environmental field too. In less happy days, e.g. during the difficult ratification of the Maastricht Treaty in the early 1990s, member states also tend to be less willing to embark upon far-reaching environmental policies. This is important to keep in mind when discussing the present state and future perspectives of EU environmental policy.

The third set of observations pertains to the mutual and dynamic relationship between regulatory goals and interests at the national and the European level. This relationship comes to the fore when policies are established in Brussels, but also when they are implemented 'at home'.

An important driving force behind national influences on European policies is the process of regulatory competition, fuelled by the member states' interest in minimizing the cost of institutional adaptation accruing from European requirements. The most effective way to pursue this interest is to push national regulatory approaches in the EU policy process from the beginning. As discussed particularly in Chapters 4–6, this can be accomplished only under certain conditions. Notably, a member state wishing to present its national policy as a model at the European level needs the support of the Commission. The Commission has the exclusive right of initiating legislation at the EU level and thus plays a central role in setting the agenda and formulating drafts. Building alliances with other member states will lend additional force to efforts to push a certain policy solution in Brussels. A successful strategy of this kind thus requires a policy concept which is innovative, but at the same time not too far away from existing preferences in the Commission and at least a number of the other member states (Liefferink and Andersen 1998).

However, national influences on European policies may result not only from countries promoting their own policies in the EU. Blocking decisions in the Council – or even just the threat of doing so – also adds to creating EU policies which are in fact blends of various national regulatory approaches. The 'patchwork' character of many EU directives (Héritier 1996) effectively reduces the cost of institutional adaptation in individual member states. It must be noted, though, that due to QMV also the blocking of decisions in the Council requires a number of member states who are willing to act as brothers-in-arms.

Despite the various strategies applied by member states to 'shape' EU policies as much as possible according to their own wishes, EU policies in turn do not fail to have a sometimes considerable impact at the national level when it comes to implementing them. This phenomenon has come to be known as 'Europeanization'. Obviously, European obligations may have an impact on the substance of national policies, e.g. the level of emission standards or environmental quality objectives. Beyond that, EU policies may – explicitly or implicitly – require institutional adaptations. These may amount to, for instance, the change of existing agencies or bureaucratic procedures, or even the establishment of wholly new ones. Especially in the longer term, the adaptation of institutional working routines may also lead to shifts in national policy culture and policy style, although this effect has been reported to be fairly limited so far (Jordan and Liefferink 2004).

If there is indeed a certain degree of Europeanization of national policies taking place, does this also lead to a gradual convergence between the member states? Given the fact that EU rules are in principle the same for all member states, this would be a reasonable assumption. With the exception of the concrete substance of policies, however, this is hardly confirmed by the literature. Alongside instances of the convergence of national institutional structures and styles, tendencies toward persistence of national differences or even divergence can also be observed (Knill 1998, 2001; Knill and Lenschow 1998; Cowles, Caporaso and Risse 2001; Jordan and Liefferink 2004; Liefferink and Jordan 2005).

There appear to be two main explanations for the in fact highly differential pattern of Europeanization and convergence of national environmental policies. First, the implementation gaps, which are particularly large in this policy area, suggest that member states actively try to restrict the cost of institutional adaptation required by European directives to a minimum. They do so not just by failing to implement those directives altogether (full non-implementation is in fact the a-typical case), but rather by integrating European requirements as much as possible (or in fact just a bit more than that!) into existing national policy structures. Second, as far as an adequate adaptation of national structures does take place, this does not necessarily lead to convergence. This is due not only to the fact that directives allow a certain amount of flexibility to the member states. More importantly, national adaptations are always 'path-dependent' in the sense that they build upon a vast foundation of well-established legal and institutional structures and traditions. Historically, these structures and traditions are very different among the member states. The result is what Cowles, Caporaso and Risse (2001, 1) aptly describe as 'domestic adaptation with national colours'.

Fourth and finally, it has to be acknowledged that EU environmental policy suffers from a considerable and fairly persistent implementation deficit. Considering only legislative output, the EU's problem-solving capacity in the environmental field may appear impressive. This pertains not only to the broad scope and variety of environmental policies, referred to above, but also to the generally high level of protection embodied in those policies. This is remarkable particularly if one realizes that much of this was built up under very difficult institutional conditions, notably the lack of any formal Treaty basis and the dominance of unanimity voting in the Council up to 1987.

Turning to the question of the transposition and actual implementation of EU environmental policy at the national level, however, the picture becomes less rosy. Environmental policy notoriously suffers the largest implementation gap of all areas of EU activity. On the one hand, this gap can be related to the character of the European decision-making process. The diversity of national interests and preferences often results in vague and open-ended provisions which offer ample room for interpretation when it comes to implementing them. On the other hand, this tendency does not change the fact that EU policies often require far-reaching and costly adaptations of policies and policy structures at the national level. Hence, as pointed out above, member states generally attempt to integrate EU requirements into existing national structures, a strategy which easily leads to poor, 'minimalistic' and ineffective implementation. As we have seen, this holds for traditional 'command-and-control' regulation as much as for 'new', supposedly more flexible policy approaches.

Future perspectives

Although the main aim of this book has been to give an analytical account, rather than a political evaluation, of the making and implementation of EU environmental policy, we will conclude this final chapter by discussing some of the major challenges facing the policy field at this moment and, on that basis, venturing a look into the future.

As we have seen, EU environmental policy has over the years evolved into a mature area of European integration, covering a wide range of environmental issues, making use of a broad repertoire of both 'old' and 'new' approaches, and exerting profound influence on national environmental policies in the member states. Nevertheless, the problem-solving capacity of EU environmental policy leaves something to be desired, to say the least. In most cases decision-making remains a long and difficult process with uncertain outcomes. In addition, there continues to be reason for serious concern about the implementation and enforcement of policies at the national level.

Both problems are already a heavy burden on EU environmental policy in themselves, but they appear to have become even more complicated due to two major developments: the recent enlargement of the EU to twenty-five members (and probably more in the near future) and the present sense of serious political crisis prevalent in the EU.

The 2004 enlargement with ten Central and Eastern European countries has not been the first to take place, to be sure. From the 1970s the EU has been extended step-by-step from the original six to fifteen members in 1995, and twenty-five today. In the foreseeable future, a number of countries is likely to follow, including Bulgaria, Romania and, somewhat further ahead, maybe Turkey. Without playing down the political benefits – or the 'historical necessity', as some would say – of this process, it must be realized that every accession has further increased not only the sheer number of member states, in itself already putting additional stress on the functioning of the EU institutions, but also the diversity among them. This diversity pertains to various factors, including geography, demography, economic development and economic structure, culture and politics. They can all give rise to serious differences between the member states around specific environmental issues – or other issues, for that matter. Thus, for instance, environmental and economic interests may differ among countries and so may regulatory preferences. Increased diversity within the EU, in other words, is likely to lead not only to increased conflicts between opposed interests, but also to a higher level of regulatory competition. This brings with it the risk of an even more 'patchy' character of European environmental policy, more watered-down compromises and exemptions, and – despite the increased use of framework directives and procedural instruments – more problems in adapting national structures to European requirements in all member states.

More or less parallel to the latest enlargement (but not necessarily caused by it) an already existing dip in the European integration process further deepened. Crisis had already been lurking in the background since the disappointing Treaty revisions adopted in Nice in 2000, but was really sparked off by the

Conclusions   221

French and Dutch 'no' to the Constitutional Treaty in 2005. It may be true that crises have been part and parcel of the European integration process from the very beginning, but the present one seems to be in fact quite fundamental. The rejection of the Constitution in two of the EU's founding members is an indication not just of the usual clash of interests between member states (which can be serious and time-consuming, but normally fades away under increased political pressure), but rather of a deep-seated scepticism among the population regarding the state and destination of the European project. Although some optimistically argue that it is only a matter of better communication to the public, others call for a more rigorous restriction to the EU's 'core business', i.e. the creation and maintenance of the Internal Market and issues directly related to that. Even when it comes to purely economic goals, however, the EU is currently not performing particularly well. The 'Lisbon' process of improving the EU's global competitiveness, for example, meets with growing criticism for not being too well on track.

How will all this affect EU environmental policy in the years to come? The consequences of enlargement in terms of increased stress on the institutions and increased diversity are being felt in each and every policy area of the EU. Also in the environmental field it will make decision-making and implementation more complex. For the overall level of environmental protection this can hardly be expected to work out positively. Particularly in combination with a protracted crisis in the EU at large, it may lead to a stagnation also of environmental policy. Although it is not likely that important parts of the environmental *acquis communautaire* will be turned back or re-nationalized, the combined effect of enlargement and lasting crisis may be a general reluctance on the part of both the member states and the Commission to take new steps. This in turn may force member states, or at least some of them, to take their own initiatives. Parallel to that, it may lead to increased international activity outside the EU, i.e. in other existing international fora or by way of *ad hoc* arrangements.

However, there is also a slightly different scenario conceivable. Among the population, environmental protection is generally valued as an important priority of European cooperation.[1] This may give additional legitimacy to EU activity in this field, even if other areas of European policy come under increasing attack. One complication here may be that several of today's pressing environmental problems, notably climate change, but also for instance biodiversity or hazardous waste, are very much global in character. An active role of the EU in these issues thus requires an active role in the global arena. Reaching EU-wide consensus on foreign policy positions, however, has always been problematic and will be even more so in a period of general 'Euro-sclerosis'. The end effect may again be that in issues which typically transcend the borders of the EU, member states will go their own way, either individually or in coalitions independent of the EU. Conversely, however, the environment may develop into one of the few areas where European cooperation goes on to bear fruit. Obviously, this story is to be continued in the next edition of this book!

Notes

1 See the results of an EU-wide Eurobarometer survey, carried out in November 2004: http://europa.eu.int/comm/environment/barometer /report_ebenv_2005_04_22_en.pdf (accessed 6 October 2005).

References

Alder, J. 1993, 'Environmental impact assessment: the inadequacy of English law', *Journal of Environmental Law*, 5:2, 203–20.

Alter, K. J. and S. Meunier-Aitsahalia 1994, 'Judicial politics in the European Community: European integration and the pathbreaking Cassis de Dijon decision', *Comparative Political Studies*, 26:4, 535–61.

Andersen, M. S. and D. Liefferink 1997, *European Environmental Policy: The Pioneers*. Manchester: Manchester University Press.

Andersen, M. S. and L. N. Rasmussen 1998, 'The making of environmental policy in the European Council', *Journal of Common Market Studies*, 36:4, 585–97.

Arp, H. A. 1993, 'Technical regulation and politics: the interplay between economic interests and environmental policy goals in EC car emission legislation', in D. Liefferink, P. D. Lowe and A. P. J. Mol (eds), *European Integration and Environmental Policy*. London: Belhaven Press, 150–71.

Aspinwall, M. and J. Greenwood 1998, 'Conceptualising collective action in the European Union: an introduction', in J. Greenwood and M. Aspinwall (eds), *Collective Action in the European Union*. London: Routledge, 1–30.

Bach, M. 1992, 'Eine leise Revolution durch Verwaltungsverfahren: Bürokratische Integrationsprozesse in der Europäischen Gemeinschaft', *Zeitschrift für Soziologie*, 21:1, 16–30.

Baier, V. E., J. G. March and H. Sætren 1990, 'Implementierung und Ungewissheit', in J. G. March (ed.), *Entwicklung und Organisation: Kritische und konstruktive Beiträge, Entwicklungen und Perspektiven*. Wiesbaden: Gabler, 170–84.

Bailey, P. 1997, 'The implementation of EU environmental policy in France', in C. Knill (ed.), *The Impact of National Administrative*

Traditions on the Implementation of EU Environmental Policy.
Florence: European University Institute, 1–35.

Bauer, S. and F. Biermann 2004, *Does Effective International Environmental Governance Require a World Environment Organization? The State of the Debate Prior to the Report of the High-Panel on Reforming the United Nations.* Global Governance Working Paper No. 13. Amsterdam / Berlin / Oldenburg / Potsdam: The Global Governance Project.

Bennett, C. 1991, 'What is policy convergence and what causes it?', *British Journal of Political Science*, 21:2, 215–33.

Bennett, G. (ed.) 1991, *Air Pollution Control in the European Community: Implementation of the EC Directives in the Twelve Member States.* London: Graham and Trotman.

Benz, A. and K. H. Götz 1996, 'The German public sector: national priorities and the international reform agenda', in A. Benz and K. H. Götz (eds), *A New German Public Sector? Reform, Adaptation and Stability.* Aldershot: Dartmouth, 1–26.

Berman, P. 1980, 'Thinking about programmed and adaptive implementation: matching strategies to situations', in H. Ingram and D. Mann (eds), *Why Policies Succeed or Fail.* London: Sage, 205–27.

Bodiguel, M. (ed.) 1996, *La Qualité des Eaux dans l'Union Européenne.* Paris: Edition L'Harmattan.

Boehmer-Christiansen, S. and J. Skea 1991, *Acid Politics. Environmental and Energy Policies in Britain and Germany.* London: Belhaven Press.

Boehmer-Christiansen, S. and H. Weidner 1992, *Catalyst vs. Lean-burn: A Comparative Analysis of Environmental Policy in the Federal Republic of Germany and Britain with Reference to Exhaust Emission Policy for Passenger Cars 1970–1990.* WZB Discussion Paper FS II 92–304. Berlin: Wissenschaftszentrum für Sozialforschung.

Boemare, C., P. Quirion and S. Sorrell 2003, 'The evolution of emissions trading in the EU: tensions between national trading schemes and the proposed EU directive', *Climate Policy*, 3:S2, 105–24.

Börzel, T. A. 2000, 'Improving compliance through domestic mobilisation? New instruments and the effectiveness of implementation in Spain', in C. Knill and A. Lenschow (eds), *Implementing EU Environmental Policy: New Directions and Old Problems.* Manchester: Manchester University Press, 222–50.

Börzel, T. A. 2001, 'Non-compliance in the European Union: pathology or statistical artefact', *Journal of European Public Policy*, 8:5, 303–24.

Börzel, T. A. 2002, 'Pace-setting, foot-dragging, and fence-sitting: member state response to Europeanization', *Journal of Common*

Market Studies, 40:2, 193–214.

Börzel, T. A. and T. Risse 2003, 'Conceptualising the domestic impact of Europe', in K. Featherstone and C. Radaelli (eds), *The Politics of Europeanization*. Oxford: Oxford University Press, 57–80.

Bouma, J. J. 2000, 'Environmental management systems and audits as alternative environmental policy instruments', in C. Knill and A. Lenschow (eds), *Implementing EU Environmental Policy: New Directions and Old Problems*. Manchester: Manchester University Press, 116–33.

Brauch, H. G. (ed.) 1996, *Klimapolitik. Naturwissenschaftliche Grundlagen, internationale Regimebildung und Konflikte, ökonomische Analysen sowie Problemerkennung und Problemumsetzung*. Berlin: Springer.

Breuer, R. 1990, 'EG-Richtlinien und deutsches Wasserrecht', *Wirtschaft und Verwaltung, Vierteljahresbeilage zum Gewerbearchiv*, 2, 79–117.

Bugdahn, S. 2005, 'Of Europeanization and domestication: the implementation of the Environmental Information Directive in Ireland, Great Britain and Germany', *Journal of European Public Policy*, 12:1, 177–99.

Caddy, J. 2000, 'Implementation of EU environmental policy in Central European applicant states: the case of EIA', in C. Knill and A. Lenschow (eds), *Implementing EU Environmental Policy: New Directions and Old Problems*. Manchester: Manchester University Press, 197–221.

Cerych, L. and P. Sabatier 1986, *Great Expectations and Mixed Preferences: The Implementation of European Higher Education Reforms*. Stoke on Trent: Trentham Books.

Christiansen, A. C. and J. Wettestad 2003, 'The EU as a frontrunner on greenhouse gas emission trading: how did it happen and will the EU succeed?', *Climate Policy*, 3:1, 3–18.

Christiansen, T. 2006, 'European Commission: the European executive between continuity and change', in J. Richardson (ed.), *European Union: Power and Policy-making*. Milton Park: Routledge, 99–120.

Christiansen, T. 2006a, 'The Council of Ministers: facilitating interaction and developing actorness in the EU', in J. Richardson (ed.), *European Union. Power and Policy-making*. Milton Park: Routledge, 147–70.

Cini, M. 1996, *The European Commission. Leadership, Organisation and Culture in the EU Administration*. Manchester: Manchester University Press.

Coen, D. 1997, 'The evolution of the large firm as a political actor in the European Union', *Journal of European Public Policy*, 4:1, 91–108.

Cohn, M. 2001, 'Fuzzy legality in regulation: the legislative mandate revisited', *Law and Policy*, 23:4, 469–97.

Collier, U. 1996, *Implementing a Climate Change Strategy in the European Union: Obstacles and Opportunities*. EUI Working Paper RSC No. 96/1. Florence: European University Institute.

Collier, U. and J. Golub 1997, 'Environmental policy and politics', in M. Rhodes, P. Heywood and V. Wright (eds), *Developments in West European Politics*. New York: St. Martin's Press, 226–42.

Collins, K. and D. Earnshaw 1992, 'The implementation and enforcement of European Community environment legislation', *Environmental Politics*, 1:4, 213–49.

Corcelle, G. 1985, 'L'introduction de la "voiture propre" en Europe', *Revue du Marché Commun*, 258–63.

Corcelle, G. 1989, 'La "voiture propre" en Europe: le bout du Tunnel est en vue!', *Revue du Marché Commun*, 513–26.

Cowles, M. G., J. Caporaso and T. Risse (eds) 2001, *Transforming Europe: Europeanisation and Domestic Change*. Ithaca / London: Cornell University Press.

Cram, L. 1997, *Policy-Making and the European Union: Conceptual Lenses and the Integration Process*. London: Routledge.

Damro, C. and P. Luaces Méndez 2003, 'Emissions trading at Kyoto: from EU resistance to Union innovation', *Environmental Politics*, 12:2, 71–94.

de la Porte, C. and P. Pochet (eds) 2002, *A New Approach to Building Social Europe: The Open Method of Coordination*. Brussels: PIE Peter Lang.

Demmke, C. 1997, 'National officials and their role in the executive process: "comitology" and European environmental policy', in C. Demmke (ed.), *Managing European Environmental Policy. The Role of the Member States in the Policy Process*. Maastricht: European Institute of Public Administration, 23–39.

de Montricher, N. 1996, 'France: in search of relevant changes', in J. P. Olsen and B. G. Peters (eds), *Lessons from Experience: Experimental Learning and Administrative Reform in Eight Democracies*. Oslo: Scandinavian University Press, 243–77.

Dietz, F., J. van der Straaten and M. van der Velde 1991, 'The European Common Market and the environment: the case of the emission of NO_X by motor cars', *Review of Political Economy*, 3:1, 62–78.

Dilling, R. 2000, 'Improving implementation by networking: the role of the European Environment Agency', in C. Knill and A. Lenschow (eds), *Implementing EU Environmental Policy: New Directions and Old Problems*. Manchester: Manchester University Press, 62–86.

DiMaggio, P. J. and W. W. Powell 1991, 'The iron cage revisited: institutionalised isomorphism and collective rationality in organizational fields', in W. W. Powell and P. J. DiMaggio (eds), *The New*

Institutionalism in Organizational Analysis. Chicago: Chicago University Press, 63–82.

Duina, F. 1997, 'Explaining legal implementation in the European Union', *International Journal of the Sociology of Law,* 25:2, 155–79.

Earnshaw, D. and D. Judge 1995, 'Early days. The European Parliament, co-decision and the European Union legislative process post-Maastricht', *Journal of European Public Policy,* 2:4, 624–49.

Eichener, V. 1993, *Social Dumping or Innovative Regulation? Processes and Outcomes of European Decision-Making in the Sector of Health and Safety at Work Harmonization.* EUI Working Papers SPS No. 92/28. Florence: European University Institute.

Eichener, V. 1996, 'Die Rückwirkungen der europäischen Integration auf nationale Politikmuster', in M. Jachtenfuchs and B. Kohler-Koch (eds), *Europäische Integration.* Opladen: Leske und Budrich, 249–80.

Eichener, V. 1997, 'Effective European problem-solving: lessons from the regulation of occupational safety and environmental protection', *Journal of European Public Policy,* 4:4, 591–608.

European Commission 1984, *10 Jahre Umweltpolitik.* Brussels: Commission of the European Communities.

European Commission 1996, *Implementing Community Environmental Law: Communication to the Council of the European Union and the European Parliament.* Brussels: Commission of the European Union.

European Commission 1999, *Sechzehnter Jahresbericht über die Kontrolle der Anwendung des Gemeinschaftsrechts (1998).* Luxembourg: Office for Official Publications of the European Communities.

European Commission 2001, *European Governance: a White Paper,* COM(2001)428, Brussels, European Commission, 25 July 2001.

European Commission 2004, *Einundzwanzigster Jahresbericht über die Kontrolle der Anwendung des Gemeinschaftsrechts (2003).* Luxembourg: Office for Official Publications of the European Communities.

European Communities 1992, *Die Europäische Union.* Luxembourg: Office for Official Publications of the European Communities.

European Environment Agency 2001, *Annual Report 2000.* Luxembourg: Office for Official Publications of the European Communities.

European Environment Agency 2005, *Environmental Policy in Integration in Europe: State-of-play and Evaluation Framework.* Technical Report no. 2/2005. Copenhagen: EEA.

Fairbrass, J. and A. Jordan 2001, 'European Union, environmental policy and the UK government: a passive observer or a strategic manager?', *Environmental Politics,* 10:2, 1–21.

Falkner, G. 2000, 'Problemlösungsfähigkeit im europäischen Mehrebenensystem: die soziale Dimension', in E. Grande and M. Jachtenfuchs (eds), Wie problemlösungsfähig ist die EU? Regieren im europäischen Mehrebenensystem. Baden-Baden: Nomos, 283–311.

Favoino, M., C. Knill and A. Lenschow 2000, 'New structures for environmental governance in the European Commission: the institutional limits of governance change', in C. Knill and A. Lenschow (eds), Implementing EU Environmental Policy. New Directions and Old Problems. Manchester: Manchester University Press, 39–61.

Felsenthal, D. S. and M. Machover 1997, 'The weighted voting rule in the EU's Council of Ministers 1958–1995: intentions and outcomes', Electoral Studies,16:1, 33–47.

Garrett, G. 1995, 'From the Luxembourg compromise to codecision: decision making in the European Union', Electoral Studies, 14:3, 289–308.

Garrett, G. and G. Tsebelis 1996, 'An institutional critique of intergovernmentalism', International Organization, 50:2, 269–99.

Genschel, P. and T. Plümper 1997, 'Regulatory competition and international co-operation', Journal of European Public Policy, 4:4, 626–42.

Golub, J. 1996, 'State power and institutional influence in European integration: lessons from the packaging waste directive', Journal of Common Market Studies vol. 34, no. 3, pp. 313–39.

Golub, J. 1997, 'Recasting EU environmental policy: subsidiarity and national sovereignty', in U. Collier, J. Golub and A. Kreher (eds), Subsidiarity and Shared Responsibility: New Challenges for EU Environmental Policy. Baden-Baden: Nomos.

Golub, J. (ed.) 1998, New Instruments for Environmental Policy in the EU. London: Routledge.

Grant, W., D. Matthews and P. Newell 2000, The Effectiveness of European Union Environmental Policy. Houndmills: Macmillan.

Green Cowles, M. 1998, 'The changing architecture of big business', in J. Greenwood and M. Aspinwall (eds), Collective Action in the European Union. London: Routledge, 109–25.

Greenwood, J. 1997, Representing Interests in the European Union. Houndmills: Macmillan.

Haas, E. B. 1958, The Uniting of Europe: Political, Economic and Social Forces, 1950–1957. Stanford: Stanford University Press.

Haas, P. 1992, 'Introduction: epistemic communities and international policy coordination', International Organization, 46:1, 1–35.

Haigh, N. (ed.) 2000, The Manual of Environmental Policy: The EC and Britain. London: Catermill Publishing.

Haigh, N. and D. Baldock 1989, Environmental Policy and 1992. London: IEEP.

Haigh, N. and C. Lanigan 1995, 'Impact of the EU on UK policy-making', in T. Gray (ed.), *UK Environmental Policy in the 1990s*. Houndmills: Macmillan, 18–37.

Hall, P. A. 1993, 'Policy paradigms, social learning and the state: the case of economic policymaking in Britain', *Comparative Politics*, 25:3, 275–96.

Hall, P. A. and R. C. R. Taylor 1996, *Political Science and the Three New Institutionalisms*. MPIFG Discussion Paper 96/6. Köln: Max-Planck-Institut für Gesellschaftsforschung.

Hanf, K. and F. W. Scharpf (eds) 1978, *Interorganizational Policy Making. Limits to Coordination and Central Control*. London: Sage.

Haverland, M. 1998, *National Autonomy, European Integration and the Politics of Packaging Waste*. Amsterdam: Thela Thesis.

Haverland, M. 2000, 'National adaptation to European integration: the importance of veto points', *Journal of Public Policy*, 20:1, 83–103.

Haverland, M. 2005, 'Does the EU cause domestic developments? The problem of case selection in Europeanization research', *European Integration Online Papers*, 9:2.

Hayes-Renshaw, F. and H. Wallace 1997, *The Council of Ministers*. London: Macmillan.

Heinelt, H., E. Athanassopoulou, P. Getimis, K. H. Haunhorst, M. MacIntosh, T. Malek, R. Smith, N. Staeck, J. Taeger and A. E. Töller 2000, *Prozedurale Umweltpolitik. Umweltverträglichkeitsprüfungen und Öko-Audits im Ländervergleich*. Opladen: Leske und Budrich.

Héritier, A. 1993, 'Policy-Netzwerkanalyse als Untersuchungsinstrument im europäischen Kontext', in A. Héritier (ed.), *Policy-Analyse: Kritik und Neuorientierung, PVS Sonderheft 24/1993*. Opladen: Westdeutscher Verlag, 432–50.

Héritier, A. 1996, 'The accommodation of diversity in European policy-making and its outcomes: regulatory policy as a patchwork', *Journal of European Public Policy*, 3:2, 149–67.

Héritier, A. 2002, 'New modes of governance in Europe: policy making without legislating?', in A. Héritier (ed.), *The Provision of Common Goods. Governance Across Multiple Arenas*. Boulder: Rowman and Littlefield, 185–206.

Héritier, A., C. Knill and S. Mingers 1996, *Ringing the Changes in Europe. Regulatory Competition and the Transformation of the State*. Berlin: de Gruyter.

Hey, C. 2000, 'Zukunftsfähigkeit und Komplexität – Institutionelle Innovation in der Europäischen Union', in V. von Prittwitz (ed.), *Institutionelle Arrangements in der Umweltpolitik, Zukunftsfähigkeit durch innovative Verfahrenskombination?* Opladen: Leske und Budrich, 85–101.

Hey, C. and U. Brendle 1994, *Umweltverbände und EG*. Opladen: Westdeutscher Verlag.

Hildebrand, P. M. 1993, 'The European Community's environmental policy, 1857 to 1992: from incidental measures to an international regime', *Environmental Politics* vol. 1, no. 4, pp. 13–44.

Hill, M. 1997, 'Implementation theory: yesterday's issue?', *Policy and Politics*, 25:4, 375–85.

Hix, S. 1999, *The Political System of the European Union*. Houndmills: Macmillan.

Holzinger, K. 1991, 'Does legal harmonization really "harmonize" the quality of the environment in the European Community?', in L. A. Pal and R. Olfa-Schultze (eds), *The Nation State versus Continental Integration*. Bochum: Brockmeyer, 297–313.

Holzinger, K. 1994, *Politik des kleinsten gemeinsamen Nenners? Umweltpolitische Entscheidungsprozesse in der EG am Beispiel des Katalysatorautos*. Berlin: Edition Sigma.

Holzinger, K. 1997, 'The influence of the new member states on EU environmental policy-making. A game-theoretic approach', in M. S. Andersen and D. Liefferink (eds), *The Innovation of European Environmental Policy*. Kopenhagen: Scandinavian University Press, 59–82.

Holzinger, K. 2000, 'Optimal regulatory units: a concept of regional differentiation of environmental standards in the European Union', in K. Holzinger and P. Knoepfel (eds), *Environmental Policy in a European Union of Variable Geometry? The Challenge of the Next Enlargement*. Basel: Helbing und Lichtenhahn, 65–107.

Holzinger, K. 2002, 'The provision of transnational common goods: regulatory competition for environmental standards', in A. Héritier (ed.), *Commons Goods: Re-inventing European and International Governance*. Lanham: Rowman and Littlefield, 57–79.

Holzinger, K. and C. Knill 2002, 'Path dependencies in European integration: a constructive response to German Foreign Minister Joschka Fischer', *Public Administration*, 80:1, 125–52.

Holzinger, K. and C. Knill 2005, 'Causes and conditions of cross-national policy convergence', *Journal of European Public Policy*, 12:5, 775–96.

Holzinger, K., C. Knill, D. Peters, B. Rittberger, F. Schimmelfennig and W. Wagner 2005, *Die Europäische Union: Theorien und Analysekonzepte*. Paderborn: Schöningh.

Holzinger, K., C. Knill and A. Schäfer 2006, 'Rhetoric or reality? "New Governance" in EU environmental policy', *European Law Journal*, 12:3.

Howlett, M. and M. Ramesh 2003, *Studying Public Policy: Policy Cycles and Policy Subsystems*. Oxford: Oxford University Press.

Ingram, H. and A. Schneider 1990, 'Improving implementation through framing smarter statutes', *Journal of Public Policy*, 10:1, 67–88.

Jachtenfuchs, M. 1996, 'Umweltpolitik', in B. Kohler-Koch and W. Woyke (eds), *Lexikon der Politik, Band 5: Die Europäische Union*. München: C.H. Beck, 254–8.

Jachtenfuchs, M. and M. Huber, 1993, 'Institutional learning in the European Community: the response to the greenhouse effect', in D. Liefferink, P. D. Lowe and A. P. J. Mol (eds), *European Integration and Environmental Policy*. London: Belhaven Press, 36–58.

Jänicke, M. 1998, 'Umweltpolitik – global am Ende oder am Ende global. Thesen zu ökologischen Determinanten des Weltmarktes', in U. Beck (ed.), *Perspektiven der Weltgesellschaft*. Frankfurt am Main: Suhrkamp, 332–44.

Jänicke, M. 2001, *Grundlagen der Umweltpolitik. Teil 2: Determinanten und Erfolgsbedingungen von Umweltpolitik*. Hagen: FernUniversität Hagen.

Jänicke, M. and H. Weidner (eds) 1997, *National Environmental Policies: A Comparative Study of Capacity-Building*. Berlin: Springer.

Joerges, C. and J. Neyer 1997, 'Transforming strategic interaction into deliberative problem-solving: European comitology in the foodstuffs sector', *Journal of European Public Policy*, 4:4, 609–25.

Johnson, E. and R. Heinen 2004, 'Carbon trading: time for industry involvement', *Environment International*, 30:2, 279–88.

Johnson, S. P. and G. Corcelle 1989, *The Environmental Policy of the European Communities*. London: Graham and Trotman.

Jordan, A. 1993, 'Integrated pollution control and the evolving style and structure of environmental regulation in the UK', *Environmental Politics*, 2:3, 405–28.

Jordan, A. 1999, 'Editorial introduction: the construction of a multilevel environmental governance system', *Environment and Planning C: Government and Policy*, 17:1, 1–17.

Jordan, A. 1999a, 'The implementation of EU environmental policy: a problem without a political solution?', *Environment and Planning C: Government and Policy*, 17:1, 69–90.

Jordan, A. 2004, 'The United Kingdom: from policy "taking" to policy "shaping"', in A. Jordan and D. Liefferink (eds), *Environmental Policy in Europe: The Europeanization of National Environmental Policy*. London: Routledge, 205–23.

Jordan, A., R. Brouwer and E. Nobel 1999, 'Innovative and responsive? A longitudinal analysis of the speed of EU environmental policy making, 1967–1997', *Journal of European Public Policy*, 6:3, 376–98.

Jordan, A. and D. Liefferink (eds) 2004, *Environmental Policy in Europe: The Europeanization of National Environmental Policy.* London: Routledge.

Jordan, A., R. Wurzel and A. Zito (eds) 2003, *New Instruments of Environmental Governance.* London: Frank Cass.

Judge, D., D. Earnshaw and N. Cowan 1994, 'Ripples or waves: the European Parliament in the European Community policy process', *Journal of European Public Policy,* 1:1, 27–52.

Kenis, P. and V. Schneider 1987, 'The EC as an international corporate actor: two case studies in economic diplomacy', *European Journal of Political Research,* 15, 437–59.

Kern, K. 2000, *Die Diffusion von Politikinnovationen. Umweltpolitische Innovationen im Mehrebenensystem der USA.* Opladen: Leske und Budrich.

Kern, K., H. Jörgens and M. Jänicke 2000, 'Die Diffusion umweltpolitischer Innovationen: ein Beitrag zur Globalisierung von Umweltpolitik', *Zeitschrift für Umweltpolitik und Umweltrecht,* 23:4, 507–46.

Kickert, W. J. M. (eds) 1997, *Public Management and Administrative Reform in Western Europe.* Cheltenham: Edward Elgar.

Kimber, C. 2000, 'Implementing European environmental policy and the directive on access to environmental information', in C. Knill and A. Lenschow (eds), *Implementing EU Environmental Policy: New Directions and Old Problems.* Manchester: Manchester University Press, 168–96.

Kingdon, J. W. 1984, *Agendas, Alternatives and Public Policies.* Boston: Little, Brown.

Kirchner, E. J. 1992, *Decision-Making in the European Community: The Council Presidency and European Integration.* Manchester: Manchester University Press.

Klok, J. 2002, *Negotiating EU CO2/Energy Taxation: Political Economic Driving Forces and Barriers.* Copenhagen: AKF Forlaget.

Knill, C. 1995, *Staatlichkeit im Wandel: Großbritannien im Spannungsfeld innenpolitischer Reformen und europäischer Integration.* Opladen: Deutscher Universitätsverlag.

Knill, C. 1998, 'European policies: the impact of national administrative traditions on European policy-making', *Journal of Public Policy,* 18:1, 1–28.

Knill, C. 2001, *The Europeanization of National Administrations: Patterns of Institutional Change and Persistence.* Cambridge: Cambridge University Press.

Knill, C. 2003, *Europäische Umweltpolitik: Steuerungsprobleme und Regulierungsmuster im Mehrebenensystem.* Opladen: Leske und Budrich.

Knill, C. 2005, 'Introduction: cross-national policy convergence: concepts, approaches and explanatory factors', *Journal of European Public Policy*, 12:5, 764–74.

Knill, C. and A. Héritier 1996, 'Neue Instrumente in der europäischen Umweltpolitik: Strategien für eine effektivere Implementation', in G. Lübbe-Wolff (ed.), *Der Vollzug des europäischen Umweltrechts*. Berlin: Erich Schmidt Verlag, 209–34.

Knill, C. and D. Lehmkuhl 1998, 'Integration by globalization: the European interest representation of the consumer electronics industry', *Current Politics and Economics in Europe*, 8:2, 131–53.

Knill, C. and D. Lehmkuhl 2000, 'Mechanismen der Europäisierung: Nationale Regulierungsmuster und europäische Integration', *Schweizerische Zeitschrift für Politikwissenschaft*, 6:4, 19–50.

Knill, C. and D. Lehmkuhl 2002, 'Private actors and state: internationalization and changing patterns of governance', *Governance*, 15:1, 41–64.

Knill, C. and A. Lenschow 1998, 'Coping with Europe: the implementation of EU environmental policy and administrative traditions in Britain and Germany', *Journal of European Public Policy*, 5:4, 595–614.

Knill, C. and A. Lenschow 1999, 'Neue Konzepte – alte Probleme? Die institutionellen Grenzen effektiver Implementation', *Politische Vierteljahresschrift*, 40:4, 591–617.

Knill, C. and A. Lenschow (eds) 2000, *Implementing EU Environmental Policy: New Directions and Old Problems*. Manchester: Manchester University Press.

Knill, C. and A. Lenschow 2000a, 'On deficient implementation and deficient theories: the need for an institutional perspective in implementation research', in C. Knill and A. Lenschow (eds), *Implementing EU Environmental Policy: New Directions and Old Problems*. Manchester: Manchester University Press, 9–38.

Knill, C. and A. Lenschow 2000b, 'Do new brooms really sweep cleaner? Implementation of new instruments in EU environmental policy', in C. Knill and A. Lenschow (eds), *Implementing EU Environmental Policy: New Directions and Old Problems*. Manchester: Manchester University Press, 251–86.

Knill, C. and A. Lenschow 2001, 'Adjusting to EU environmental policy: change and persistence of domestic administrations', in M. G. Cowles, J. Caporaso and T. Risse (eds), *Transforming Europe. Europeanization and Domestic Change*. Ithaca: Cornell University Press, 116–36.

Knill C. and A. Lenschow 2004, 'Modes of regulation in the governance of the EU: towards a comprehensive evaluation', in J. Jordana and D. Levi-Faur (eds), *The Politics of Regulation. Institutions and*

Regulatory Reforms for the Age of Governance. Cheltenham: Edward Elgar, 218–44.

Knill, C. and A. Lenschow 2005, 'Compliance, competition and communication: different approaches of European governance and their impact on national institutions', *Journal of Common Market Studies*, 43:3, 583–606.

Knill, C. and D. Winkler 2006, 'Convergence or divergence of national legal and administrative structures? Europeanisation effects of the Environmental Impact Assessment in Germany and England (Part 1)', *Journal for European Environmental & Planning Law*, 1, 43–51.

Koppen, I. 1993, 'The role of the European Court of Justice', in D. Liefferink, P. D. Lowe and A. P. J. Mol (eds), *European Integration and Environmental Policy*. London: Belhaven Press, 126–49.

Krämer, L. 1992, *Focus on European Environmental Law*. London: Sweet and Maxwell.

Krämer, L. 1996, 'Defizite im Vollzug des EG-Umweltrechts und ihre Ursachen', in G. Lübbe-Wolff (ed.), *Der Vollzug des europäischen Umweltrechts*. Berlin: Erich Schmidt Verlag, 7–36.

Krämer, L. 2000, *EC Environmental Law*. London: Sweet and Maxwell, 4th edn.

Krasner, S. D. 1988, 'Sovereignty: an institutional perspective', *Comparative Political Studies*, 21:1, 66–94.

Krislov, S., C.-D. Ehlermann and J. Weiler 1986, 'The political organs and the decision-making process in the United States and the European Community', in M. Cappelletti, M. Seccombe and J. Weiler (eds), *Integration Through Law, Methods, Tolls and Institutions: Political Organs, Integration Techniques and Judicial Process*. Berlin: de Gruyter, 3–112.

Kronsell, A. 1997, 'Policy innovation in the garbage can: the EU's Fifth Environmental Action Programme', in D. Liefferink and M. S. Andersen (eds), *The Innovation of EU Environmental Policy*. Oslo: Scandinavian University Press, 111–32.

La Spina, A. and G. Sciortino 1993, 'Common agenda, southern rules: European integration and environmental change in the Mediterranean states', in J. D. Liefferink, P. D. Lowe and A. P. J. Mol (eds), *European Integration and Environmental Policy*. London: Belhaven Press, 217–36.

Lane, J.-E. 1995, *The Public Sector: Concepts, Models and Approaches*. London: Sage.

Lascoumes, P. 1994, *L'Éco-Pouvoir*. Paris: Éditions La Découverte.

Lauber, V. and V. Ingram 2000, 'Packaging waste', in A. P. J. Mol, V. Lauber and D. Liefferink (eds), *The Voluntary Approach to Environmental Policy: Joint Environmental Policy-making in Europe*. Oxford: Oxford University Press, 104–55.

Lenschow, A. 1997, 'Variation in European environmental policy integration: agency push within complex institutional structures', *Journal of European Environmental Policy*, 4:2, 109–27.

Lenschow, A. 1997a, 'The implementation of EU environmental policy in Germany', in C. Knill (ed.), *The Impact of National Administrative Traditions on the Implementation of EU Environmental Policy*. Florence: European University Institute, 1–38.

Lenschow, A. 1999, 'The greening of the EU: the common agricultural policy and the structural funds', *Environment and Planning C: Government and Policy*, 17:1, 91–108.

Lenschow, A. 1999a, 'Transformation in European environmental governance', in B. Kohler-Koch and R. Eising (eds), *The Transformation of Governance in the European Union*. London: Routledge, 39–60.

Lenschow, A. (ed.) 2001, *Environmental Policy Integration – the Greening of Sectoral Policies in Europe*. London: Earthscan.

Liefferink, D. 1996, *Environment and the Nation State: The Netherlands, the European Union and Acid Rain*. Manchester: Manchester University Press.

Liefferink, D. and M. S. Andersen 1998, 'Strategies of the "green" member states in EU environmental policy-making', *Journal of European Public Policy*, 5:2, 254–70.

Liefferink, D. and A. Jordan 2005, 'An 'ever-closer Union' of national policy? The convergence of national environmental policy in the European Union', *European Environment*, 15:2, 102–13.

Liefferink, D., P. D. Lowe and A. P. J. Mol 1993, 'The environment and the European Community: the analysis of political integration', in D. Liefferink, P. D. Lowe and A. P. J. Mol (eds), *European Integration and Environmental Policy*. London: Belhaven Press, 1–14.

Linder, S. and B. G. Peters 1989, 'Instruments of government: perceptions and contexts', *Journal of Public Policy*, 9:1, 35–58.

Lipsky, M. 1980, *Street-Level Bureaucracy*. New York: Russell Sage.

Long, T. 1998, 'The environmental lobby', in P. D. Lowe and S. Ward (eds), *British Environmental Policy and Europe: Politics and Policy in Transition*. London: Routledge, 105–18.

Lübbe-Wolff, G. 1996, 'Stand und Instrumente der Implementation des Umweltrechts in Deutschland', in G. Lübbe-Wolff (ed.), *Der Vollzug des europäischen Umweltrechts*. Berlin: Erich Schmidt Verlag, 77–106.

Macrory, R. 1992, 'The enforcement of Community environmental laws: critical issues', *Common Market Law Review*, 29, 347–69.

Macrory, R. and R. Purdy 1997, 'The enforcement of EC environmental law against member states', in J. Holder, *The Impact of the EC Environmental Law in the UK*. Chichester: Sussex, 27–50/335–68 (addendum).

Majone, G. 1989, 'Regulating Europe: problems and prospects', in T. Ellwein (ed.), *Jahrbuch zur Staats- und Verwaltungswissenschaft*. Baden-Baden: Nomos, 159–77.

Majone, G. (ed.) 1996, *Regulating Europe*. London: Routledge.

Majone, G. 1997, 'The new European agencies: regulation by information', *Journal of Public Policy*, 17:2, 262–75.

Maloney, W. A. and J. Richardson 1995, *Managing Policy Change in Britain: The Politics of Water*. Edinburgh: Edinburgh University Press.

March, J. G. and J. P. Olsen 1989, *Rediscovering Institutions*. New York: Free Press.

Mastenbroek, E. 2003, 'Surviving the deadline: the transposition of EU directives in the Netherlands', *European Union Politics*, 4:4, 371–96.

Mastenbroek, E. 2005, 'EU compliance: still a "black hole"?', *Journal of European Public Policy*, 12:6, 1103–20.

Mayntz, R. 1983, 'Implementation von regulativer Politik', in R. Mayntz (ed.), *Implementation politischer Programme II*. Opladen: Westdeutscher Verlag, 50–74.

Mazey, S. and J. Richardson 2006, 'Interest groups and EU policy-making: organisational logic and venue shopping', in J. Richardson (ed.), *European Union: Power and Policy-making*. Milton Park: Routledge, 247–68.

Mbaye, A. D. 2001, 'Why national states comply with supranational law', *European Union Politics*, 2:3, 259–81.

McBarnet, D. and C. Whelan 1991, 'The elusive spirit of the law: formalism and the struggle for legal control', *The Modern Law Review*, 54:6, 848–73.

McCown, M. 2006, 'Judicial law-making and European integration: the European Court of Justice', in J. Richardson (ed.), *European Union: Power and Policy-making*. Milton Park: Routledge, 171–86.

Mendrinou, M. 1996, 'Non-compliance and the Commission's role in integration', *Journal of European Public Policy*, 3:1, 1–22.

Mol, A. P. J., D. Liefferink and V. Lauber 2000, 'Epilogue: conclusions and policy implications', in A. P. J. Mol, V. Lauber and D. Liefferink (eds), *The Voluntary Approach to Environmental Policy: Joint Environmental Policy-making in Europe*. Oxford: Oxford University Press, 217–26.

Mol, A. P. J., V. Lauber and D. Liefferink (eds) 2000, *The Voluntary Approach to Environmental Policy*. Oxford: Oxford University Press.

Moser, P. 1996, 'The European Parliament as a conditional agenda-setter: what are the conditions? A critic of Tsebelis', *American Political Science Review*, 90:4, 834–8.

Moser, P. 1997, 'The benefits of the conciliation procedure for the

European Parliament: comment to George Tsebelis', *Außenwirtschaft*, 52:1/2, 57–62.

Oberthür, S. 1999, 'The EU as an international actor: the protection of the ozone layer', *Journal of Common Market Studies*, 37:4, 641–59.

Olson, M. 1965, *The Logic of Collective Action, Public Goods and the Theory of Groups*. Cambridge: Harvard University Press.

O'Riordan, T. and J. Cameron (eds) 1994, *Interpreting the Precautionary Principle*. London: Earthscan.

Oshitani, S. 2005, *Global Warming Policy in Japan and Britain: Interactions Between Institutions and Issue Characteristics*. Manchester: Manchester University Press.

Ott, H. and S. Oberthür 1999, *Breaking the Impasse: Forging an EU Leadership Initiative on Climate Change*. Papers and Reports of the Heinrich Böll Foundation No. 2.

Page, E. 1997, *People Who Run Europe*. Oxford: Clarendon.

Pellegrom, S. 1997, 'The constraints of daily work in Brussels: how relevant is the input from national capitals?', in D. Liefferink and M. S. Andersen (eds), *The Innovation of EU Environmental Policy*. Oslo: Scandinavian University Press, 36–58.

Peters, B. G. 1993, 'Alternative Modelle des Policy-Prozesses. Die Sicht "von unten" und die Sicht "von oben"', in A. Héritier (ed.), *Policy-Analyse: Kritik und Neurorientierung, PVS Sonderheft 24/1993*. Opladen: Westdeutscher Verlag, 289–306.

Peterson, J. 1995, 'Decision-making in the European Union: towards a framework for analysis', *Journal of European Public Policy*, 2:1, 60–93.

Pijnenburg, B. 1998, 'EU lobbying by ad hoc coalitions: an exploratory case study', *Journal of European Public Policy*, 5:2, 303–21.

Pollack, M. A. 1997, 'Delegation, agency and agenda setting in the European Union Community', *International Organization*, 51:1, 99–134.

Pressman, J. and A. Wildavsky 1973, *Implementation*. Berkeley: University of California Press.

Rehbinder, E. 1991, *Das Vorsorgeprinzip im internationalen Vergleich*. Düsseldorf: Werner-Verlag.

Rehbinder, E. and R. Stewart 1985, *Environmental Protection Policy: Integration Through Law*. Berlin: de Gruyter.

Rhodes, R. A. W. 1996, *The New European Agencies: Agencies in British Government: Revolution or Evolution?* EUI Working Papers RSC No. 96/51. Florence: European University Institute.

Risse, T. 2000, 'Let's argue: communicative action in world politics', *International Organization*, 54:1, 1–40.

Rüdig, W. and R. A. Krämer 1994, 'Networks of cooperation: water policy in Germany', *Environmental Politics*, 3:4, 52–79.

Sabatier, P. A. 1986, 'Top-down and bottom-up approaches to implementation research', *Journal of Public Policy*, 6:1, 21–48.

Sabatier, P. A. 1993, 'Advocacy-Koalitionen, Policy-Wandel und Policy-Lernen: eine Alternative zur Phasenheuristik', in A. Héritier (ed.), *Policy-Analyse: Kritik und Neurorientierung*, PVS Sonderheft 24/1993. Opladen: Westdeutscher Verlag, 116–48.

Sbragia, A. M. 1998, 'Institution-building from below and above: the European Community in global environmental politics', in A. Stone Sweet and W. Sandholtz (eds), *European Integration and Supranational Governance*. Oxford: Oxford University Press, 283–303.

Sbragia, A. M. 2000, 'Environmental policy', in H. Wallace and W. Wallace (eds), *Policy-Making in the European Union*. Oxford: Oxford University Press, 4th edn, 293–316.

Scharpf, F. W. 1988, 'The joint decision trap: lessons from German federalism and European integration', *Public Administration*, 66:3, 239–78.

Scharpf, F. W. 1993, *Autonomieschonend und gemeinschaftsverträglich. Zur Logik der europäischen Mehrebenenpolitik*. MPIFG Discussion Paper 93/9. Köln: Max-Planck-Institut für Gesellschaftsforschung.

Scharpf, F. W. 1994, *Mehrebenenpolitik im vollendeten Binnenmarkt*. MPIFG Discussion Paper 94/4. Köln: Max-Planck-Institut für Gesellschaftsforschung.

Scharpf, F. W. 1996, 'Politische Optionen im vollendeten Binnenmarkt', in M. Jachtenfuchs and B. Kohler-Koch (eds), *Europäische Integration*. Opladen: Leske und Budrich, 109–40.

Scharpf, F. W. 1997, *Games Real Actors Play: Actor-Centred Institutionalism in Policy Research*. New York: Westview.

Scharpf, F. W. 1997a, 'Introduction: the problem-solving capacity of multi-level governance', *Journal of European Public Policy*, 4:4, 520–38.

Scharpf, F. W. 1999, *Regieren in Europa: Effektiv und Demokratisch?* Frankfurt am Main: Campus.

Scharpf, F. W. 2000, *Interaktionsformen: Akteurzentrierter Institutionalismus in der Politikforschung*. Opladen: Leske und Budrich.

Schmidt, S. K. 1997, *Behind the Council Agenda: The Commission's Impact on Decisions*. MPIFG Discussion Paper 97/4. Köln: Max-Planck-Institut für Gesellschaftsforschung.

Schneider, G. 1984, 'Die europäische Umweltpolitik steht noch vor der Bewährung: von der Reglementierung über die Implementation zur tatsächlichen Umweltverbesserung', in G. Schneider and R. U.

Sprenger (eds), *Mehr Umweltschutz für weniger Geld*. München: Ifo-Institut für Wirtschaftsforschung, 601–42.

Schröder, M. 1998, 'Aktuelle Entwicklungen im europäischen Umweltrecht', *Natur und Recht*, 20:1, 1–6.

Schwarze, J. 1996, 'Deutscher Landesbericht', in J. Schwarze (ed.), *Administrative Law under European Influence*. Baden-Baden: Nomos, 123–227.

Scott, J. and D. M. Trubek 2002, 'Mind the gap: law and new approaches to governance in the European Union', *European Law Journal*, 8:1, 1–18.

Siedentopf, H. and J. Ziller (eds) 1988, *Making European Policies Work: L'Europe des Administrations? Vol. 2, National Reports, Rapports Nationaux*. London: Sage.

Sjöstedt, G. 1998, 'The EU negotiates climate change: external peformance and internal structural change', *Cooperation and Conflict*, 33:3, 227–56.

Skjaerseth, J. B. 1994, 'The climate policy of the EC: too hot to handle?', *Journal of Common Market Studies*, 32:1, 25–45.

Snyder, F. 1993, 'The effectiveness of European Community law: institutions, processes, tools and techniques', *Modern Law Review*, 56:1, 19–54.

SRU (Rat von Sachverständigen für Umweltfragen) 1998, *Umweltgutachten 1998. Umweltschutz, Erreichtes sichern, neue Wege gehen*. Stuttgart: Metzler-Poeschel.

Steunenberg, B. 1994, 'Decision-making under different institutional arrangements: legislation by the European Community', *Journal of Institutional and Theoretical Economics*, 150:4, 642–69.

Steunenberg, B. 1997, 'Codecision and its reform. A comparative analysis of decision-making rules in the European Union', in B. Steunenberg and F. van Vught (eds), *Political Institutions and Public Policy*. Amsterdam: Kluwer, 205–29.

Steunenberg, B. 2005, *Turning Swift Policymaking into Deadlock and Delay: National Policy Coordination and the Transposition of EU Directives*. Paper prepared for the ECPR Joint Sessions, Granada, Spain, 14–19 April 2005.

Stevis, D. and S. Mumme 2000, 'Rules and politics in international integration: environmental regulation in NAFTA and the EU', *Environmental Politics*, 9:4, 20–42.

Stewart, R. B. 1993, 'Environmental regulation and international competitiveness', *Yale Law Journal*, 102:8, 2039–106.

Sverdrup, U. 2004, 'Compliance and conflict management in the European Union: nordic exceptionalism', *Scandinavian Political Studies*, 27:1, 23–43.

Tallberg, J. 1999, *Making States Comply: The European Commission, the European Court of Justice and the Enforcement of the Internal Market*. Lund: Studentliteratur.

Tallberg, J. 2002, 'Paths to compliance: enforcement, management, and the European Union', *International Organization*, 56:3, 609–43.

Thelen, K. and S. Steinmo 1992, 'Historical institutionalism in comparative politics', in K. Thelen, S. Steinmo and F. Longstreth (eds), *Structuring Politics: Historical Institutionalism in Comparative Analysis*. Cambridge: Cambridge University Press, 1–32.

Toonen, T. A. J. 1992, 'Europe of the administrations: the challenges of 1992 (and beyond)', *Public Administration Review*, 52:2, 108–15.

Tsebelis, G. 1994, 'The power of the European Parliament as a conditional agenda-setter', *American Political Science Review*, 28:1, 128–42.

Tsebelis, G., C. B. Jensen, A. Kalandrakis and A. Kreppel 2001, 'Legislative procedures in the European Union: an empirical analysis', *British Journal of Political Science*, 31:4, 573–601.

Tsekouras, K. 2000, 'Exploiting the implementation potential of alternative instruments: design options for environmental liability funds', in C. Knill and A. Lenschow (eds), *Implementing EU Environmental Policy: New Directions and Old Problems*. Manchester: Manchester University Press, 134–67.

Veenman, S. and D. Liefferink 2005, 'Different countries, different strategies. "Green" member states influencing EU climate policy', in F. Wijen, K. Zoeteman and J. Pieters (eds), *A Handbook of Globalization and Environmental Policy: National Government Interventions in a Global Arena*. Cheltenham: Edward Elgar, 519–44.

Vogel, D. 1986, *National Styles of Regulation: Environmental Policy in Great Britain and the United States*. Ithaca: Cornell University Press.

Vogel, D. 1995, *Trading Up: Consumer and Environmental Regulation in the Global Economy*. Cambridge: Harvard University Press.

Vogel, D. 1997, 'Trading up and governing across: transnational governance and environmental protection', *Journal of European Public Policy*, 4:4, 556–71.

Wallace, H. 2000, 'The institutional setting', in H. Wallace and W. Wallace (eds), *Policy-Making in the European Union*. Oxford: Oxford University Press, 4th edn, 3–38.

Weale, A. 1992, *The New Politics of Pollution*. Manchester: Manchester University Press.

Weale, A. 1996, 'Environmental rules and rule-making in the European Union', *Journal of European Public Policy*, 3:4, 594–611.

Weale, A. 1999, 'European environmental policy by stealth. The dysfunctionality of functionalism', *Environment and Planning C*:

Government and Policy, 17:1, 37–52.

Weale, A., G. Pridham, M. Cini, D. Konstadakopulos, M. Porter and B. Flynn 2000, *Environmental Governance in Europe: An Ever Closer Ecological Union*. Oxford: Oxford University Press.

Webster, R. 1998, 'Environmental collective action: stable patterns of cooperation and issue alliances at the European level', in J. Greenwood and M. Aspinwall (eds), *Collective Action in the European Union*. London: Routledge, 176–95.

Weidner, H. 1987, *Clean Air Policy in Great Britain: Problem Shifting as Best Practicable Means*. Berlin: Edition Sigma.

Weidner, H. 1996, *Umweltkooperation und alternative Konfliktregelungsverfahren in Deutschland*. Schriften zu Mediationsverfahren im Umweltschutz 16, Berlin: Wissenschaftszentrum für Sozialforschung.

Weiler, J. H. H. 1988, 'The White Paper and the application of Community law', in R. Bieber, R. Dehousse, S. Pinder and J. H. H. Weiler (eds), *One European Market?* Baden-Baden: Nomos, 337–58.

Wessels, W. 1990, 'Administrative interaction', in W. Wallace (ed.), *The Dynamics of European Integration*. London: Pinter, 229–41.

Wessels, W. 2001, 'Nice results: the millenium IGC in the EU's evolution', *Journal of Common Market Studies*, 39:2, 197–219.

Wessels, W. and D. Rometsch 1996, 'German administrative interaction and the European Union: the fusion of public policies', in Y. Mény, P. Muller and J.-L. Quermonne (eds), *Adjusting to Europe: The Impact of the European Union on National Institutions and Policies*. London: Routledge, 73–109.

Wilkinson, D. 1997, 'Towards sustainability in the European Union: steps within the European Commission towards integrating the environment into other policy sectors', *Environmental Politics*, 6:1, 153–73.

Windhoff-Héritier, A. 1987, *Policy-Analyse: Eine Einführung*. Frankfurt: Campus.

Winter, G. 1996, 'Freedom of environmental information', in G. Winter (ed.), *European Environmental Law: A Comparative Perspective*. Aldershot: Dartmouth, 81–94.

Woerdman, E. 2004, 'Path-dependent climate policy: the history and future of emissions trading in Europe', *European Environment*, 14:5, 261–75.

Wright, R. 2000, 'Implementing voluntary policy instruments: the experience of the EU ecolabel award scheme', in C. Knill and A. Lenschow (eds), *Implementing EU Environmental Policy: New Directions and Old Problems*. Manchester: Manchester University Press, 87–115.

Wright, V. 1994, 'Reshaping the state: the implications for public administration', *West European Politics*, 17:2, 102–37.

Wurzel, R. K. W. 1996, 'The role of the EU Presidency in the environmental field: does it make a difference which Member State runs the Presidency?', *Journal of European Public Policy*, 2:2, 272–91.

Wurzel, R. K. W. 2002, *Environmental Policy-making in Britain, Germany and the European Union: The Europeanisation of Air and Water Pollution Control*. Manchester: Manchester University Press.

Wurzel, R. K. W. 2004, 'Germany: from environmental leadership to partial mismatch', in A. Jordan and D. Liefferink (eds), *Environmental Policy in Europe: The Europeanization of National Environmental Policy*. London: Routledge, 99–117.

Wynne, B. and C. Waterton 1998, 'Public information on the environment: the role of the European Environment Agency', in P. D. Lowe and S. Ward (eds), *British Environmental Policy and Europe. Politics and Policy in Transition*. London: Routledge, 119–28.

Young, A. R. and H. Wallace 2000, 'The Single Market', in H. Wallace and W. Wallace (eds), *Policy-Making in the European Union*. Oxford: Oxford University Press, 4th edn, 85–114.

Zito, A. 1995, 'Integrating the environment into the European Union: the history of the controversial carbon tax', in C. Rhodes and S. Mazey (eds), *The State of the European Union*. Boulder: Lynne Rienner Publishers, 431–48.

Zito, A. R. 1999, 'Task expansion: a theoretical overview', *Environment and Planning C: Government and Policy*, 17:1, 19–36.

Zürn, M. 1997, 'Positives Regieren jenseits des Nationalstaates: zur Implementation internationaler Umweltregime', *Zeitschrift für internationale Beziehungen*, 4:1, 41–68.

Index

accessions to the EU, 220
acidification and acid rain, 4–5, 10–11, 31, 49, 52, 78, 114, 122–3
action at source principle, 15, 29, 36, 42
adaptation pressure on institutions, 173–7, 185–94
administrative implications of new policies, 182
administrative traditions and capacities of EU member states, 110–11, 156, 159, 179, 184–90 *passim*
Agenda 21, 74
agenda-setting, 57–8, 78–83, 92, 112, 217
air pollution, 4–5, 10, 29, 36–7, 43–4, 49–52, 93, 107, 198, 202, 206, 210
Alder, J., 192
Amsterdam Treaty (1999), 2, 20–2, 25, 34, 65, 96, 216
Arp, H. A., 86
Austria, 19, 91, 115, 211
automobile emissions, 4, 29, 40, 49, 104–5, 122, 152; *see*

also catalytic converters

bathing water, quality of 32, 108, 201–3, 206–7
Belgium, 91, 211
best available technology (BAT), use of, 36–8, 43
best available technology not entailing excessive cost (BATNEEC), 37
best practice, dissemination of, 176
'bottom-up' measures, 39, 153–4, 166
Bouma, J. J., 171
Brundtland, Gro-Harlem, 73
Bulgaria, 220

California, 104–5
Canada, 135
Caporaso, J., 218
carbon tax, proposed, 135–8
catalytic converters, 99, 122–9, 133, 140–3
Cerych, L., 168
chemicals control, 4, 10, 29, 50–2, 107–8

China, 134
climate change, 31, 49, 52,
74–5, 133–5, 142, 210,
215, 222; *see also* global
warming
co-decision procedure, 21, 65,
96–100, 139
Cohesion Funds, 94
Collins, Ken, 66
comitology, 61
'command-and-control' form of
regulation, 22, 33, 38–9,
156, 180, 194, 209, 215,
219
Committee of Permanent
Representatives
(COREPER), 63–4, 87–8,
92–3, 116
common environmental policy,
15, 21–4
legislation for, 45–6
'Common Market relevance'
criterion, 16–18, 52
compensation payments, 107,
118
competition policy, 4, 204
competitiveness, economic, 103,
107–10, 132, 135
conciliation committee procedure, 98
consensus-seeking, 88, 91–2,
109, 128
conservation of natural
resources, 30
Constitutional Treaty of the EU,
22, 214–16, 220–1
consultation procedure, 65,
96–9, 141
context-oriented environmental
governance, 38, 41, 55,

157, 163, 166–8, 172, 179,
194
convergence in national regulatory structures and patterns,
117, 119, 218
cooperation procedure, 17–21,
65, 96–9, 124, 126, 129, 141
cooperative arrangements for
environmental protection,
39, 46, 164
costs and benefits, analysis of,
35–7
Council of Environmental
Ministers, 3, 6, 62
Council of Ministers of the EU,
9, 12, 16–21, 25, 58–66,
70, 79, 82, 85–99, 109,
113, 117, 123–9, 132–5,
139, 142–3, 197, 208, 219
Presidency of, 64, 73, 92–3,
139
Cowan, N., 66
Cowles, M. G., 218
'creative compliance', 177
criticisms of EU environmental
policy, 199–204
cross-border pollution, 4–5, 9,
52, 78

Damro, C., 136
data, environmental, 158–9
'daughter directives', 44–50
decision-making in the EU:
procedures for, 16–21, 25,
43–4, 54, 87–101, 196–9
quality of, 197, 199–204
'decisions' on environmental
policy, 46–7
deliberative problem-solving,
116–17

Denmark, 11, 95, 115, 123–8, 131, 135–42, 211
dialogue groups, 34
directives of the EU, 29–30, 36–52, 111, 131, 164, 170, 180–4, 187–92, 201–8, 217–18
diversity within the EU, 220
'double majority' principle, 90
drinking water, quality of, 11, 108, 159, 180–91 *passim*, 194, 205, 207

Earnshaw, D., 66
eco-label scheme, 44, 47, 108, 165, 170, 172
Economic Commission for Europe, 122
emission limits, 38, 40, 48–9, 99, 114, 122–7
emissions trading, 39, 44, 49, 74–5, 134–42
'end-of-pipe' technologies, 28
energy tax, proposed, 34, 63, 84–5
enlargement of the EU, 220–1
Environmental Action Programmes, 3, 5, 15, 27, 30, 45–6
First, 6, 9, 14–15, 31, 33, 73
Third, 163
Fourth, 33, 130, 141
Fifth, 19, 33–4, 38, 53, 137, 163–4, 210
Sixth, 44, 53
'environmental dumping', 118–19
environmental impact assessment (EIA), 29–30, 43, 47, 108, 111, 164–5, 169–70,

181–93 *passim*, 203–4
Environmental Management and Audit Scheme (EMAS), 39, 44, 47, 108, 114, 165, 169, 171
environmental quality objectives (EQOs), 43, 164
epistemic communities, 116
Euro-feds, 70
European Commission, 3, 5, 11, 13, 23, 34–8, 46, 49, 53–4, 57–61, 70–3, 79–87, 92–3, 96–88, 112–14, 118–19, 123–30, 138–43, 146–50, 156–9, 164, 167, 199, 203–5, 208, 210, 217, 221
DG Environment, 22, 34–5, 59–61, 72, 84–5, 136–7, 216
other DGs, 84–5
Presidency of, 84
working groups, 85–7, 117
European Commissioners, college of, 59, 84, 148
European Court of Justice (ECJ), 6–7, 46, 61, 66–8, 128, 148, 150, 184, 205
European Environment Agency (EEA), 2, 20, 22, 25, 68–9, 209, 211
European Environmental Bureau (EEB), 71–2, 125
European Information and Observation Network (EIONET), 22, 69
European Parliament (EP), 13, 17, 21, 58, 61, 63–6, 70, 79, 87, 95–9, 113, 119, 122, 125–9, 141–3, 208;

Environment Committee, 66, 130
Europeanization, 173, 217–18
external shocks, 194

federal structures, 159
Finland, 19, 115, 211
'first mover' advantages, 112–13, 138
'forerunner' role in environmental matters, 110, 113, 115, 129, 133, 138, 141–2, 200
framework directives, 40, 43–52, 93
France, 22, 91, 123, 127–8, 131, 138, 179, 182–93 *passim*, 203, 211, 220–1
'free-market environmentalism', 136

genetically-modified products, 51, 215
Germany, 10–11, 31, 36–7, 49, 68, 78–9, 90–1, 111–15, 122–5, 128–35, 140–1, 159–60, 166, 170, 179, 182–90 *passim*, 202, 205–7, 211
global warming, 134
   see also climate change
'goodness-of-fit', 173
governance, environmental, 36–44, 53–5
   see also context-oriented environmental governance
Governance in the European Union (White Paper), 53
Greece, 12, 91, 124–5, 128, 135, 211

greenhouse gases, 39, 44, 49, 74, 85, 134–9 *passim*

habitats, protection of, 51
harmonization, 7–8, 16, 24, 30, 104–7, 118, 122, 177, 200
Héritier, A., 54, 112, 114, 169
Hey, C., 53–4
Hix, S., 83
Holzinger, K., 18, 94–5, 104, 199, 201
Huber, M., 134

implementation deadlines, 205
implementation deficits, 40, 95, 143, 145–61, 177–8, 183, 193, 204–8, 212, 218
   extent of 151–60
implementation of environmental measures: effectiveness of, 146–60, 162, 165–9, 172–6, 179–80, 184–6, 193–5, 197
   as an empirical and political problem, 160–1
implementation theory and implementation research, 166–9
incentive structures, 44, 140, 157, 165, 176
India, 134
information, environmental, access to, 18, 22, 39, 44, 47, 108, 113–14, 129–33, 140–2, 164, 170, 181–9, 194, 206–7
infringement proceedings, 147–9, 157–60
Ingram, H., 168

institutional adaptation,
110–12, 132
institutional theories, 172–5
integrated pollution prevention
and control (IPPC), 30, 37,
47, 202
integration agenda, European,
220
integration correspondents, 59
integration of environmental
policy with other EU policy
areas, 15, 22, 29–30, 33–5,
62
interest groups, 69–72, 81–2,
99, 119, 166, 191
intergovernmental negotiations,
82, 77, 96, 116
internal market policies, 216, 221
international environmental
regimes, 72–5
Ireland, 91, 133, 206, 211
Italy, 91, 123, 211

Jachtenfuchs, M., 134
Japan, 134–5
Joerges, C., 116
Johannesburg Summit on
Sustainable Development
(2002), 75
Jordan, A., 1, 17, 148, 158
Judge, D., 66

Kimber, C., 170
Knill, C., 112, 114, 169, 174
Krämer, L., 205
Kyoto Protocol, 49, 74–5,
134–6, 140

legislation, environmental,
forms of, 45–6

legislative procedures, 95–101
legitimacy of environmental
policy, 12–13
Lenschow, A., 53, 174
'Lisbon' process, 221
living conditions, improvement
in, 5–6
Luaces Méndez, P., 136
Luxembourg, 90–1, 131, 135,
211
Luxembourg compromise
(1985), 123–6

Maastricht Treaty, 2, 20–1, 25,
31–2, 41, 63, 65, 71, 94,
96, 148, 197, 216
see also Treaty on European
Union (TEU)
Majone, G., 69, 82
'Mediterranean syndrome',
155–6
Mingers, S., 112, 114, 169
mixed agreements, 74–5
multi-level governance, 119,
214–19

national interests, 77, 86–8, 92,
95, 105–6, 109, 116–18,
129, 219
national regulatory structures
and styles, 110–11, 117,
119, 174, 185, 193–4
nature protection, 51–2, 81, 199
Netherlands, the, 11, 22, 91,
115, 123–8, 131, 138, 206,
211, 220–1
Neyer, J., 116
Nice Treaty (2000), 22, 89–90,
216, 220
noise control, 49, 52

non-governmental organizations (NGOs), 69

Open Method of Coordination (OMC), 176–7, 195
'opinions' on environmental policy, 46
optimal management of the environment, 36
'Our Common Future' report (1987), 73
overarching measures, 46–8
ozone depletion, 73

package deals, 94, 118, 127
paradigms, 35
path-dependence, 218
peer review, 176–7
performance indicators, 168
planning authorities, 192
policy content linked to institutional arrangements, 181
policy instruments, 41–5; 'new' form of, 156–7, 162–72, 176, 181, 184, 215; *substantive* and *procedural*, 42–4, 140, 171
policy output and policy outcome, 151–5, 167, 208
policy proposals, drafting of, 83–6
'polluter pays' principle, 28, 33–4, 191
poor member states of the EU, 106–11, 118
Portugal, 12, 91, 135, 211
precautionary principle, 15, 31, 36
Pressman, J., 145
prevention, principle of, 28–31

principles of European environmental policy, 27–8, 53
privatization, 190
problem-solving capacity, 197, 199, 204, 208, 211, 218–19
procedural regulation, 42–4, 54, 164, 169–71, 176, 181–2
product standards, 7, 43, 49, 52, 106, 118, 140
production methods, regulation of, 104–8, 118
programme formulation, 83–6

qualified majority voting (QMV), 17–18, 21–2, 25, 63, 88–91, 95–8, 109, 112, 118, 124–8, 139, 141, 197, 217
quality of decision-making, 197, 199–204
quality-oriented environmental policy, 36–7, 40–3

'race to the bottom', 103–5, 115
'race to the top', 104
reasoned opinions, 147–8, 157–8
'recommendations' on environmental policy, 46, 49
regulations of the EU, 45–50
regulatory approaches and styles, 35–41, 180
regulatory capture, 82
regulatory competition, 36, 102–15, 214–17, 220
    advantage of the 'first move', 110–15

effects of market integration, 103–9
reminder letters, 147–8, 157–8
renewable sources of energy, 75
rich member states of the EU, 106–11, 118
Rio de Janeiro Conference on Environment and Development (1992), 74–5
Ripa di Meana, Carlo, 125
Rise, T., 218
Romania, 220
Rome Treaty (1957), 1–2, 5, 12, 215–16
Russia, 135

Sabatier, P., 168
Sbragia, A. M., 23, 58, 62, 69, 200
Scharpf, F. W., 41, 104, 106
Schneider, A., 168
Schneider, G., 202
Schröder, M., 21
sector-specific measures, 48–53
Seveso incident, 52, 81
Shapley-Shubik Index, 90–1
'shared responsibility', 163
shellfish water, 201, 207
Single European Act (SEA), 2, 9, 12–17, 20–1, 24–5, 30–4, 41, 63–73 *passim*, 96, 124–7, 150, 197, 216
Small Cars Directive, 122, 127–9
Spain, 12, 91, 159, 179, 182–93, 203–5, 211
standards, environmental, 3, 30–1, 40–3
product and production types, 43, 104–9, 118

Stockholm Conference on the Human Environment (1972), 4, 73
subsidiarity, 15, 32–3, 41
sustainable development, concept of, 21–2, 75
Sweden, 19, 115, 138, 211

target-oriented perspectives, 153–7
technological developments, response to, 40
technological measures to prevent pollution, 35–7, 53
Thatcher, Margaret, 131, 187, 194
'top-down' measures, 152–3, 169, 175–6
trade barriers, 2–4, 7, 13, 103–6, 123
transitional periods, 202, 212
transposition of EU law into national legislation, 45, 146–50, 157–60, 162, 184, 193, 204–6, 212
Treaty on European Union (TEU), 5–6, 21, 24
Article 18, 14, 16
Article 30, 68, 104, 106
Article 94, 67
Article 95, 7–9, 14–21, 106, 124
Articles 174–176, 13–17, 21
Article 226, 147
Article 249, 45
Article 308, 8–9, 16, 18, 67
see also Maastricht Treaty
Tsebelis, G., 97
Turkey, 220

Union des Industrie de la
    Communauté Européenne
    (UNICE), 72
United Kingdom (UK), 5, 11,
    32, 36–8, 78, 91–4,
    113–15, 123–33 *passim*,
    137–42, 160, 166, 179,
    182–3, 186–7, 190–4,
    201–3, 206, 211
United Nations, 73;
    Environment Program
    (UNEP), 73
    Framework Convention on
    Climate Change
    (UNFCCC), 74–5, 134
United States, 74–5, 104–5,
    123, 134–6

veto powers, 16–21, 98, 124,
    200

Vogel, David, 104
voluntary agreements for
    environmental protection,
    39–40, 44, 47, 49, 54–5,
    108, 164–5, 170, 172, 177,
    191, 206

Wallace, H., 88
waste management policies, 10,
    29, 36, 49–52, 107–8, 198,
    210
water pollution, 10–11, 29, 37,
    48, 52, 107–8, 191, 198,
    201, 206, 210
Weale, A., 2, 27–8, 31, 34, 67,
    79, 83, 99, 208, 215
Weiler, J. H. H., 86, 95
Wessels, W., 85
Wildavsky, A., 145
Wright, R., 170